GUNS, CRIME,

AND FREEDOM

GUNS, CRIME, AND FREEDOM

WAYNE R. LAPIERRE

FOREWORD BY TOM CLANCY

REGNERY PUBLISHING, INC.
Washington, D.C.

Library of Congress Cataloging-in-Publication Data

LaPierre, Wayne. 1949–
Guns, crime, and freedom / Wayne LaPierre : foreword by Tom Clancy.
p.   cm.
Includes bibliographical references and index.
ISBN 0-89526-477-3
1. Gun control—United States.   2. Firearms—Law and legislation—
United States.   I. Title.
HV7436.L365   1994   94-19160
363.3'3'0973—dc20   CIP

Published in the United States by
Regnery Publishing, Inc.
An Eagle Publishing Company
422 First St., SE, Suite 300
Washington, DC 20003

Distributed to the trade by
National Book Network
4720-A Boston Way
Lanham, MD 20706

Printed on acid-free paper.

Manufactured in the United States of America.

10   9

Books are available in quantity for promotional or premium use. Write to
Director of Special Sales, Regnery Publishing, Inc., 422 First Street, SE, Suite
300, Washington, DC 20003, for information on discounts and terms or call
(202) 546-5005.

*To Our Founding Fathers Who Guaranteed Me
the Freedom to Write this Book.*

ACKNOWLEDGEMENTS

I especially want to thank Marion P. Hammer and Mary Marcotte Corrigan for making this happen. I also want to thank those individuals too numerous to mention for their input and support.

CONTENTS

FOREWORD

BY TOM CLANCY

Switzerland is a land where crime is virtually unknown, yet most Swiss males are required by law to keep in their homes what amounts to a portable, personal machine gun. The same situation exists in Israel, whose armed forces are similar to the Swiss model: Many citizens keep their military weapons—the well-known Uzi submachine gun, for example—in their coat closets.

Street crime in Israel is very low by American standards. And it is plain from this evidence that the possession of firearms does not automatically foster crime.

I am a gun owner. I was introduced to shooting while a member of Troop 624 of the Boy Scouts of America over thirty years ago, and from the first, shooting was something that I have enjoyed. I own a modest number of handguns and long guns, some of them semi-automatic. All are kept securely out of reach of my children, who know not to touch my guns without my supervision. My hobby is shooting, and I have never come close to injuring anyone, even myself, because I undertake this activity responsibly, as do virtually all of my fellow shooters. Shooting, like golf, is a discipline in which one must exercise exact control at one point to achieve a goal at a distant point. And as with golf, the reward of shooting is an internal one. One is gratified by his or her own conquest of the laws of physics. Shooting is, in a word, as much fun for me as a good 5-iron shot is for someone else; and I find that shooting is effective for controlling stress, as golf or other hobbies doubt-less are for others.

I live in an area—on the Chesapeake Bay, in Maryland—where the great majority of citizens own firearms, mainly shotguns, because it is simply the way things are in the country. Guns are kept as tools in the country, much as lawn-mowers are kept as tools in the suburbs. There is very little crime where I live, another classic case of many guns but little crime, and less than an hour away from Washington, D.C., where the reverse is true.

While an insurance agent, I carried the coverage for two police forces, and I have numerous friends in the FBI. I have yet to meet a single law-enforcement officer who thinks that con-fiscating firearms from the general public will do any good at all concerning crime in the United States—not one. They all say that gun control has no demonstrable effect on crime—or that its effects appear to be negative, as can be crudely demon-strated in such restrictive cities as Washington and New York. And no firearm has ever killed anyone unless directed by a person who acted either from malice, madness or idiocy. Sadly, not all of our elected officials are willing to accept this as fact. Somehow, guns themselves—pieces of hardware, no more, no less—have become the source of evil, while the actions of depraved individuals are conveniently ignored.

I submit that the actions of criminals and lunatics are irrele-vant to my right to own and use firearms in pursuit of my personal enjoyment, or in pursuit of my legitimate right to self-defense. Personal ownership of firearms has a long history in America. The current use of firearms in hunting and sport-shooting merely echoes the time when a gun over the mantel was a means of putting food on the table. Owning a gun meant that a person could protect his or her family when the state was unable to do so, a lamentable condition that persists to this day even in areas that have large, organized police agen-cies. Having a gun today still gives the individual a degree of personal autonomy—the capacity for self-defense—that is not the anachronism many pretend it to be. Unfortunately, many people with a morbid fear of firearms seek to expand the scope of their prejudices, attempting to enforce them upon others who do not share them.

This is not a new phenomenon in America. Earlier, people who disapproved of liquor consumption decided that no one should drink alcoholic beverages. This prejudice was fundamentally un-American and, in fact, caused a great deal more harm than good, giving gangsters and criminals opportunities which, without Prohibition, they would not have enjoyed. So it is with gun control in our cities today. The very thing which these laws have tried to curb—criminal opportunity—has been increased through the disarmament of ordinary, law-abiding citizens.

As with most of the lessons of history, however, this one has been, and continues to be, in large part ignored. Politicians clamor in Washington and the state legislatures, claiming to be fighting crime by foisting their anti-gun prejudices on the general public. This is dangerous in at least two respects.

First, the lessons of gun prohibition in various cities across the United States would convince the rational person that the abolition of private firearm ownership would actually increase, not mitigate, the extent of violent criminal activity in America. Criminals seek opportunity. In this respect I suppose that they are not much different from the rest of us. If we take steps to allow them greater opportunity, that is, if we legislate the right to self-defense out of existence, we should assume that crime will increase.

The other danger we encounter, in discussing the restriction of our Second Amendment rights, is that we distract the political debate from the real issue of crime. More and more, we place the blame for violence on guns, not on individuals. We neglect to punish offenders as we debate the extent to which certain hardware items ought to be regulated. And if we allow our elected officials to continue with this line of debate, in the direction that gun control advocates want it to go, we run the risk of losing a fundamental freedom that, until recently, has been held sacrosanct along with our constitutional freedoms of press, speech, religion, and so forth.

Yet, until now, there has been no concise reference work which would enable gun owners to have the facts at their fingertips to refute the gun control argument, and participate in this discussion in a meaningful way. There has been no place for the average citizen and gun owner to turn in order to arm himself or herself with the facts and speak with authority on Second Amendment issues.

Now there is. In the pages of this book, Wayne LaPierre explores and explodes the myths which gun control advocates have used to undermine our Second Amendment rights. In the pages of this book, you will find a definitive manual for taking part in the political debate, and preserving your right to keep and bear arms.

I am grateful for the good work that Wayne LaPierre has done in writing this book, and in leading the fight to preserve one of our most important American birthrights.

Tom Clancy
Calvert County, Maryland
May 31, 1994

GUNS, CRIME,

AND FREEDOM

CHAPTER 1

"THAT'S NOT WHAT THEY MEANT"

"[The NRA] should either put up or admit there is no Second Amendment guarantee . . . We are confident in our challenge because there is no confusion in the law on this issue."

R. WILLIAM IDE III, *President*
American Bar Association
April 15, 1994

"A well-regulated Militia, being necessary to the security of a free State, the right of the people to keep and bear Arms, shall not be infringed."

SECOND AMENDMENT
U.S. CONSTITUTION

A COMMON CLAIM of the anti-gun lobby is that the Founding Fathers never meant that *individuals* should be armed; they only intended for the Second Amendment to apply to a *militia*, such as the National Guard.

These self-proclaimed interpreters of the Constitution also ignore the Second Amendment's specific reference to "the right of the people." The fact that the "rights of the people" appears in the Fourth, Ninth, and Tenth Amendments as well—and that the courts have ruled repeatedly that these rights belong to individuals—matters little to them. They retreat to their standard charge that the Founding Fathers never intended for the people to have the right to keep and bear arms.

Even a casual reading of our Founding Father's works would prove these foes of the Second Amendment wrong. Volumes upon volumes of articles, pamphlets, speeches, and documents that laid the foundation for the Bill of Rights clearly define the founders' purpose, including what they intended with the Second Amendment.

In prerevolution America, the threats posed by a standing British army loomed large in the minds of the colonists. Resistance was widespread. In response to the dissent, the British increased their military presence. Two years later, in 1770, unarmed citizens were gunned down in the streets of Boston, in what became known as the Boston Massacre.

The Boston Massacre was the fuse that lit the powder keg of debate over the right of the people to be armed. Ironically enough, the colonists did in fact have the right to be armed under English common law. John Adams, then serving as a defense counsel for one of the British soldiers who participated in the shooting, acknowledged this in his opening argument:

> Here, every private person is authorized to arm himself, and on the strength of this authority, I do not deny the inhabitants had a right to arm themselves at that time, for their defense, not for offense. . . .[1]

With the courts of the time affirming the colonists' right to keep and bear arms, the British oppressors were placed between the proverbial "rock and a hard place." From that point on, quelling dissent would involve the denial of a basic right afforded all British citizens.[2]

Nonetheless, the British proceeded down a path that could

only lead to revolution. Not only did the British strengthen their military chokehold on Boston, they instituted a program of arms confiscation. Citizens could leave the city only upon "depositing their arms with their own magistrates."[3]

British confiscation of arms focused the attention of our Founding Fathers on the threats posed by a standing army quartered among the people, and the necessity of having an armed citizenry to prevent the tyranny of such an occupying force.

No doubt inspired by the Boston arms confiscations, George Mason, the subsequent co-author of the Second Amendment, wrote in his Fairfax County Militia Plan:

> ... A well-regulated Militia, composed of the Gentlemen, Free-holders, and other Freemen was necessary to protect our ancient laws and liberty from the standing army ... And we do each of us, for ourselves respectively, promise and engage to keep a good Fire-lock in proper Order & to furnish Ourselves as soon as possible with, & always keep by us, one Pound of Gunpowder, four Pounds of Lead, one Dozen Gun Flints, and a pair of Bullet Moulds, with a Cartouch Box, or powder horn, and Bag for Balls.[4]

The anti-gun lobby devotes considerable intellectual energy to the definition of "militia" as it appears in Mason's writings. Mason, however, made a very clear distinction between a "standing army," such as a guard unit, and a "militia," composed of private citizens. The anti-gunners nevertheless claim that the militia refers to a national guard, not to the citizenry at large. To eliminate any doubt, however, Mason made his point clear in other writings as, for example, when he said, "To disarm the people [is] the best and most effectual way to enslave them."[5]

Mason's sentiments were echoed by Samuel Adams who admonished the uneasy colonists that:

> ... It is always dangerous to the liberties of the people to have an army stationed among them, over which they have no

control ... The Militia is composed of free Citizens. There is therefore no Danger of their making use of their power to the destruction of their own Rights, or suffering others to invade them.[6]

In this passage, Samuel Adams further clarified Mason's thinking on the power of government in respect to the armed citizen: rights are sacred when the beneficiaries of those rights are entrusted with their safekeeping, *and have the means to do so*.

Our Founding Fathers clearly understood that, once armed, Americans would defend their freedoms to the last breath. Nowhere was this notion more evident than in Patrick Henry's "Give me liberty, or give me death" speech. The context of that oration—the importance of an armed population—has unfortunately been lost in today's "politically correct" anti-gun climate. Yet, Henry's words are there to defend the embattled Second Amendment. When speaking of revolution, Henry proclaimed:

They tell us ... that we are weak—unable to cope with so formidable an adversary. But when shall we be stronger? ... Will it be when we are totally disarmed, and when a British guard shall be stationed in every house? ... Three million people, armed in the holy cause of liberty ... are invincible by any force which our enemy can send against us.[7]

Patrick Henry not only issued this warning, he acted upon it. Following the British attempt to seize arms and ammunition in Boston, and the subsequent historic skirmish at Lexington, the British seized gunpowder at Williamsburg, Virginia. The Hanover Independent Militia, led by Patrick Henry, was unable to retake the powder, but they forced the British to pay restitution. At this point, the British denial of the colonists' right to keep and bear arms became the driving force behind the armed resistance.[8]

This fundamental right—the importance of an American's ability to defend his liberties—became the principal argument of our Founding Fathers for independence. Following the "shot heard round the world" at Lexington, Thomas Jefferson penned these words in the Virginia Constitution of 1776: ". . . No free man shall be debarred the use of arms within his own land."[9]

Nowhere are Jefferson's thoughts about the rights and powers of the citizenry more explicit than in the Declaration of Independence, which he had such a hand in writing: "Governments are instituted among Men, deriving their just powers from the consent of the governed. That whenever any form of Government becomes destructive of these ends, it is the Right of the People to alter or abolish it."

Certainly Jefferson, and his co-authors of the Declaration, preferred peaceful changes in government. But those four words—"the Right of the People"—state in plain language that the people have the right, must have the right, to take whatever measures necessary, including force, to abolish oppressive government.

Jefferson was not alone in sounding the call to arms. Henry, Adams, Washington all called upon the colonists to arm themselves. And the call was issued to *all* Americans, not only landowners and freemen. Thomas Paine, renowned for his treatise, *Common Sense*, urged religious pacifists to take up arms in his pamphlet *Thoughts on Defensive War*:

> . . . The balance of power is the scale of peace. The same balance would be preserved were all the world not destitute of arms, for all would be alike; but since some will not, others dare not lay them aside . . . Horrid mischief would ensue were one half the world deprived of the use of them . . . the weak will become a prey to the strong.[10]

In the case of the American Revolution, however, it was the strong that became the prey of the weak. Indeed, seasoned British troops were beleaguered by the armed and resolute citizens of the colonies.

Our Founding Fathers wasted no time in attributing this

victory to the right of the people to keep and bear arms. James Madison, the father of the Second Amendment, congratulated his countrymen:

> Americans [have] the right and advantage of being armed—unlike citizens of other countries whose governments are afraid to trust the people with arms.[11]

Indeed, it was President George Washington who urged the first Congress to pass an act enrolling the entire adult male citizenry in a general militia. The father of our country further urged that "A free people ought not only to be armed, but disciplined."[12]

Washington's sentiments about the militia, and who should be included in the militia in the infant United States, were echoed by George Mason in the debate on the ratification of the Constitution before the Virginia Assembly: "I ask, sir, what is the militia? It is the whole people, except for a few public officials."[13]

"Except for a few public officials." With these six words, George Mason made explicit his deep-set belief that the individual armed citizen was the key to protection against government excesses and in defense of freedom.

James Madison expanded on this point in *The Federalist Papers*, number 46, where he downplayed the threat of seizure of authority by a federal army, because such a move would be opposed by "a militia amounting to half a million men."

In 1790, since the population of the United States was about 800,000, Madison wasn't referring to state reserves. By militia, Madison obviously meant every able-bodied man capable of bearing arms. This, undoubedly, was also the meaning of "militia" when the Second Amendment was written.

Across the nation, Federalists echoed our Founding Fathers' insistence that the right to keep and bear arms become part of the Constitution. In a pamphlet advocating Pennsylvania's ratification of the Constitution, patriot and statesman Noah Webster declared:

> Before a standing army can rule, the people must be disarmed; as they are in almost every kingdom in Europe. The supreme power in America cannot enforce unjust laws by the sword, because the whole body of the people are armed, and constitute a force superior to any band of regular troops that can be, on any pretense, raised in the United States.[14]

Not only did our Founding Fathers focus their debate on the right of the people to keep and bear arms, they devoted considerable energy to issuing a warning to future generations that the battle to defend these freedoms will take precedence over all other work.

It was Patrick Henry at the Virginia convention on the ratification of the Constitution who articulated the necessity of guarding the rights of an armed citizenry.

> Guard with jealous attention the public liberty. Suspect every one who approaches that jewel. Unfortunately, nothing will preserve it but downright force. Whenever you give up that force, you are ruined.[15]

And James Madison, in the *National Gazette*, January 19, 1792:

> Liberty and order will never be perfectly safe until a trespass on the Constitutional provisions for either, shall be felt with the same keenness that resents an invasion of the dearest rights.

Unfortunately, the invasion of our dearest rights is taking place today. As this book goes to press, there are sixteen gun-ban bills before the United States Congress, and hundreds more before the state legislatures and city councils. The politicians, in the name of fighting crime, are attacking the sacred constitutional rights of law-abiding American citizens. Today, it is politically correct to ignore the Founding Fathers and their clear intent. For the sake of political expediency, the anti-gun lobby, the anti-gun media, and the anti-gun politicians, including the president, have twisted, tangled, and reinterpreted their words. The anti-gunners would do well to pay heed to the words of Benjamin Franklin:

> They that can give up essential liberty to purchase a little temporary safety, deserve neither liberty not safety.[16]

Unfortunately, a large part of this tragedy—the wanton disregard of our essential liberties—can be laid at the feet of Americans who have not taken action to protect their freedoms. To quote C.S. Lewis: "We laugh at honor and are shocked to find traitors in our midst."[17]

Every American must leap to the defense of his or her liberties. We must answer, word for word, the vicious attacks that pour out from the TV screen and newspaper pages around the country. We must attend town meetings in protest and we must hold our elected officials accountable. We must not allow them to misinterpret our Founding Fathers' directives. Then, and only then, will freedom be safe for future generations.

In the words of Dwight D. Eisenhower, "Freedom has its life in the hearts, the actions, the spirit of men and so it must be daily earned and refreshed—else like a flower cut from its life-giving roots, it will wither and die."[18]

CHAPTER 2

THE SECOND AMENDMENT

"THE RIGHT OF THE PEOPLE TO KEEP AND BEAR ARMS"

COLUMNIST DON SHOEMAKER dismisses as "idiocy" the belief that the Second Amendment prevents government from banning guns.[1]

Leonard Larsen of Scripps-Howard News Service says "only gun nut simpletons [and] NRA propagandists ... defend against gun controls on constitutional grounds."[2]

Such rhetoric, including the suggestion that the constitutional right to keep and bear arms applies only to the state militia and National Guard, is commonly heard in the media's anti-gun campaign.

Some columnists, however, are willing to concede that their views on the Second Amendment don't square with scholarship on the issue. In a column in the *Washington Post*,

March 21, 1991, George Will wrote concerning Sanford Levinson's *Yale Law Journal* article, "The Embarrassing Second Amendment":

> The National Rifle Association is perhaps correct and certainly is plausible in its "strong" reading of the Second Amendment protection of private gun ownership. Therefore gun control advocates who want to square their policy preferences with the Constitution should squarely face the need to deconstitutionalize the subject by repealing the embarrassing amendment.

Anti-gun lawyer-activist Michael Kinsley, co-host on CNN's "Crossfire" and formerly editor-in-chief of the *New Republic*, regularly calls for gun control and proudly holds membership in Handgun Control, Inc. But in an op-ed article in the *Washington Post*, January 8, 1990, Kinsley wrote:

> Unfortunately, there is the Second Amendment to the Constitution.
> The purpose of the First Amendment's free-speech guarantee was pretty clearly to protect political discourse. But liberals reject the notion that free speech is therefore limited to political topics, even broadly defined. True, that purpose is not inscribed in the amendment itself. But why leap to the conclusion that a broadly worded constitutional freedom ("the right of the people to keep and bear arms") is narrowly limited by its stated purpose, *unless you're trying to explain it away?* My *New Republic* colleague Mickey Kaus says that *if liberals interpreted the Second Amendment the way they interpret the rest of the Bill of Rights, there would be law professors arguing that gun ownership is mandatory.* [Emphasis added.]

Despite an occasional admission that the Second Amendment means what it says, many columnists, with little or no understanding of the roots of the Constitution, rush to embrace a view that finds virtually no support among high-ranking constitutional scholars.

According to an article in the *Encyclopedia of the American Constitution* summarizing Second Amendment literature in 1986, of the thirty-six law review articles published since 1980, only four support the anti-gun position, while thirty-two articles support the individual right position advocated by the National Rifle Association.[3]

The individual rights authors include leading constitutional scholars who don't own guns and who "never expected or desired the evidence to crush the anti-gun position."[4] (Citations for all the articles appear in the Appendix.)

Professor Sanford Levinson of the University of Texas Law School, co-author of the standard law school text on the Constitution, *Processes of Constitutional Decision Making*, is a ACLU stalwart. In his 1989 *Yale Law Journal* article, cited by George Will, Professor Levinson admits his own embarrassment at having to conclude from his research that private gun ownership *cannot* be prohibited—he must have hoped to find the opposite.

Like Levinson, Yale Law Professor Akhil Amar, a visiting professor of constitutional law at Columbia University, is held in high repute by liberal constitutional scholars. Yet Amar trounces the anti-gun states' right theory, emphasizing again and again that the Second Amendment guarantees the right to arms to "the people," not "the states":

> [W]hen the Constitution means "states" it says so ... The ultimate right to keep and bear arms belongs to "the people," not the "states." ... Thus the "people" at the core of the Second Amendment [a]re [the] Citizens—the same "We the People" who "ordain and establish" the Constitution and whose right to assemble ... [is] at the core of the First Amendment. ... Nowadays, it is quite common to speak loosely of the National Guard as "the state militia," but [when the Second Amendment was written] ... "the militia" referred to all Citizens capable of bearing arms. [Thus] "the militia" is identical to "the people" ...[5]

Are these eminent constitutional scholars "gun nut simpletons, [and] NRA propagandists"? Activist Michael Kinsley doesn't think so.

After reviewing a *Michigan Law Review* article by Professor Don Kates, Kinsley wrote in an op-ed piece, February 8, 1990, in the *Washington Post:*

> If there is a reply, the [gun] controllers haven't made it . . . Establishing that a flat ban on handguns would be [unconstitutional,] Kates builds a *distressingly* good case.

Kinsley is distressed because "a flat ban on handguns," preferably all guns, is precisely what he wants. His article concludes:

> Gun nuts are unconvincing (at least to me) in their attempts to argue that the individual right to bear arms is still as vital to freedom as it was in 1792. *But the right is still there.* [Emphasis added.]

Two major contributors to constitutional scholarship are neutral historians with no personal interest in the "gun control" debate. One is Professor Joyce Malcolm, a political historian whose work on the English and American origins of the right to arms has been underwritten by the American Bar Foundation, Harvard Law School, and the National Endowment for the Humanities. In *To Keep and Bear Arms: The Origins of an Anglo-American Right* (Harvard University Press, 1994), Professor Malcolm writes:

> The Second Amendment was meant to accomplish two distinct goals. . . . First, it was meant *to guarantee the individual's right to have arms for self-defense and self-preservation . . . These privately owned arms* [emphasis added] were meant to serve a larger purpose [militia service] as well . . . and it is the coupling of these two objectives that has caused the most confusion. The customary American militia necessitated an armed

public ... the militia [being] ... the body of the people ... The argument that today's National Guardsmen, members of a select militia, would constitute the *only* [emphasis hers] persons entitled to keep and bear arms has no historical foundation.

Professor Robert Shalhope, a non-gun-owning intellectual historian, whose interest is the philosophy of the Founding Fathers, agrees. In the 1982 edition of the *Journal of American History*,[6] Professor Shalhope writes:

When James Madison and his colleagues drafted the Bill of Rights they ... firmly believed in two distinct principles: (1) *Individuals had the right to possess arms to defend themselves and their property*; and (2) states retained the right to maintain militias *composed of these individually armed citizens* ... Clearly, these men believed that the perpetuation of a republican spirit and character in their society depended upon *the freeman's possession of arms* as well as his ability and willingness to defend *both himself and his society*. [Emphasis added.]

As Professor Kates put it, "Historical research shows that our Founding Fathers out NRAed the NRA."[7]

Thomas Paine believed it would be better for "all the world to lay [arms] aside ... and settle matters by negotiation"— "but unless the whole will, the matter ends, and I take up my musket and thank Heaven He has put it in my power."[8]

Paine clearly doubted that criminals could be disarmed and deemed it important that decent people be armed against them:

The peaceable part of mankind will be continually overrun by the vile and abandoned while they neglect the means of self-defense.... [Weakness] allures the ruffian [but] arms like laws discourage and keep the invader and plunderer in awe and preserve order in the world. . . . Horrid mischief would ensue were [the good] deprived of the use of them . . . [and] the weak will become a prey to the strong.[9]

Or, simply stated—criminals prefer unarmed victims. Consider the similar views of the great eighteenth-century Italian criminologist Cesare Beccaria, which could be described as an older rendition of today's slogan "when guns are outlawed only outlaws will have guns."

Thomas Jefferson translated the following from Beccaria's Italian and laboriously copied it in longhand into his own personal compilation of great quotations:

False is the idea of utility that sacrifices a thousand real advantages for one imaginary or trifling inconvenience; that would take fire from men because it burns, and water because one may drown in it; that has no remedy for evils, except destruction. The laws that forbid the carrying of arms are laws of such a nature. They disarm those only who are neither inclined nor determined to commit crimes. Can it be supposed that those who have the courage to violate the most sacred laws of humanity, the most important of the code, will respect the less important and arbitrary ones, which can be violated with ease and impunity, and which, if strictly obeyed, would put an end to personal liberty—so dear to men, so dear to the enlightened legislator—and subject innocent persons to all the vexations that the quality alone ought to suffer? Such laws make things worse for the assaulted and better for the assailants; they serve rather to encourage than to prevent homicides, for an unarmed man may be attacked with greater confidence than an armed man. They ought to be designated as laws not preventive but fearful of crimes, produced by the tumultuous impression of a few isolated facts, and not by thoughtful consideration of the inconveniences and advantages of a universal decree.[10]

The Founders unanimously agreed. "The great object," thundered Anti-Federalist Patrick Henry, "is that every man be armed."[11] James Madison, Federalist author of the Bill of Rights, reviled tyrants for being "afraid to trust the people with arms" and extolled "the advantage of being armed, which the Americans possess over the people of almost every other nation."[12]

The Anti-Federalists endorsed Madison's Bill of Rights while claiming it was their own idea. They characterized the Second Amendment as a mere rewording of their Sam Adams' proposal "that the [federal] Constitution be never construed to prevent the people who are peaceable citizens from keeping *their own* arms."[13] The Federalist analysis said the amendment confirmed to the people "their *private* arms."[14]

LIMITATIONS ON THE RIGHT TO ARMS

Are there any limits on either the kinds of arms the Second Amendment guarantees or the kinds of people it protects?

Neither felons nor children under eighteen, of course, have the right to own arms—any more than they have the right to vote. This restriction is based on solid historical reasons. The National Rifle Association, moreover, has for over seventy years supported laws to prohibit gun ownership by those who have been convicted of violent felonies.

By the same token, the NRA has for decades supported and helped pass tough penalties to keep those who misuse guns in prison where they belong. The NRA was among the earliest and strongest proponents of "Three Strikes and You're Out" laws which would put repeat violent offenders in jail *permanently*.

Yet the anti-individual rights crowd accuse the NRA of claiming the Second Amendment guarantees guns for all—including criminals—and all weapons—including weapons of war like bazookas and bombs. Such has never been the case, and there is no reason for anyone to believe otherwise—the facts have been available to all. Prominent constitutional scholar Professor Stephen Halbrook has summed it up:

"[A]rtillery pieces, tanks, nuclear devices and other heavy or-dinances," he said, "are not constitutionally protected" arms which civilians have a Second Amendment right to possess; neither are "grenades, bombs, bazookas and other devices . . . which have never been commonly possessed for self-defense. . . ."[15]

But the right to arms *does* protect ordinary small arms—handguns, rifles, and shotguns—including "assault weapons." Indeed, "assault weapons" are just ordinary semi-automatic firearms like those that have existed in this coun-try for over a century. They fire no faster than revolvers or pump action rifles and shotguns. As Rutgers law professor Robert Cottrol notes:

> It has been argued that "assault weapons" are far more deadly than 18th Century arms. Actually, modern medical technology makes them far less deadly than blunderbusses were in the 18th Century. (In fact, "assault weapons" are less deadly—and far less often used in crime—than ordinary shotguns or hunting rifles.)[16]

Professors Cottrol and Don Kates agree that if the many changes in conditions since 1792 when the Second Amend-ment was enacted could justify ignoring it, other rights pro-tected by the Bill of Rights would also be endangered: *"changing times affect many constitutional rights, not just the right to arms."*[17]

Take, for instance, radio, TV, and the movies. These didn't exist when the Bill of Rights was written, yet all three are now embraced by its free speech and press clauses. The Supreme Court enforces that stand. The media's First Amendment rights are soundly defended even though it is widely accepted that they may exert far more influence than a book or newspaper—even prompting some suggestible people to com-mit violent acts.

By the same token, sensationalized national network cover-age can spread new crimes. Car-jacking, first confined to

Michigan, caught on nationwide as other criminals picked up on the idea. Freedom of the press in our modern era has many other drawbacks, but we continue to expand our constitutional free press protections to cover new forms of disseminating news and opinion.

To quote Professors Cottrol and Kates:

> If the Bill of Rights is to continue, we must apply its spirit even as conditions change. That is the nub of the Second Amendment controversy: Modern intellectuals who tend to feel self-defense is barbaric—that government should have a monopoly of arms with the people being dependent on it for protection—have difficulty accepting the Founders' diametrically opposite views.[18]

The Warren Court had this to say when its decisions vindicating the privilege against self-incrimination were assailed as inconsistent with the government's need to detect modern criminals and subversives:

> If it be thought that the privilege is outmoded in the conditions of this modern age, then the thing to do is to [amend] it out of the Constitution, not to whittle it down by the subtle encroachments of judicial opinion. [*Ulmann v. United States*, 350 U.S. 422, 427–8 (1956)]

CAN AN ARMED PEOPLE RESIST TYRANNY?

Those who claim that the *only* purpose of the right to arms is to enable citizens to resist a military takeover of our government sometimes argue that the Second Amendment is obsolete since a populace armed with only small arms cannot defeat a modern army. That is doubly wrong. Even if overthrowing tyranny were the amendment's only purpose, the claim that an armed populace cannot successfully resist assault stems from an unproved theory.

The twentieth century provides *no example* of a determined

populace with access to small arms having been defeated by a modern army. The Russians lost in Afghanistan, the United States lost in Vietnam, and the French lost in Indo-China. In each case, it was the poorly armed populace that beat the "modern" army. In China, Cuba, and Nicaragua, the established leaders, Chiang Kai-shek, Battista, and Somoza lost. Modern nations like Algeria, Angola, Ireland, Israel, Mozambique, and Zimbabwe only exist because guerrilla warfare can triumph over modern armies. While we may not approve of all the resulting governments, each of these triumphs tells a simple truth: a determined people who have the means to maintain prolonged war against a modern army can battle it to a standstill, subverting major portions of the army or defeating it themselves or with major arms supplied by outside forces.

The Founders' purpose in guaranteeing the right to keep and bear arms was not merely to overthrow tyrants. They saw the right to arms as crucial to what they believed was a prime natural right—self-defense.

Those who claim that the right to arms is outmoded tend to think of armed personal self-defense as does former Attorney General Ramsey Clark, who described it as "anarchy, not order under law—a jungle where each relies on himself for survival."[19]

Handgun Control, Inc. (HCI) chairperson Sarah Brady claims that "the only reason for guns in civilian hands is for sporting purposes," i.e., not self-defense. "Pete" Shields, Brady's predecessor as HCI head, in the book titled *Guns Don't Die*, advised victims *never* to resist rape or robbery: "give them what they want or run."[20]

Not surprisingly, HCI has proposed a national licensing law confining gun ownership to sportsmen—self-defense not being considered proper grounds for ownership. In an October 22, 1993, editorial, the *Los Angeles Times* agreed.

But author Jeff Snyder points out in his essay, "A Nation of Cowards," in *Public Interest* quarterly/Fall 1993:

As the Founding Fathers knew well, a government that does not trust its honest, law-abiding, taxpaying citizens with the means of self-defense is not itself worthy of trust. Laws disarming honest citizens proclaim that the government is the master, not the servant of the people . . .

The Bill of Rights does not *grant* rights to the people, such that its repeal would legitimately confer upon government the powers otherwise proscribed. The Bill of Rights is the list of the fundamental, inalienable rights, endowed in man by his Creator, that define what it means to be a free and independent people, the rights which must exist to ensure that government governs only with the consent of the people.

CHAPTER 3

SELF-DEFENSE

THE RIGHT AND THE DETERRENT

DURING THE EMOTIONAL firestorm surrounding the 1993 murders in Florida of a German tourist near the airport in Miami and a British tourist in the rest area on I–10 near Tallahassee, TV "news magazine" programs visited juvenile detention facilities in south Florida to find out why violent juvenile predators were targeting foreign tourists.

Part of the answers were predictable, but the principal reason stunned the media and gun control proponents.

With total candor, the jailed juveniles said *they knew that tourists didn't have guns*. Since Florida allows law-abiding people to carry guns, these young criminals were afraid to attack residents. Tourists are considered easy marks; they not only have cash and expensive video and camera equipment, they are unarmed and defenseless.

Most shocking, these juveniles offenders had committed to

memory—and actually recited on camera—the airline arrival schedules of flights from abroad. Their procedure is to wait near the airport and follow the tourists as they come out of the airport.

From the mouths of these young criminals came the strongest reason for allowing law-abiding people to carry firearms—protection. These juveniles may be criminals but they're not stupid—they don't want to be shot and so they avoid people who may be armed and might defend themselves.

Many have characterized criminals as fearless, but, in fact, they do fear being killed or injured by armed citizens.

Self-defense works—criminals fear armed citizens. Self-defense, the most basic of all human reactions, is triggered by the threat or fear of harm. The survival instinct is not exclusive to law-abiding people, it is just as basic to criminals.

As many as 2.45 million crimes are thwarted each year in the United States by average citizens using firearms, and in most cases the potential victim never has to fire a shot, according to a survey conducted early in 1993 by nationally recognized Florida State University criminologist Gary Kleck.[1]

The findings of Kleck's National Self-Defense Survey are consistent with a dozen previous studies which generally show that the use of guns for defensive purposes is relatively common, as well as effective. Crimes are frustrated because criminals flee when confronted with a firearm.

Kleck's study went beyond previous studies by excluding situations where respondents used a gun to investigate some suspicious noise or occurrence which turned out to be harmless. He included only defensive uses of a gun, such as when there was an actual confrontation between the intended victim and an offender.

Consider, for a moment, what the carnage on our streets and in our homes might be like if law-abiding citizens were not allowed to exercise their right to self-defense with firearms. There could potentially be as many as 2.5 million *more* crimes each year listed in the national crime data banks with an additional incalculable cost in loss of property, health, and life.

An analysis of a U.S. Justice Department victimization study found that in the categories of robbery and assault, "victims who used guns for protection were less likely either to be attacked or injured than victims who responded in any other way, including those who did not resist at all," and "victims who resisted robbers with guns . . . were less likely to lose their property. . . . When victims use guns to resist crimes, the crimes usually are disrupted and the victims are not injured."[2]

Self-defense is generally viewed today as it was in 1765 when Sir William Blackstone's *Commentaries* was first published in England. Blackstone described the use of arms for self-defense as among the "Absolute Rights of Individuals."

Blackstone's *Commentaries* is the basis of the American legal system and as such is used by the U.S. Supreme Court in its decisions involving common law and in its understanding of the roots of our constitutional rights.

But despite Blackstone's authorization of our rights to self-defense and the overwhelming proof of the deterrence of firearms, many people who exercise their right and deter violent crimes against themselves are ironically victimized and persecuted by law enforcement, the criminal justice system, or other branches of the government.

Take the case of twenty-two-year-old Rayna Ross. Ms. Ross is the Marine lance corporal who shot and killed her bayonet-wielding ex-boyfriend, Corporal Anthony Goree—also a Marine—in June of 1993. Goree had broken into her apartment at least twice before, and after further beatings, stalking, and threats, Ms. Ross finally went to military authorities and pressed charges.

The Marine Corps did little to protect Ms. Ross. They confined Goree to the brig for six days, put him on base restriction, and ordered him to stay away from Ross. Almost immediately after being released from the brig, he disobeyed orders and left the base.

The Marine Corps and civilian police couldn't find Goree,

but he found Rayna Ross. Wielding a bayonet, he broke into her apartment at 3:00 A.M. and entered her bedroom, where she was sleeping with her infant daughter. Forced to defend herself and her baby, she shot and killed him with a handgun she had purchased three days before.

Remember, Ms. Ross purchased the gun only after repeated failures by the Marine Corps and civilian police to protect her.

Police ruled the act a justifiable homicide and filed no charges, but months later, to the outrage of many, the Marine Corps charged Ms. Ross with first degree murder. Forced to defend herself from the government, in this case the military, she faced a possible court-martial and life in prison.

The *Washington Times* wrote on February 22, 1994, "Why the military is weighing a murder case against her now is unclear. . . . It is also not clear why feminists haven't rallied to her cause the way they did for Lorena Bobbitt [who cut off her husband's penis]. In some respects, Ms. Ross is the dream of the politically correct: She is a black woman, a single mother and wittingly or unwittingly, a symbol of 'progress' in a putatively reactionary, hidebound (and so on) military. And no doubt that would have made a fine epitaph, except that Ms. Ross wasn't much interested in dying."

It was the National Rifle Association that came forward with legal assistance and funds to defend Ms. Ross, and stood by her until the Marine Corps finally dropped all charges against her.

But why was it all necessary? What has gone so terribly wrong with the government? Has the arrogance of power so corrupted the system that government, including the military, targets victims of crime rather than the perpetrators of crime?

There are currently no laws that prohibit self-defense, but the gun control and gun ban zealots are clearly moving in that direction. Some courts have ruled that victims have "a duty to retreat" rather than stand their ground in their own homes and defend themselves. These absurd rulings defy logic and fly in the face of the Constitution.

No would-be victim should be required to surrender his or her dignity, safety, property, or life to a criminal; no person should be required to retreat in the face of attack.

Counterattack—self-defense—has proved to be a more effective deterrent to crime than any of the laws on the books. Criminals don't fear the law—but they do fear armed citizens.

Research gathered by Professors James Wright and Peter Rossi, co-authors of "The Armed Criminal in America" in 1985, a National Institute of Justice three-year study of criminal acquisition and use of firearms in America, points to the armed citizen or threats from the armed citizen as perhaps the most effective crime deterrent in the nation.

Wright and Rossi questioned over 1,800 prisoners serving time in prisons across the nation. They found:

- 81 percent agreed that the "smart criminal" will attempt to find out if a potential victim is armed
- 74 percent felt that burglars avoided occupied dwellings for fear of being shot
- 57 percent felt that the typical criminal feared being shot by citizens more than he feared being shot by police
- 57 percent of "handgun predators" had encountered armed citizens
- 39 percent did not commit a specific crime for fear that the victim was armed
- 69 percent of "handgun predators" personally knew other criminals who were scared off or shot at by armed victims.

One glaring statistic: burglars who choose, either unintentionally or otherwise, to enter an occupied home are twice as likely to be shot or killed as they are to be caught, convicted, and imprisoned by America's criminal justice system.

While Rayna Ross actually had to shoot her gun to save her life, Sonya Dowdy did not, but both are alive today because each had a firearm and exercised the right of self-defense when attacked by a violent criminal.

Sonya Dowdy's father was deeply concerned for his daughter's safety and gave her a handgun that he had purchased on the day she was attacked. It saved her life only fifteen minutes after he had given it to her. When Ms. Dowdy went to the post office to pick up her mail, she was followed back to her car by an armed drifter who had raped a twelve-year-old girl that same day. The man told her he wouldn't hurt her but lunged toward her before she could close her car door. He stuck a .25 caliber pistol in her face and said, "I'm going to kill you, bitch!"

When he attempted to get into the back seat of the car, she pulled her gun, cocked the hammer, and said, "No, I'm going to kill you." He threw down his gun and ran. He was captured by the police four hours later.

The right of self-defense and the right to use firearms for defense of self and family are the cornerstone of individual rights enumerated in the U.S. Constitution. If the gun licensers and gun banners succeed in subverting and eroding that cornerstone—the most basic of natural rights—then surely all other individual rights will fall. The freedom of all Americans is in jeopardy.

Nationally syndicated columnist Charley Reese, in his column appearing in the *Orlando Sentinel* March 31, 1994, put it succinctly:

It is both illogical and inconsistent for a government to say people have a right to life and a right to self-defense but no right to own the tools necessary to defend their lives.

It is illogical for a government that says its police have no obligation to provide individual protection to deny people the means to protect themselves.

It is immoral for a government that repeatedly releases predators to prey on people to tell those victims they cannot have a weapon for self-defense.

It's stupid for a government that can't control criminals, drugs or illegal immigrants to claim it can take guns away from criminals only if honest folks will give up theirs.

Gun-control proposals are also an insult. Gun control by definition affects only honest people. When a politician tells you he wants to forbid you from owning a firearm or force you to get a license, he is telling you he doesn't trust you. That's an insult.

The government trusted me with a M–48 tank and assorted small arms when it claimed to have need of my services. It trusts common Americans with all kinds of arms when it wants them to go kill foreigners somewhere—usually for the financial benefit of some corporations.

But when the men and women take off their uniforms and return to their homes and assume responsibility for their own and their families' safety, suddenly the politicians don't trust them to own a gun. This is pure elitism. Elitists think we common folk are stupid or mad and that if we have a firearm, we are going to shoot the checkout girl at the supermarket when she makes a mistake on the register. Or, knowing what they intend for our future, maybe they fear we would shoot them.

The fact that gun control is an elitist effort at people control is easily verifiable. Go to New York or any big city and see who gets the gun permits. The small shopkeeper or the retail clerk actually exposed to crime? NO, the elite, like William F. Buckley and the publisher of *The New York Times*.

Gun control is not about guns or crime. It is about an elite that fears and despises the common people. . . .

More than ever before, politicians are clamoring to restrict Americans' constitutional right to own guns and the right of self-defense. Yet we, individually as armed citizens, are the best deterrent to violent criminal attack. We, collectively as an armed law-abiding populace, are the best protection against the taking-over of America by criminals, or, should it come to that, the tyranny of government.

[Self-defense is] justly called the primary law of nature, so it is not, neither can it be in fact, taken away by the laws of society.
—Sir William Blackstone

CHAPTER 4

CARRYING CONCEALED FIREARMS

WHO WILL PROTECT THE PEOPLE?

IN DECEMBER 1991, Thomas Terry was in a Shoney's restaurant in Anniston, Alabama, when three armed robbers entered the restaurant.

As the gunmen were herding the nearly two dozen restaurant patrons and employees into a walk-in freezer, Terry hid from the armed bandits. Attempting to escape the building to summon police by opening a locked door, he triggered an audible alarm. Alerted to his presence, one gunman ran out of the restaurant and the remaining two went after Terry who was legally carrying a .45 caliber handgun tucked under his sweater in the small of his back.

In the ensuing battle, Terry sustained a graze-wound to his

hip but killed one gunman and severely wounded the other. None of the patrons or employees was injured.

Terry was licensed to carry a concealed firearm.

Alabama has a concealed carry law that allows its citizens to carry concealed firearms for protection.

On October 16, 1991, Suzanna Gratia, a thirty-two-year-old chiropractor, was having lunch with her mother and father at a Luby's cafeteria in Killeen, Texas. Suddenly, George Hennard drove his truck through the front window of Luby's and began randomly shooting customers. Gratia was unarmed. Her gun was outside in her car.

Gratia and her parents turned their table over hoping it would shield them from Hennard's deadly assault. But Hennard shot Gratia's father, then shot her mother as she held his head in her arms, while Gratia crouched helplessly, unable to protect her parents or herself.

The gunman shot and killed twenty-two helpless, innocent people that day before turning the gun on himself.

Up until several months before Hennard's deadly rampage, Gratia had carried a handgun in her purse for protection. But fearing she would lose her professional chiropractic license if she were caught carrying a gun, Gratia had left her handgun in her car.

Texas *does not* allow its citizens to carry concealed firearms for self-protection.

No one will ever know if Suzanna Gratia could have stopped George Hennard's senseless slaughter of her mother and father and the other twenty innocent people in Luby's cafeteria that day—but we do know that Texas lawmakers never gave her a chance.

For years, the citizens of Texas had fought to reform the Texas carry law, but top brass law enforcement administrators had bullied the legislature into reserving the right to carry firearms—to protect themselves—to law enforcement officials only. Gratia would later testify before the Texas House Public Safety Committee: "I am not saying I could have stopped this guy, but I would have had a chance. The fact is, you can't go up against an armed man unless you're armed. Someone legislated me out of the right to protect myself and my loved ones."[1]

Compare the two cases of terrorism in restaurants in two different states. Surely, every American would prefer the outcome in Alabama, a state where legislators and law enforcement officials trust law-abiding citizens to carry concealed firearms to protect themselves and their families.

Anti-gun forces say that the job of protecting the people rightfully belongs to the police. But we all know that simply is not true or possible. The courts around the nation, including the U.S. Supreme Court, have repeatedly and consistently ruled that police have *no duty* to protect individuals—their duty is only to the community at large.

On December 1981, for example, a federal appeals court in Washington, D.C., ruled that police have a duty only to the "public at large and not to individual members of the community." And further, that "a government and its agents are under no general duty to provide public services, such as police protection, to any particular individual citizen" (*Warren v. District of Columbia* (D.C. App. 1981). This ruling stemmed from a case in which police were called by two women because two intruders were attacking a third woman living in the same house. The dispatcher promised that police were on the way, but nothing eventuated. All three women were subsequently abducted at knife point and repeatedly raped and beaten for fourteen hours. The "no duty to protect individuals" rulings go back as far as 1856 in a U.S. Supreme Court ruling in *South v. Maryland* and as recently as 1993 in *Rogers v. City of Port Huron* (*Michigan*).

Where were the Texas police when Suzanna Gratia, her parents, and twenty other innocent unarmed people needed them?

The basic and fundamental right of self-defense is rarely disputed. But the right to carry a firearm has been a bone of contention.

Refusal by legislators and law enforcement officials to trust their law-abiding citizens with guns is not new or exclusive to Texas. Colorado has a history of the same type of elitism. Colorado's top brass law enforcement administrators have consistently tried to drive a wedge between citizens and law-makers on this issue. But this "listen to us because we're the police" attitude doesn't wash in mainstream America. In a Gallup survey published by the U.S. Department of Justice, citizens were asked, "How much confidence do you have in the ability of the police to protect you from violent crime?" Only 17 percent of the Americans polled responded "a great deal," while 46 percent responded "not very much."[2]

In many states, legislators have been told that a vote *for* carrying a concealed firearm is a vote *against* law enforcement. Why? And what of these other questions:

- Why would law enforcement officials position themselves against the people they are supposed to serve?
- Why are they afraid of law-abiding people carrying firearms to protect themselves and their families?
- Why do they try to wedge themselves between legislators and the people they were elected to represent?
- Why do law enforcement administrators lobby against the needs, the rights, and the protection of the people?

This is not a law enforcement issue; this is a fundamental human rights issue. Law-abiding people carrying firearms have never been a threat to law enforcement; and there is overwhelming evidence to support the positive results of carrying concealed firearms.

In March 1994, Colorado's law enforcement administrators distributed a document, rife with emotion and bare of facts, opposing "concealed carry" in that state. In the document they asked, "If carrying concealed weapons is such a great crime fighting strategy, then why is all of Colorado's law enforcement opposed?" A good question—*with no convincing answer*.

Law enforcement's opposition to concealed carry has never been defended with logic, common sense, or fact. It is political, ideological, and elitist. And it lays bare a basic distrust of the law-abiding people they are sworn to serve—and a contempt for the basic and fundamental right of every citizen to self-defense.

Other than a bodyguard or a law enforcement officer at one's side twenty-four hours a day, the most effective deterrent to criminal attack is the criminal's fear that the prospective victim is armed and prepared to defend himself or herself.

Florida crime data, presented by Colorado law enforcement administrators, were deliberately skewed and selectively used in an effort to distort perception. By excerpting and isolating statistics, they attempted to establish that the law had caused a new increase in crime in Florida. But although they said that Florida's violent crime had risen 17.8 percent between 1987 and 1992, they failed to report that Florida's increase was considerably below the national average, which was 24 percent for the same time period. They also failed to report that Florida's comparison rate in 1992 was 59 percent above the national average, a decrease from the 1980 comparison of 69 percent. The Florida Department of Law Enforcement's *Crime in Florida, Annual Report*,[3] reveals the truth:

- Florida's *homicide* rate dropped from 37 percent above the national average to 3 percent below the national average after the state changed its concealed carry law in 1987.
- In 1987, Florida's murder rate was 11.4 per 100,000 compared with a national rate of 8.2. By 1992 the national rate had risen to 9.3 per 100,000 while Florida's had dropped to 9, and in 1993, it continued to drop another .3 to 8.7 per 100,000.
- Between 1987 and 1992, *rape* increased nationally by 14.4 percent. But in Florida it only increased 2.9 percent and in 1993 rape in Florida *decreased* .2 percent.
- Florida's *property* crime is also falling. In 1992, property crimes were 4.7 percent below their 1980 level and the rate fell each year between 1989 and 1992 (7.4 percent over that period).
- Florida's overall crime rate in 1993 dropped 1 percent.

During the fight for passage of Florida's landmark licensing reform legislation, there was a steady drumbeat in the media about the new Dodge City, frontier-style justice, the O.K. Corral for guns, a Wild West mentality, blood on the hands of those who vote for passage, and on and on—mostly from a few isolated law enforcement administrators. Yet the media focused on those few as though they represented the whole universe of law enforcement. Quite the opposite was true, but law enforcement officers who supported concealed carry were virtually ignored.

The sort of material the media produced, like this editorial in the *Sun Tattler,* was long on creativity and short on facts:

> [A] state law that welcomes virtually everyone to pack a rod would increase lawlessness—and death. Forget that a pistol-packing citizenry will mean itchier trigger fingers ... Forget that South Florida's climate of smoldering fear would flash like napalm when every stranger totes a piece, and every mental snap in traffic could lead to the crack of gunfire.[4]

On March 14, 1982, the *Miami Herald* reported that North Miami Police Chief Thomas O'Connor had sent a telegram to the governor "warning that he would take appropriate steps to protect his officers if the [concealed carry] bill becomes law: He would arm his men with machine guns."

Such hysterical rhetoric was as disturbing to rank-and-file police as it was to citizens and legislators.

Finally, in order to set the record straight on Florida's pending concealed carry bill, its sponsors called a press conference with law enforcement representatives from the Florida Sheriff's Association, Florida Police Benevolent Association, Florida Department of Law Enforcement, Florida Fraternal Order of Police, and Florida Police Chief's Association. All joined NRA and Unified Sportsmen of Florida in ratifying the reform bill, which was passed and quickly signed into law by a new governor.

The legislation went into effect on October 1, 1987, and the blood and gore predictions were soon disproved. Florida's carry law required statistical tracking and reporting as the state was prepared to set the example—good or bad, success or failure of such law—based on facts.

A few opponents of the legislation, like the chief of the Dade County Department of Public Safety, were not satisfied. Following passage of the law, he directed that all police interactions with license holders be monitored. For two-and-a-half years, law enforcement officers were required to fill out a form every time a person they came in contact with—as either a victim or a suspect in any crime, including traffic violations— had a concealed firearms license.

During that time, eighteen thousand permit holders were tracked. Three involved gun-related crimes and ten involved instances where license holders successfully used their guns to fend off criminal attackers. *There was not one single case in which a license holder had his gun taken away by a criminal, shot someone by accident, or was killed defending himself or herself.*

If an increase in the number of those legally carrying firearms was going to have an adverse effect anywhere, it would have been Dade County, with the highest violent crime rate of any county in Florida. But it didn't happen there, or anywhere else in the state.

A Dade County resident, among the first to apply for a carry license, was also the first to exercise his right of self-protection. A few short months after receiving his license, Miami police reported that on March 5, 1988, a thirty-three-year-old Miami cab driver was attacked and forced to defend himself. He shot and killed a robber who had pointed a firearm at him, had demanded and received money, and then had told the cab driver he was going to kill him.

The robber, a twenty-nine-year-old ex-convict, tried to fire a Smith & Wesson 9mm semi-automatic handgun at the cabby at point blank range. But he had forgotten to disengage the safety. In the few split seconds during which the robber was distracted, the cab driver pulled and fired his own gun—a Colt .45 caliber semi-automatic handgun—killing his attacker.

The ex-convict's past included an arrest for armed robbery, gun violations, and attempted first degree murder of a police officer. In 1981, he shot out the windshield of a Hialeah patrol car, causing it to crash. He also shot at Miami Springs police during a chase. He was sentenced to twelve years in prison, but seven years later he was back on the street pulling the trigger on the law-abiding cab driver.

The criminal justice system failed to protect the cabby, but Florida's new concealed weapons licensing law made it possible for him to protect himself, his very life. As reported in the *Miami Herald*, March 6, 1988, following the incident, the cab driver "used the weapon correctly to defend himself. Without the law in effect, he would be a dead man this morning." The Miami police sergeant on the scene told reporters that the incident "sends a message to the rest of the robbers out there."

Florida issued 204,108 licenses during the first six-and-a-half years that the law was in effect. Only seventeen licenses have been revoked for unlawful conduct that involved possession of a firearm—that is .008 percent (eight thousandths of 1 percent). If every law ever passed had that kind of success rate, we would have virtually no crime.

Three typical cases of licenses being revoked occurred in Miami. One involved a license holder who was arrested for drunk driving and had his gun impounded. Another was an inadvertent technical violation—a woman forgot she had her gun in her purse and carried it into an airport. And the third was an intentional technical violation—a man was arrested trying to bring his gun into a court building.

A year after the law took effect, the executive director of the Florida Police Chiefs Association told the press, as reported in the *Palm Beach Post*, July 26, 1988, "The minute the bill was passed, we asked our chiefs in the state to be particularly alert for any cases in their jurisdiction that would give us knowledge of the fact that there was some abuse. At this point, it would appear the law is working very well. There are no horror stories that can be attributed to the passage of the law."

The general counsel for the Florida Sheriff's Association

agreed, said the *Post*. "I haven't seen where we have had any instance of persons with permits causing violent crimes, and I'm constantly on the lookout," he said.[5]

Even Robert Creighton, agent in charge of the U.S. Bureau of Alcohol, Tobacco and Firearms (BATF) in Florida, acknowledged that the popular concealed weapons permits aren't a factor in crime, adding, "The criminal element has no permits."[6]

Three years after the concealed carry reforms in Florida were implemented, critics were forced to recant their dire predictions. They were forced to abandon their parades of horribles. In November 1990, the press revisited the issue in an interview with state Representative Ron Silver. Silver, an ardent supporter of Handgun Control, Inc., and the organization's chairwoman Sarah Brady, told the press, as reported in the Associated Press, November 4, 1990: "There are lots of people, including myself, who thought things would be a lot worse as far as that particular situation [people being licensed to carry firearms for protection] is concerned. I'm happy to say they're not."

Silver also said, the AP story added, that Florida had a long way to go to rid itself of its "Wild West" reputation and the "GUNshine state" label that he and HCI had helped create with their emotional predictions of misuse and abuse of firearms. He added, "All of us are trying to do away with that image. . . ."

Almost seven years after implementation of the gun law, Silver, by then a state senator, was asked, this time on a national TV news program (CBN 4/1/94), about his original opposition to passage of the law, and he responded: "I am pleasantly surprised to find that I think it's working pretty well. . . . We have found very few instances whereby [license holders] have actually gone out and committed a crime afterwards." (Seventeen out of 204,000 in almost seven years.)

On the same TV program, John Russi, director of the licensing program under the Florida Department of State, told viewers that "people obtain [licenses] for legitimate purposes and they are not the people committing crimes. People who commit crimes are crooks and are not going to obtain a concealed weapons license."

Florida's success should come as no surprise. A study conducted by Don B. Kates, Jr., at the St. Louis University School of Law[7] found that armed citizens were very responsible about carrying handguns on the street. The study reported that while police were successful in shooting or driving off criminals 68 percent of the time, private citizens succeeded 83 percent of the time. Most importantly, while 11 percent of the individuals involved in police shootings were later found to be innocents misidentified as criminals, only 2 percent of those in civilian shootings were so misidentified. Since private citizens in urban areas encounter and kill up to three times as many criminals as do law enforcement authorities, the track record of the private citizen is very impressive. And Florida's experience proves it once again.

Oregon has also experienced unqualified success with its concealed carry law. Over sixty thousand licenses have been issued—none has been revoked. Simply put, concealed carry is a right and a necessity that in no way diminishes the importance or challenges the competence of police.

Nor does competent research in other areas support the predictions of the anti-gun forces—that allowing law-abiding citizens fair protection against the criminal element in society increases violence. A government-funded survey of 1,874 felons by respected criminologists Peter Rossi and James Wright, designed to determine the "experiences" of convicted felons with firearms and their "perceptions" of gun laws, found that about 40 percent of the felons sampled said they decided not to commit a crime because they feared the victim was carrying a firearm. Thirty-four percent had been "scared off, shot at, wounded or captured by an armed victim."

Given the preponderant evidence, how is it that a handful of anti-gun groups continues to influence legislation and regulations that abridge the rights of the people to defend themselves?

The answers are rooted in the media, which spotlight sensational cases that will aid the cause to ban firearms. For example, in the case in which George Hennard savagely murdered Suzanna Gratia's parents and twenty other law-abiding citizens, the media made firearms the scapegoat. Why did the media not blame George Hennard? Why the failure to come to grips with the stark reality that there are mean, vicious, and violent people in our society who roam about freely threatening innocent people?

If Suzanna Gratia had carried her pistol in her purse on that tragic day in Luby's cafeteria, her parents might be alive today. But then, she would probably have been prosecuted by the Texas police for unlawfully carrying a concealed firearm.

By a geographical quirk of fate, Thomas Terry, legally armed, was able to save his own life and maybe the lives of some two dozen customers and employees in a restaurant in Alabama. But Suzanna Gratia, unarmed, crouched and watched helplessly as Hennard slaughtered the patrons in a restaurant in Texas—a victim not only of George Hennard but of the Texas legislature and Texas "top cops."

In drafting the Bill of Rights, the Founding Fathers confirmed that self-protection was a prime right in the Second Amendment. Thomas Jefferson, quoting criminologist Casare Beccaria, renowned for his *On Crimes and Punishments* (1764), said:

Laws that forbid the carrying of arms . . . disarm only those who are neither inclined nor determined to commit crimes . . . Such laws make things worse for the assaulted and better for the assailants; they serve rather to encourage than to prevent homicides, for an unarmed man may be attacked with greater confidence than an armed man.

CHAPTER 5

WAITING PERIODS

THE FIRST STEP

THE HEARING ROOM was jammed—packed full with spectators, media, lobbyists, and aides to members of the U.S. House of Representatives.

Attention was riveted on Sarah Brady, wife of former White House press secretary, James Brady, felled by an assassin's bullet intended for President Ronald Reagan on March 30, 1981.

Now, many years after Mrs. Brady launched her campaign to rid America of firearms, she had gained the national spotlight.

Although she presented herself as a suburban housewife, Mrs. Brady had in fact become a hired lobbyist for Handgun Control, Inc. (HCI), and would earn upwards of $96,000 annually from the national gun ban group to drum up support for a federal waiting period on handgun purchases. Though her testimony during repeated appearances on Capitol Hill never failed to make the headlines, it failed, by any objective standard, to tell the real story. Then, as now, Sarah Brady and HCI misled the public. But few seemed to care. The show was on and Sarah Brady, as reported in the *Chicago Sun-Times* (6/5/88), would make an additional $5,000 per appearance traveling the nation giving speeches promoting gun control. "[Mrs. Brady's] fees," the *Times* reported, "are expected to increase substantially in the near future when Brady himself begins making joint appearances with her."

In 1986, New Jersey Representative Bill Hughes held "road show" hearings around the country designed, in part, to pass the Kennedy-Rodino Bill that called for a fifteen-day national waiting period. These "road shows" provided a stage for the anti-gun mythology. The hearings were stacked: pro-gun authorities were denied the opportunity to present contrary facts or express their dissenting views.

At one of those hearings, Sarah Brady referred once again to her standard story of the assassination attempt, saying:

> The case of John Hinckley is a vivid reminder of how easy it is for a handgun to fall into the wrong hands. He walked into a Dallas pawnshop, purchased a cheap "Saturday Night Special"—no questions asked, no waiting period to see if he had a criminal or mental illness record—and a few minutes later was on his way, ready to shoot the president of the United States . . .

John Hinckley, of course, could not have been stopped by a waiting period. In addition to the gun he used in the assassination attempt, Hinckley had bought a handgun in California with no problem, despite the fifteen-day waiting period. No waiting period ever devised would have stopped Hinckley. But passage of a law demanding a waiting period would only be a "symbolic victory" that would lay the groundwork for a massive government intrusion into the lives of ordinary, decent Americans.

John Hinckley purchased the gun he used in the assassination attempt nearly six months before he shot the president and James Brady. He purchased the .22 caliber revolver on October 13, 1980, from a Dallas, Texas, pawn shop. It was a lawful purchase. He had no felony convictions and no adjudications or record of commitment for mental illness or incompetence. No background check or waiting period of any length would have found anything to prevent the purchase. Hinckley actually bought two .22 caliber revolvers, and the federally mandated multiple purchase form was filed by the dealer with the Bureau of Alcohol, Tobacco and Firearms (BATF). BATF had a prime opportunity to conduct a background check—but there was nothing to find.

Because of the assassination attempt, the federal waiting period bills became known as "The Brady Bill." The number of days to wait would change, as would its provisions and its sponsors, but one fact did not change—the bill was a first step.

The multiple dangers of waiting periods were obvious, but many citizens seemed to close their minds to the truth—they would be the only ones forced to comply with the red tape, regulations, and costs, while criminals sat by and laughed. They pay no attention to laws, or rules, or regulations. They never have. And this has never been more true than with waiting periods.

The saga of waiting periods leaves a fifty-year-old trail of emotionalism and deception.

Promoted as a "crime control" measure, waiting periods, backers claim, will keep guns out of the hands of criminals, will stop "crimes of passion," will keep guns away from "people who shouldn't have them," and on and on. But in reality, waiting periods do none of those things—because they don't work. California's history, replete with waiting period failures, proves the point.

In 1940, the imposition of a forty-eight-hour waiting period on handguns took effect in California. Touted as a "crime control" measure, it failed to control crime, so in 1958, legislators increased the wait to three days. More failure. In 1965, they increased it again, this time to five days. Still more failure. The state legislature upped it to fifteen days in 1976—longer than any other state—but California's crime rate continued to soar, and finally, in 1990, the waiting period was expanded to cover all handguns, rifles, and shotguns, and all transfers, including private transfers between family members. Today, a man cannot give his wife or daughter a firearm for protection without registering the transfer with police and waiting fifteen days.

But California didn't stop there. Next came a ban on many semi-automatic handguns, rifles, and shotguns. And currently attempts are being made to impose registration of all *law-abiding gun owners, but not felons* (felons are exempt from registration under the Fifth Amendment of the U.S. Constitution—*Haynes v. U.S. 85 (1968)*).

Yet waiting periods don't deter crime—as pro- and anti-gun scholars now agree. A U.S. Department of Justice-sponsored study of criminals reveals the reason: Criminals don't undergo background checks and waiting periods because firearms are readily available through other, unregulatable sources.[1]

In addition, the Centers for Disease Control has produced evidence that waiting periods have no effect on suicide, a favorite but unsubstantiated argument of the anti-gun crowd.[2]

So what *do* waiting periods prevent? Waiting periods prevent law-abiding people from purchasing handguns without delay when they need firearms the most—for self-protection.

In the 1980s, during the Liberty City riots in Dade County, Florida, law enforcement leaders publicly informed citizens that police could not protect them. They were told to protect themselves—but this was all but impossible since a county waiting period kept law-abiding citizens from purchasing the handguns needed to protect themselves.

In 1990 mass murderer Danny Rolling mutilated five college students in Gainesville, Florida. Fear gripped the college town—there were no suspects. But because that county had a waiting period, the sheriff's department advised residents to go to neighboring counties that had *no waiting periods*, to buy guns for protection.

In Los Angeles, during the riots resulting from the Rodney

King case in 1992, people were outraged because the fifteen-day waiting period prevented them from immediately acquiring firearms to protect their homes and families. As a result, many lost their homes and businesses to rioters and looters.

Following the riots, gun shops did a brisk business for weeks. Law-abiding people were frightened and sought to defend themselves and their homes from mobs. They had watched media coverage of Korean-American business owners who saved some of their life's work by standing guard and shooting as rioters and looters approached.

And the example set by Floridians following Hurricane Andrew was unprecedented. The "YOU LOOT—WE SHOOT" sign scrawled on a piece of building debris that flashed across TV screens during the aftermath coverage of the massive destruction left a clear message. Hurricane Andrew had damaged and destroyed much of what Dade County residents owned, and they did not intend to lose anything more to looters and roving street gangs.

During one news report, the screen moved to a woman sorting through rubble looking for salvageable possessions. The reporter stopped and asked, "Do you have a gun?" She answered, "Yes." The reporter continued, "Would you really shoot somebody?" The answer was straightforward and unflinching: "Yes, I would." The reporter went on to observe that many Dade County residents were protecting their property with guns.

Throughout, the television showed many people standing guard over the rubble of their homes to protect what little they had left. One incoming report from Miami informed us a police officer had been on local TV telling residents that if they needed security, they'd better get a gun—the police couldn't help them.

Nine days after Hurricane Andrew hit South Florida moderator Stone Phillips of "Dateline NBC" (9/1/92) asked Jon Scott, who was broadcasting live from Homestead, Florida: "Has anyone actually had to use their weapon?" Scott responded that two looters had been shot in the neighborhood they had just profiled. Phillips asked, "And the police response to this?" Scott reported, "Police have said do what you have to do. Police are acknowledging that they can't be everywhere in this kind of crisis."

Even after the National Guard arrived, residents reported that they had to continue to protect themselves because when the sun went down the soldiers disappeared and residents were once again on their own.

During this TV coverage the overwhelming majority of firearms that were being used for protection by residents were semi-automatic firearms—guns that have been around for over a hundred years, and guns that "assault weapons" legislation seeks to ban. Guns that, in fact, have already been banned in California—"the waiting period state."

Such tragic disasters make folks open their eyes to the importance of firearms for protection and the outrageous restriction of waiting period laws, like the Brady Bill, that stand in the way of this protection.

One of the most profound admissions of the dangers of waiting periods came from Myriam Marquez, an anti-gun editorial writer for Florida's *Orlando Sentinel*. Ms. Marquez felt compelled to write about her revised views on waiting periods after talking to a friend in Miami who had been hit by the disaster. The friend, returning after the storm to check on the house, found looters rummaging through what was left and shocked the reporter by talking about needing a gun. The following are excerpts from Ms. Marquez's column on August 31, 1992:

My friend's call to arms shocked me. She has always been a laid-back, peace-and-love type. But when the going gets tough, it seems even softies like my friend get tough.

I've written about why waiting periods can save lives . . . I've also written about the futility of the national seven-day waiting period in the Brady Bill unless all the loopholes in it are closed. But now all of these safeguards against gun abuse seem useless to me. . . .

You can't apply civilized rhetoric when you're in a survival mode. . . . Nerves are shot, tempers are high and thousands of decent, hard-working people are armed and ready to protect what few material things are left of their lives. . . . When the going gets tough, even softies like me start talking tough.

From the victims of riot-torn Los Angeles and the victims of hurricane devastation in South Florida comes a clear, unmistakable message—the need to protect self, family, and property.

Those whose anti-gun philosophy emanates from air-conditioned offices or homes with electronic security systems should take heed. Their cohorts in Los Angeles and Miami, now victims of disaster, have a new perspective on the importance of the Second Amendment's guarantee of the right of the people to keep and bear arms. For them the ice cold reality of need has doused their anti-gun ideology. The striking differences between the destructive riots in Los Angeles, where citizens couldn't get firearms for protection when they desperately needed them, and the disastrous hurricane in south Florida, where citizens could get firearms and succeeded in protecting themselves and their property, surely should have convinced any reasonable person that waiting periods are dangerous.

But the anti-gun media and politicians have soft-pedaled the waiting period and argued that such measures will keep guns out of the hands of criminals. Their arguments, however, are shallow and fictional.

Take the "crimes of passion" argument, a situation when a law-abiding person gets angry and buys a gun to kill somebody. When an individual kills another in an outburst of anger or uncontrollable emotion with whatever weapon he or she has at hand—whether it's a gun, knife, or a golf club—it is often classified as a "crime of passion." But in reality, when an individual gets angry, buys a gun, and kills someone, it is premeditated murder. We have laws against murder in every state in the nation—but they certainly haven't stopped murder. It is illogical to assume that another law—a waiting period—will stop it either.

Statistics show the most frequent time for passion murders is between 8:00 P.M. and 3:00 A.M., long after gun shops are closed. How then could a waiting period stop a crime that does not involve a legal purchase through a regulatable source?

Advocates of waiting period legislation have claimed, however, that it will stop passion slayings in "matrimonial situations." Yet a Kansas City study concerning spouse slayings shows that in 90 percent of these murders, police had been called at least once for wife beating or some other disturbance, and in 50 percent of these cases police had been called at least five times. This is hardly a case of spontaneous passion. Rather it is a predictable situation in which the participants have a propensity for murder that law enforcement and the judicial system have failed or are unable to control.

If these "matrimonial situation" slayings are justifiable, self-defense homicides, then a waiting period could actually prevent a battered spouse from being able to get a firearm for protection when the abuse intensifies and police cannot take action against the abuser. It is not uncommon for police to tell battered victims to purchase a gun for protection because the law does not always allow the police to take action. Waiting period proponents inevitably resort to the emotions: "If it will save one life, isn't one life worth saving?" While completely agreeing that one life is worth saving, we do not ignore the fact that a waiting period is far more likely to cause the loss of a life by denying a person a firearm for protection than it is to save one.

Waiting periods, moreover, aren't needed for background checks. Many states currently require an instantaneous criminal records check on firearms purchasers. Like credit card checks, it only takes minutes—not three, or seven, or fifteen days.

Waiting periods not only do not keep criminals from getting guns, they create an immense drain on law enforcement resources by diverting police from the job of apprehending violent criminals to handling forms and reports about law-abiding citizens. And who ultimately pays for moving mountains of meaningless paperwork? You, the law-abiding taxpayer.

Another fundamental fact also seems to elude waiting period proponents. Criminals do not obtain firearms from legitimate sources, and never have. Professor Philip Cook of Duke University confirmed in a study that there is ". . . no convincing empirical evidence that a police check on handgun buyers reduces violent crime . . . most felons and other ineligibles who obtain guns do so not because the state's screening system fails to discover their criminal record, but rather because the people find ways of circumventing the screening system entirely."[3] In fact, in states restricted by waiting periods, crime rates climb faster than the national average.[4]

Douglas Murray of the University of Wisconsin conducted a study for that state's Council on Criminal Justice on the effect of gun control laws, waiting periods in particular, in all fifty states and concluded: "The severity of handgun control laws has no significant effect on violent crime rates . . . thus far, the relationship between gun laws and crime is nonexistent."[5]

John Lennon's murderer purchased a handgun in Hawaii, a state already awash in gun bans, permit requirements, and registration schemes. Neither John Hinckley, President Reagan's assailant, nor Lennon's murderer could have been "found out" under any waiting period yet devised. Laws cannot—and never could—read minds.

This brings us back to the real intent behind waiting periods. Waiting periods are only a first step. Regardless of what they promise to do or not to do, they are nothing more than the first step toward more stringent "gun control" measures.

Some people call it "the camel's nose under the tent," some call it "the slippery slope," some call it "a foot in the door," but regardless of what you call it, it's still the same—the first step.

On May 8, 1991, the U.S. House of Representatives passed a

version of the "Brady Bill" that mandated a seven-day waiting period. While the anti-gun supporters of waiting periods once denied the "first step" charge, Congressman Ed Feighan (D-OH), during passage of the Brady Bill, revealed the real agenda to Ted Koppel on ABC "Nightline" (5/8/91) just hours after the vote:

> TED KOPPEL: Congressman Feighan, is the Brady Bill then merely a first step or should it be viewed as just a first step?
>
> REP. FEIGHAN: Well, I think, Ted, it has to be viewed as part of the overall strategy for dealing with crime in America. We have a lot more that we have to do, not only in gun control, with "assault weapons" and other dimensions of the gun proliferation problem in America.
>
> TED KOPPEL: But limit it just for one moment for me—forget about the crime package for a moment—in terms of gun control, is this only a first step or would this be enough?
>
> REP. FEIGHAN: It's only a first step. It's not going to be enough. The Brady Bill will give us the opportunity now, if it passes the Senate and is signed into law . . . it will have a significant impact but it will not be enough. We've got to go beyond that, and I hope we'll do it this session of Congress, to stop the proliferation of "assault weapons" in America, and other dimensions of the gun problem as well.

The anti-gun crowd not only confirmed the "first step" charge on national TV, they bragged about it for days. As it turned out, they celebrated too soon. The Brady Bill never moved out of the Senate that year.

But in 1993, with a new sponsor, New York Representative Charles Schumer, and a new president, Bill Clinton, in the White House, the Brady Bill waiting period passed the U.S. Congress and was signed into law on November 30.

It didn't take long for the "second step" to be unveiled. Eight days later, on December 8, 1993, Sarah and Jim Brady of Handgun Control, Inc., and Representative Charles Schumer called a press conference to announce their intention to file "Brady Bill II." Jim Brady read his prepared statement:

> A little more than a week ago, President Clinton signed into law the *foundation of America's national gun control policy*. Today, we begin building on that foundation. Handgun Control Inc. has put together a package . . . that is what we are offering here today—*a combination of steps* . . . And we have staying power. [Emphasis added.]

Then they unveiled their next step. Brady Bill II:

- Requires a license to buy a handgun
- Requires fingerprinting to buy a handgun
- Requires gun training for a license to buy a handgun
- Requires a permanent seven-day waiting period
- Requires national registration of gun transfers to track guns and gun owners
- Requires a special license to own a "gun arsenal" (search for guns)
- Requires a special license to own 1,000 rounds of ammunition
- Requires gun dealers to pay an annual license fee of $1,000
- Limits sale to one gun a month to any individual
- Requires a separate federal license to sell ammunition
- Bans firearms sales at Gun Shows
- Bans semi-automatic "assault weapons"
- Bans "Saturday Night Special" handguns
- Bans all "non-sporting" ammunition
- Requires surtax of 30 percent on handguns
- Requires surtax of 50 percent on handgun ammunition
- Prohibits certain misdemeanants from possessing firearms
- Allows victims of gun violence to sue gun sellers

Richard Aborn, Handgun Control, Inc. president, was jubilant:

> [NRA] claimed that they vigorously fought [the Brady bill] at every turn and every step . . . because it was the nose of the camel [under the tent] . . . Today we would like to tell you what the rest of the camel looks like.

Those who intend to ban guns in America will never settle for Brady Bill II either. It is just one more step in the march toward national disarmament.

CHAPTER 6

"ASSAULT WEAPONS"

A CLASSIC CASE OF BAIT AND SWITCH

WITHOUT THE HELP of the media, the "assault weapons" issue never would have found favor with the public. The issue, stemming from an understandable revulsion of monstrous criminal acts, was tailor-made for media "bait and switch."

THE BAIT: News headlines—a violent and senseless tragedy perpetrated by a psychotic killer in a schoolyard, or in a fast food restaurant, or in the work place, horrifies America. In interviews, tearful victims and families of victims ask why. Viewers are moved and shocked—whom will they blame for the sickening tragedy brought home on the TV screen? The stage is set.

THE SWITCH: The reporter recounts that police say the victims were "assaulted" with a "rapid fire military-style weapon." A common semi-automatic rifle was used, but instead of the traditional wood stock, it has a black plastic stock. The camera switches to file footage of guns being fired on a police range—"rapid fire military-style" guns. Targets are shown being obliterated with explosive bursts of fully automatic fire. The guns actually being demonstrated? Fully automatic firearms, commonly called "machine guns," not the type of gun used in the tragedy. They are look-alikes. The seed of deceit has been planted.

The focus has been successfully diverted from the vicious perpetrator—to the gun.

Politicians grandstand before the cameras and the press, pledging to do something to stop these senseless tragedies by promising to ban "rapid fire assault weapons that are only used to kill people."

Politicians make statements such as "if the assault weapons weren't available to walk-in off the street killers, this tragedy would never have happened."

On hearing such rhetoric and viewing such pictures, and having little technical knowledge of firearms, the public is hoodwinked into believing that the gun is to blame. The semi-automatic firearm used by the criminal has now been branded an "assault weapon" and those menacing two words are indelibly linked with fully automatic "machine guns." The bait and switch is complete.

What the public doesn't know is that fully automatic "assault rifles" have been virtually banned for over fifty years under the National Firearms Act of 1934. They don't know that semi-automatic firearms have been around for over a hundred years and are owned and lawfully used by millions of law-abiding people. They don't know that some semi-automatic firearms only look different from other semi-automatic firearms. And the media certainly aren't going to tell them.

During the late 1960s, the cosmetics of firearms began to change. Manufacturers of firearms, looking for new ways to keep costs down, turned to modern technology. As traditional woods suitable for gun stocks became expensive, the miracle of plastics made it possible to produce replicas of wood stocks economically. Plastic stocks first appeared on popular, less expensive models of firearms. At a distance, they looked like very expensive fine quality wood.

Some firearms owners rejected the cosmetic changes; others welcomed them. For utility in hunting and for recreational shooting, plastic stocks have benefits. They don't warp and crack from moisture. Scratches and dents on plastic don't matter as they do on expensive wood stocks. With acceptance of plastic and the evolution of better grades of plastic, less traditional stocks—more convenient and easier to carry and handle than conventional stocks—emerged. The look of fake wood on some stocks was replaced with color—black or green or even camouflage.

This cosmetic transformation in appearance gave birth in the 1980s to a deception concerning semi-automatic guns and their owners. The black color, utilitarian shape, convenient pistol grip, and barrel shroud gave rise to the "assault weapons" description of the gun control crowd. No one could have predicted that innocent cosmetics would be used to symbolize criminal intent and tragedy, or to evoke fear and disgust in the uninformed.

The bait and switch accomplished, gun prohibitionists swung into action, capitalizing on national anger over the senseless tragedy in a schoolyard in Stockton, California, in 1989. Patrick Purdy's AKM–47 semi-automatic rifle, used by him against innocent schoolchildren, became an excuse to ban all semi-automatic rifles, handguns, and shotguns, all under the guise of banning "assault weapons."

The focus had been switched from Patrick Purdy, a deranged and dangerous criminal who had been pampered by the criminal justice system, to his semi-automatic rifle. By all rights, Purdy should have been in jail instead of stalking the schoolyard in Stockton, but the criminal justice system had unconscionably put Purdy back on the streets seven times through reduced charges, plea bargains, and dropped charges.

The blame for this tragedy lies in the failure of the criminal justice system—not in the lawful private ownership of semi-automatic firearms.

But for irresponsible politicians and bureaucrats to admit the error of putting Patrick Purdy back on the street would have been tantamount to admitting their failure to reform the criminal justice system. It was much easier, with media backing, to attack the gun, gun ownership, and the Second Amendment.

So the subterfuge and the attack against "assault weapons" began. Definitions of so-called "assault weapons" proposed in state legislatures and in the U.S. Congress would ban literally millions of semi-automatic rifles, shotguns, and handguns now owned and used by millions of honest and decent Americans.

"Assault weapon" is nothing more than a contrived term that now applies to all semi-automatic firearms. Their distinguishing feature is that after firing a single shot by one pull of the trigger, a mechanism reloads another cartridge. This mechanism is equivalent to, and often slower than, some other commonly used methods for loading additional shots, such as in pump-action shotguns.

Under some legislative schemes proposed, a firearm would be classified as an "assault" firearm if it looks like a military firearm, with features such as carrying handles, two-piece stocks, and high sights. Attempts to define and outlaw a firearm based on its appearance are absurd—a civilian jeep looks like a military jeep; a civilian tent looks like a military tent. Firearms owners, like other consumers, are attracted by state-of-the-art products. These firearms are popular because they resemble military rifles, which—as the government demands—offer the latest in firearm technology. The fact is, practically every type of popular firearm in existence at some time has been used by the military.

In the 1700s, for example, flintlock rifles and smoothbore muskets were used by the military. Using some of the terminology and definitions that are being tossed around, they could correctly be called "assault weapons" today.

Firearms with semi-automatic mechanisms have been man-ufactured in this country longer than the automobile. In fact, semi-automatic firearms remain an American standard—as much a part of our heritage as Henry Ford's horseless carriage.

All the gun ban rhetoric doesn't change facts. Rifles that look like (but don't function like) fully automatic military firearms are involved in less than one-half of 1 percent of violent crimes. Guns with military cosmetics are rarely ever seen, much less seized, in connection with crime.

The facts have been virtually ignored by the media which continue to promote the agenda of the gun banners. The U.S. Treasury Department testified on February 10, 1989, before the U.S. Congress that the AKS, a so-called "assault weapon," is functionally identical and, except for looks, "is no different from other semi-automatic rifles." In fact, Treasury officials testified that "the identical firearm [AKS] with a sport stock is available and, in appearance, [is] no different than other so-called sporting weapons."[1]

Gun prohibitionists claim that firearms that are "readily convertible" to fully automatic should be banned. But it is already a federal felony—carrying a ten-year prison term—to convert a semi-automatic to fully automatic fire. Apparently it is easier to propose a new law than to push for enforcement of existing ones.

Moreover, the "look-alike" and "readily convertible" defini-tions that have been used are hopelessly ambiguous and inac-curate; they are clearly designed to help ban all semi-automatic firearms by terming them "assault weapons."

Although a few top brass law enforcement administrators around the country seized media opportunities to promote banning semi-automatic firearms from private possession, rank-and-file policemen, like ordinary citizens, have a stake in this debate. These policemen and women disapprove of the position taken by their superiors, but many fear for their jobs should they speak out. Some have nevertheless decided that upholding freedom and constitutional protections is over-ridingly important, and they have come forward—but they have not been given the same media coverage as gun-banning administrators.

Deputy Police Chief Joseph Constance of the Trenton, New Jersey, Police Department testified before the Maryland Senate Judicial Proceedings Committee that "assault weapons" legislation, like New Jersey's legislation, had nothing to do with crime or apprehending criminals:

> At best, it was mere window dressing for frightened politicians to say they did something, when rank-and-file officers in New Jersey knew perfectly well that criminals would continue to obtain their guns illegally and won't fill out applications, for permission with superintendents or anyone else. Most frightening, this bill breaks down the trust between law enforcement and the citizens we're sworn to protect. Many of the guns outlawed are used by police as well as citizens for protection and recreation. Our citizens are ignoring this law and so are many police officers who privately own many of these firearms.[2]

The thought of law enforcement officials supporting measures to take firearms from law-abiding citizens conjures up images of a police state. In fact, police and their families and friends also privately own a wide range of semi-automatic firearms, and they are no more willing to surrender or register their firearms than the rest of the law-abiding community.

But the voices of dissent of these police have been largely disregarded by a media that refuse to hear the truth and record facts.

Law enforcement officers are not particularly vulnerable to semi-automatic firearms. They are vulnerable to criminals who have guns—any kind of gun—and who roam our streets. Our streets aren't safe for anybody—citizens and law enforcement alike. Why? Not because of guns, but because of violent criminals who are repeatedly turned back out on the streets by a lenient criminal justice system.

The news media, along with violent movies and TV shows, perpetuate the myth that "high tech" semi-autos are the choice of criminals and enhance the danger for enforcement officers. But there is simply no evidence to show that criminals prefer to use semi-automatic firearms for illegal purposes. In fact, Trenton Deputy Chief Constance told the Senate Judiciary Committee in August 1993 (as reported by the *Wall Street Journal*, January 6, 1994):

> Since police started keeping statistics, we now know that assault weapons are/were used in an underwhelming .026 of 1 percent of crimes in New Jersey. This means that my officers are more likely to confront an escaped tiger from the local zoo than to confront an assault rifle in the hands of a drug-crazed killer on the streets.

In 1985, the most comprehensive study ever conducted of criminal experiences with firearms was released by the U.S. Department of Justice. This survey of over 1,800 incarcerated felons found that criminals prefer guns *other than* semi-automatic firearms.[3]

Since that date, nothing has changed. On December 29, 1993, *USA TODAY* published a full-page graphic of the ten most popular crime guns as reported by the U.S. Treasury Department's Bureau of Alcohol, Tobacco and Firearms. Only one so-called "assault weapon" appeared on the list and it was in the number nine position. The list is as follows:

1. Smith & Wesson .38 Special Revolver
2. Raven Arms .25 caliber
3. Davis P–380
4. Smith & Wesson .357 Revolver
5. Ruger .22 caliber (commonly used for target shooting)
6. Lorcin L–380
7. Smith & Wesson semi-automatic handgun
8. Mossberg 12 gauge shotgun
9. TEC DC–9
10. Remington 12 gauge shotgun

Yet one week later, on January 5, 1994, Florida Attorney General Robert Butterworth stood before the Florida House of Representative's Criminal Justice Committee and told lawmakers that "assault weapons" are the weapons of choice of criminals and must be banned from private possession.[4]

Gun control fanatics from Florida to California continue to claim that "assault weapons" are the weapon of choice of criminals, despite the evidence from law enforcement agencies around the country that disproves the contention.

In 1989, the Florida Assault Weapons Commission, created by the Florida legislature, surveyed 415 Florida law enforcement agencies in the state on the use of "assault weapons" in crimes over the past four years.[5] Responding jurisdictions said that "assault weapons" were used in fewer than fifty crimes, while other weapons (guns, knives, hands, etc.) were used in 108,600 crimes. Even the Metro Dade Police survey showed that no "assault weapons" were used in 1986–1988 and only five were used in over 36,000 weapons crimes during 1989. Moreover, data from cities such as Los Angeles, San Francisco, and New York suggest that military "look alikes" constitute only 2 to 3 percent of guns seized by the police.

A 1994 review of the two major population areas of Florida found that the use of "assault weapons" by criminals continues relatively unchanged despite the claims of gun prohibitionists. The Orange County Sheriff's Department reported that 1.9 percent of the guns confiscated in 1993 were "assault weapons." Metro Dade County Police Firearms ID Department reported that "assault weapons" accounted for only 3.2 percent of the firearms that came into their possession in 1993.

While the media continue to exploit the few tragedies that have occurred, there is no criminological evidence to support the claim that semi-automatics are "evil" firearms. But such factual and empirical data run contrary to the gun-banning agenda. Their minds are made up and they don't want to be confused by the truth.

In short, then, gun ownership doesn't cause crime. Criminals do. Whether a firearm has a long or short barrel, fires single or multiple rounds, its capacity for "good" or "evil" rests solely with the user. No gun ban has ever kept guns out of the hands of criminals—only prisons do.

The most effective means of deterring crime is the promise of swift, certain, and severe punishment for criminal behavior, including mandatory sentencing without hope of probation or parole. Controlling crime by legislating against semi-automatics on the basis of appearance is a false issue. Such perceptions—that "guns cause crime" or that there are "good guns" and "evil guns"—not only defy reason, but also distract energies from the real issue: stopping crime.

Like all previous attempts at "gun control," restrictive legislation targeted at semi-automatic firearms will have no effect on criminals. But it will have dread implications for the civil rights of millions of America's law-abiding gun owners.

The continuing and vicious attack against semi-automatic firearms has outraged millions of decent Americans who own and use the popular guns. Some 60 percent of this nation's 20 million hunters own semi-automatic rifles and shotguns. Millions of additional citizens own semi-automatic target rifles and pistols. Together they constitute a strong part of this country's vast shooting and outdoor tradition. These men and women are responsible, hard-working, tax-paying, law-abiding citizens.

When the press and anti-gun advocates insinuate that semi-auto owners are, by association, no better than common criminals, law-abiding gun owners resent it. As they should.

CHAPTER 7

COMPARING GUNS TO VEHICLES

A FLAWED TACTIC OF THE ANTI-GUN CROWD

CAR BUFFS BEWARE: "More than 70 percent of all felony crimes involve the use of a motor vehicle."[1] That finding, highlighted in legislation (HB–2171) dealing with motor vehicles in Florida's legislature in 1994, could have terrible consequences.

Using the logic of gun prohibitionists, shouldn't lawmakers consider banning the following motor vehicles?

- BLACK BMWs (assault cars) are the vehicles of choice of drug dealers with their menacing looks and dark-tinted windows that hinder law enforcement visual searches.
- SPORTS CARS (machine racers) with speedometers that register 100 or more mph are designed to exceed the speed

limit—nobody needs to go that fast except to "out-car" police.

- COMPACT CARS (SNS—small nifty size) are small, inexpensive, and easy to park out of sight of police.
- VANS (high-capacity vehicle) are able to hold large numbers of people and frequently are used by street gangs for drive-by shootings.
- PICK-UP TRUCKS (thief sweepers) offer a bed on which thieves can put the valuables stolen from homes and businesses and then speed away.

Consequently, no one should have anything other than a big all-purpose station wagon, designed to haul children and groceries.

Since motor vehicles are used far more frequently in felony crimes than firearms, banning "crime vehicles" can have a much greater impact on reducing crime than banning guns.

Absurd? Of course it is.

Yet, the anti-gun medical people at the Centers for Disease Control and Prevention (CDC) and the National Center for Health Statistics have compared firearms to motor vehicles and herald the results as the latest "evidence" showing a need for gun control. They have spent taxpayer dollars working up "scientific" studies promoting gun control to stop the "epidemic" of gun deaths.

Major newspapers recently reported the release of the studies with headlines that read "Guns Gaining on Cars as Bigger Killer in U.S." (*New York Times*, 1/28/94) and "Firearms Gain on Car Crashes as Top Killer" (*Wall Street Journal*, 1/28/94). Those headlines conveyed the news that studies had determined that deaths from motor vehicle *accidents* were declining, while deaths from firearms were increasing.

But these "studies" drew conclusions by comparing statistics that are totally irrelevant to each other—the "apple to oranges" syndrome. Any true comparison has of course to be made with comparable statistics.

These studies compared deaths in motor vehicle accidents, and *only* accidents, with the combined total gun deaths, which included murders, justifiable homicides (self-defense), suicides, and accidents. Clearly, had they compared accidents to accidents they could not have made the political point they were attempting to make.

Accidental death statistics:

Year	Motor Vehicles	Firearms
1910	1,900	1,900
1920	12,500	2,700
1930	32,900	3,200
1940	34,501	2,375
1950	34,763	2,174
1960	38,137	2,334
1970	54,533	2,406
1980	53,172	1,955
1990	46,800	1,400

Gun owners, as can be seen above, have a far better safety record than motor vehicle owners. And these statistics compare "apples to apples." They come from the National Safety Council 1992 edition of *Accident Facts*.[2]

In 1910, the number of motor vehicle accidents and gun accidents were the same. In 1990 there were thirty-six times more motor vehicle accidents than gun accidents. Motor vehicle accidents have gone up; gun accidents have gone down. Quite an accomplishment for gun owners considering the increase in population and the increase in the number of gun owners.

It could be argued, moreover, that all the laws regulating motor vehicles have not reduced their deadly accident rate— licensing, registration, vehicle tags, ownership titles, traffic lights, stop signs, double yellow lines, school zones, and so on.

When people commit the crime of driving while drunk and

cause accidents injuring and killing people, they are individually held accountable for their actions. Nobody demands or sponsors legislation to ban motor vehicles.

But when criminals commit crimes with firearms, anti-gun zealots hold all gun owners accountable and demand legislation to ban firearms.

In their zeal to control guns, anti-gunners make absurd comparisons that just don't wash. Individuals must be held accountable for their crimes—whether they concern motor vehicles or firearms.

Tough sentences and locking up criminals who use firearms to commit violent crimes will reduce gun crime and make our streets safer. Regulating honest, law-abiding gun owners will do nothing to reduce crime.

The studies of the Centers for Disease Control and Prevention and the National Center for Health Statistics, referred to above, were seriously flawed.

The CDC report stated: "Prevention strategies to reduce firearm death rates must be tried and evaluated." And again: "The same level of attention that was, and continues to be, paid to the reduction of motor vehicle death rates must be directed toward lowering firearm mortality."

Dr. Jim Mercy, acting director of the Division of Violence Prevention for the National Center for Health Statistics, told the *New York Times* (January 28, 1994):

> If the death rate for automobiles was what it was in the 1960s, 250,000 Americans wouldn't be here today. Our changes [i.e., new legal and policy regulations on cars and driving] have saved 250,000 lives. Now we just need to do that kind of work in the area of firearm deaths.

Dr. Mercy apparently didn't get his statistics from the nation's foremost authority on accident statistics—the National Safety Council. A quick look at the 1960 through 1990 statistics shows that motor vehicle accident deaths over the past thirty years have been considerably higher than they were in

1960. That is, the "new legal and policy regulations on car and driving" have not produced the results he claims.

Secretary of Health and Human Services Donna Shalala, whose department supervised release of the report, condoned the "apples to oranges" comparisons in her introduction to the CDC report. She wrote:

> It is appalling that in the world's strongest and wealthiest country death by firearms is increasing at the alarming rate these studies find.

What is really appalling is that agencies of the U.S. government misled the public with these studies, in this instance to support those who would deprive Americans of their gun rights.

Another defect of these studies—aside from the actual statistical information—is their logic and the interpretation of them by their sponsors.

Their numbers show that from 1980 through 1985, deaths from motor vehicles and from firearms declined, but from 1985 through 1991, deaths from motor vehicles continued to fall (by 10 percent) while fatalities from firearms increased (by 14 percent). Should these trends continue, the CDC report concluded, fatalities from firearms will displace fatalities from motor vehicles as the leading cause of injury death in the country by the mid–1990s.

As columnist Samuel Francis wrote in a column analyzing the CDC figures:

> If you're going to make comparisons, you don't compare the apples of car accident fatalities with the oranges of all fatalities from guns. You compare the apples of accidental deaths in cars with the apples of accidental deaths from guns, and when you make that comparison, you find that car accidents are 28 times as lethal as gun accidents—a factoid conveniently omitted from the statistical colossus compiled by the CDC. [Mr. Francis used CDC numbers rather than National

Safety Council's which show cars are thirty-six times as lethal as firearms.][3]

The CDC study concludes with a virtual endorsement of gun control legislation as well as other legislative and policy measures, the desirability and effectiveness of which are dubious.

While many of the measures and procedures the CDC enumerates as contributing to the decline of motor vehicle fatalities have no doubt been effective, the report did not investigate why the number of fatalities from firearm accidents declined. Indeed, since the fact of the decline was never mentioned, there was no reason for the report to consider the reasons for the decline.

In ignoring both the fact of the decline and possible explanations of it, the CDC failed to inform the public of important issues relating to its own expanded concept of "public health" encompassing the ownership and use of firearms.

Instead, the CDC, in reference to declining motor vehicle deaths, mentioned "legal proscriptions," the obvious analogy to gun deaths being to outlaw certain kinds of firearms or ammunition.

Another favorite comparison between firearms and motor vehicles, which has become a staple feature of the rhetoric of gun control, is the oft-repeated insistence that just as citizens are required to register their cars and pass a test to get a driver's license, so they should be required to register firearms and pass certain tests or meet certain criteria before they can buy, keep, or fire a gun. As in the other comparisons, there are several flaws in this one.

The Second Amendment to the Constitution guarantees the right to keep and bear arms; there is no comparable constitutional guarantee of a right to keep and drive cars. Hence, governments may constitutionally regulate the sale, ownership, and operation of motor vehicles in ways that they are not free to do with respect to firearms.

Even given the obvious need to regulate motor vehicles, no

one seriously advocates that motor vehicles be outlawed or banned, nor does anyone regularly denounce motor vehicles as unmitigated social evils, lethal relics from America's past, or dangerous toys that cater to dark psychic urges of aggression and power—language that is frequently used about firearms.

Indeed, even under existing motor vehicle codes, virtually anyone, regardless of age, mental stability, or criminal history, can buy a car whereas the same cannot be said of the right to buy a gun. Nor is there any movement in support of laws that would restrict citizens to buying only one car a month, passing a driver's test to buy (as opposed to operating) a car, or prohibit minors from buying cars.

In short, existing legal controls on firearms and gun ownership in some jurisdictions are already far more restrictive than any such controls on motor vehicles.

When those who insist that gun laws conform to motor vehicle laws begin to call for holding the individual accountable for gun-related crimes, as they do with drunk driving, then we will have a true comparison between motor vehicles and firearms.

CHAPTER 8

GUNS-FOR-CASH

OR GOOD INTENTIONS— BAD RESULTS

IT IS 1:30 A.M. and a cold rain slants across the street as paramedics work deliberately but without haste to load a young black man, no more than seventeen years old, onto a stretcher. The rain splashes into the man's half-closed eyes, but he doesn't blink. Shot twice in the back of the head, execution style, he's dead.

A gentle breeze causes the yellow tape surrounding the crime scene to flutter in an almost festive manner, but there is no joy here. In a few hours, a police officer will tell the boy's disbelieving mother that her worst nightmare has become a grim reality. For those involved, this is serious business.

Across town, another mother huddles with her children on the floor of their tiny apartment as bullets fly through the air outside. Armed thugs wander the streets, engaged in a form of urban warfare, threatening and intimidating citizens who only want to be left alone to raise their children in safety.

Bosnia? Somalia? No. These scenes are being played out in cities all across the United States. Despite massive crime prevention programs, the land of the free is being held hostage by criminals who are increasingly violent and, shockingly, younger and younger.

Daily, the cry, "Stop the gun violence!" grows louder and more strident. Although the problem is plain, it is also complex. A pervasive sense of lawlessness has settled on our society, especially among young people. The real problem is more a matter of heart than of hardware. Yet some hope to stem the tide of crime by limiting the availability of guns through gun turn-in programs, a matter of placing symbolism over substance. Citizen's groups, churches, and sports luminaries in a number of cities have urged the public to turn in guns in exchange for money, concert tickets, athletic shoes, grocery vouchers, even credits for heating bills. In St. Louis, San Francisco, and Baltimore, taxpayers' money was actually used to buy guns from citizens.

In Washington, D.C., Riddick Bowe took a different approach. Instead of taxpayers' money, he offered to use his own. A professional boxer from the D.C. area, who briefly reigned as heavyweight champion of the world, Bowe put up $100,000 to purchase guns from those willing to turn them in.

Citizens who responded to the offer received a double reward. First, a significant incentive for many of them, they had a chance to meet Bowe personally. Second, they received up to $100 for each firearm turned in irrespective of whether it was serviceable or junk.

At the end of the day, a total of 3,600 guns were in boxes ready to be taken to the smelter and Riddick Bowe had reportedly spent over $200,000, double his original commitment. Those are impressive figures by any standard, but although his motives may have been pure, few of the guns, if any, came "off the street."[1]

One published photograph of the event showed an old Thompson submachine gun of World War II vintage. This firearm, the venerated "tommy gun," dates back to the 1930s and, being fully automatic, was virtually banned from public possession by the National Firearms Act in 1934. It has often been depicted in movies as the intimidating gun of choice in the days of Al Capone and other Prohibition-era mobsters. But where were the Sig Sauers, MAC 10s, Uzi's, Glocks, PPKs, or "assault weapons" such as the AK–47? It is unlikely that any such firearms were turned in.

Far more likely, the guns that were surrendered came off dusty shelves in closets, out of packing boxes or other places where law-abiding citizens had kept them, unused, for years. While some guns may have still been serviceable, these folks felt that taking the money and meeting a real live superstar was more important than the potential protection afforded by their guns. Time will tell if they made the right choice.

Detractors say that these programs are a sham, and certainly the experience in St. Louis demonstrates the point. At least twice, this city has tried a "guns-for-cash" program. As reported in the *St. Louis Post-Dispatch* in October 16, 1991, nearly twelve hundred guns were turned in during one of these campaigns. For each gun, the owner received two $25 cash certificates redeemable at a Boatmen's National Bank and a $10 food certificate redeemable at any Shop 'N Save store.

Now, twelve hundred guns is a lot of hardware, but did these guns come "off the street"? Consider the following, as reported the same day by the *Post Dispatch*: One man turned in a box of over one hundred old pistols—$5,000 worth. "Obviously, the guy is some kind of gun dealer," said a police officer. In another instance, a forty-four-year-old insurance salesman had five old pistols to sell. "I'm doing it for the money," he said. "I collect guns, and I'm a target shooter, but I know these guns are not worth $50." Another man, an admitted gun dealer, sold twelve long guns and fifteen handguns to the police. "About half of them work," he said. "They're a bunch of junk, and it's better to get money for them than to destroy them." Yet another man, forty-two years old, brought in four old rifles. "I tried selling them for $50 apiece at gun stores and couldn't find a buyer. Now, I've got a buyer." The final bit of irony was the sixty-eight-year-old man who sold his shotgun because he didn't need it. "I've already got a .38 snubnose for my protection," he said.

A similar program in Philadelphia netted 1,044 guns in two weeks. Police sergeant Ray Bencivengo was quoted as saying, "You can't really gauge if any lives were saved but we got a lot of favorable publicity, and the public was made very aware of the gun problem."[2]

Unfortunately, the publicity attendant to these programs is used by spin doctors to advance the agenda of gun control zealots. In March 1994, St. Louis authorities launched yet another "Goods for Guns" program. The day after the program started, it was reported that about sixty firearms had been exchanged for $25 cash or for $50 gift certificates good at Venture stores around the area. Of those collected, the police said that "most of the guns were old, inexpensive pistols."[3]

The picture that accompanied the story, however, displayed firearms obviously assembled for the benefit of the media. Among them were various handguns as well as a row of so-called "assault weapons." The latter included what appeared to be a "machine gun," a couple of shotguns, an AK–47, and several other "lethal looking" firearms. When it was learned that these were not turned in as part of the program, this was brushed aside as merely a case of inadequate caption space for the photo—hardly credible. The picture was staged to create an illusion.

Let's face it. The bad guys aren't stupid. They aren't going to give up their guns, their source of power, for $50 or $100.

Have these gun turn-in programs made a dent in crime? Quite the contrary; they have aided criminals everywhere.

Thousands of law-abiding citizens may now be totally dependent for their protection upon already overstressed police forces, and criminals know it. These citizens are more vulnerable than ever to attack by the predators who roam our streets.

Further, such programs increase the risk of burglaries of homes and vehicles. Youthful offenders have no compunction about stealing guns in order to turn them in for concert tickets, athletic shoes, or ready cash.

Worse yet, police are now saying these programs are interfering with their criminal investigations. Violent perpetrators have realized they can turn in their crime guns—no questions asked—and get rid of evidence. This will result in more unsolved crimes and more unprosecuted cases.

In one area, citizens were alarmed to hear that drug dealers had stationed themselves at the guns-for-cash location. With rolls of cash in hand, they stopped people as they approached and offered to buy the better guns for more money than was being offered by the program.

The problem of guns and crime in our society is far more basic and far more complex than the control zealots are willing to admit. It has both a legal and a moral aspect and will not respond to simplistic solutions.

For decades the government has adopted "feel good" approaches in dealing with society's troubles, imposing layers of regulations designed to protect us from ourselves rather than focusing on personal accountability and responsibility. Concentrating on measures that only affect the decent citizen is insulting, useless, and wrong. It has more to do with power than with controlling crime.

Recent gun control schemes, including guns-for-cash programs, may make their proponents feel better and garner headlines, but they will have a negligible impact on crime. What America needs is a moral revolution of massive proportions. Changed hearts and the restoration of traditional and stable families, combined with stricter law enforcement and a reversal of our revolving door justice system, could, over time, bring safety back to our streets.

Since money is what primarily draws people to these turn-in programs, drug dealers and black market gun traffickers have once again found a way to exploit the "good intentions of the naive." Guns from these programs are providing a new way to put more guns on the streets, and into the hands of the very people we want to deprive of guns—the criminal element.

CHAPTER 9

CHILDREN AND GUNS

"On a frosty night just before Christmas in 1990, 15-year-old Kenneth Johnson shot Edward Taylor, a cab driver who wouldn't hand over his money, in northwest Detroit.

"Taylor 43, a decorated Vietnam veteran, died in the emergency room. Johnson was tried as an adult and convicted of murder. But rather than sentence him to life in prison, the judge sent Johnson to a juvenile facility. Less than two years later he was back on the street."

—KNIGHT-RIDDER, 4/25/94

KENNETH JOHNSON WAS not a child. He was a violent perpetrator—a criminal—regardless of his age.

The notorious Crips and Bloods, Los Angeles gangs, are not boy scouts—they commit random acts of criminal violence. Their turf has expanded, moved out into many other areas of the country, escalating juvenile crime.

In Colorado, the Crips and Bloods brought a wave of terror. In January 1993, the National Rifle Association (NRA) helped draft a bill to give law enforcement officers in Colorado greater powers to deal with these armed gang members and other young thugs. That legislation called for the following reforms:

sending violent offenders fourteen years or older to adult court; considering the death penalty for juveniles convicted of murder; funding the construction of five hundred new prison beds for violent juvenile offenders; and allowing for violent juvenile records to be considered in the sentencing process for criminals over the age of eighteen.

The bill also called for prohibiting the possession of handguns by juveniles except those under adult supervision engaged in hunting, target shooting, or receiving instruction in the shooting sports.

Colorado Governor Roy Romer, who had shown no support for the crime-prevention legislation during the winter legislative session, embraced the issue only after a series of violent crimes involving gangs hit the Denver area. Governor Romer then called a special session of the legislature in August 1993 to consider a ban on juvenile gun possession, but introduced his own legislation rather than working to pass the legislation already developed.

Romer's bill made all juvenile gun possession, regardless of the reason for possession, probable cause for arrest and temporary confinement. Although Romer's bill provided that hunting and target shooting be "affirmative defenses" for handgun possession, the difference between an affirmative defense and an "exception" is much more than a matter of semantics.

With an exception, a juvenile engaged in legitimate firearms use is not subject to arrest. With an affirmative defense, regardless of activity, a juvenile in possession of a handgun is subject to arrest and confinement for a minimum of forty-eight hours.

An affirmative defense would also require that an arrested youth go to trial because only at a trial can a judge hear the evidence needed to invoke the affirmative defense provision. This turns the notion of innocent until proven guilty on its head and makes every law-abiding youth engaged in recreational firearms use subject to arrest.

Because the National Rifle Association opposed Governor Romer's bill, he launched a vicious attack against the association in televised debate, in the press, and in public appearances, claiming that the NRA was "out of touch" with Colorado and that the association "was part of the problem."[1]

To some observers, it seemed as if Governor Romer was using the issue of gang violence to make headlines and score some easy political points with voters in his 1994 reelection campaign. But would this help solve the real problem of gang violence?

Ultimately, the Colorado legislature shelved Romer's bill and passed the HB1001 bill. The governor signed it, praised it as a major achievement, and took full credit for its passage. The *Wall Street Journal* in September 28, 1993, reported that "even the NRA reluctantly gave its support." In truth, it was quite the reverse.

Street gang members in Los Angeles, Colorado, or in any area, are not children, they are criminals, and violent ones.

In Arizona and Florida, as well as Colorado and other states, some legislators along with various groups have worked hard to pass proposals that give law enforcement authorities the tools they need to deal effectively with juvenile criminals. In so doing, these bills did not toss the rights of law-abiding youngsters to the wind, tarring all youngsters with the same brush. They protect the rights of youngsters for lawful hunting, target shooting, and other sport and recreational shooting with their families and friends.

Juvenile offenders who unlawfully carry guns and commit crimes with guns should not in any case be called "children" in the legal sense. Regardless of their ages, when they commit crimes and violate the laws of society they must be held accountable.

In September 14, 1993, a thirteen-year-old along with three other teens was charged with the shooting death of a British tourist, Gary Colley, at an Interstate–10 rest area near Monticello, Florida.

The media reported that the thirteen-year-old had a lengthy record of previous charges—over fifty of them. But the small community in which he resided at the time of the shooting had no knowledge of his past record. The Department of Health and Rehabilitative Services (HRS) with jurisdiction over juvenile delinquents had moved the boy and his family out of Tallahassee to Monticello in hopes of changing his criminal ways.

Instead, the boy fell in with older juveniles in the rural community and his—and their—criminal activities escalated to murder.

This thirteen-year-old was not a child—he was a repeat juvenile offender turned loose on society by a lenient juvenile justice system that puts more weight on the age of the perpetrator than on the number or seriousness of the crimes he has committed.

Today juveniles are breaking laws at a record rate. The bleeding hearts have turned the juvenile justice system into a joke in order to protect "these poor misguided children who have a tough life." As a result, violent juveniles scoff at the system and at the very thought of punishment.

The laws must be changed. Juveniles who commit violent acts with firearms need to be locked up behind bars. They aren't children; they are terrorists running rampant in our communities. One thing is absolutely certain—when they are locked up and off the streets they can't commit crimes.

Youngsters who grow up around firearms and are taught safety and respect for firearms are not the problem. It's the "TV-educated" juveniles who emulate the gratuitous violence in the media that are causing the problem.

A new report by the Office of Juvenile Justice and Delinquency Prevention of the U.S. Justice Department has confirmed it. The report on the findings of a new study, titled "Urban Delinquency and Substance Abuse," was released in July 1993. It was prepared under the Program of Research on the Causes and Correlates of Juvenile Delinquency, and funded by the U.S. Justice Department. The report was based on three studies: the Denver Youth Survey, the Pittsburgh Youth Study, and the Rochester Youth Development Study. The following section of the report is of particular interest:

GUN OWNERSHIP AND DELINQUENCY

Adolescent ownership and use of firearms is a growing concern, and results from the Rochester study suggest the concern is well founded.

By the ninth and tenth grades, more boys own illegal guns (7 percent) than own legal guns (3 percent). Of the boys who own illegal guns, about half of the whites and African-Americans and nearly 90 percent of the Hispanics carry them on a regular basis.

Seventy-four percent of the illegal gunowners commit street crimes, 24 percent commit gun crimes, and 41 percent use drugs. Boys who own legal firearms, however, have much lower rates of delinquency and drug use and are even slightly less delinquent than nonowners of guns.

The socialization into gun ownership is also vastly different for legal and illegal gunowners. Those who own legal guns have fathers who own guns for sport and hunting. On the other hand, those who own illegal guns have friends who own illegal guns and are far more likely to be gang members. For legal gunowners, socialization appears to take place in the family; for illegal gunowners, it appears to take place "on the street."

Youngsters who have been taught safety and respect for firearms are not the problem. They should not be required to forfeit their rights and be victimized as a result of the actions of juvenile criminals.

Children who are endangered by careless adults who leave firearms where the children can easily get access to them are an entirely different issue.

Gun control zealots capitalize on accidents and tragedies involving children, and rather than look for real solutions to protect the children, they call for more gun control laws. Moreover, they criticize and attempt to block safety education programs designed to help children understand how to behave around firearms.

In July 1988, when the NRA unveiled its Eddie Eagle Gun Safety Program for preschool through sixth grade children, gun prohibitionists immediately jumped on the effort and misconstrued the contents of the program, egged on by a sympathetic press.

Reports in the press that the program was designed to "offer after-school practice for shooting rifles, shotguns and handguns," as reported in the *Sarasota Herald Tribune* on July 26, 1988, were, and are, patently untrue. No part of the program involves teaching young children how to shoot guns. Those allegations were simply attempts by the anti-gun crowd to discredit a program that has a track record of saving young lives.[2] Educators and responsible officials who are realistic about their concern about child safety see the Eddie Eagle program as a positive step in preventing tragic accidents.

The program is simple, straightforward, and effective. Utilizing the "No. Go. Tell." concept, the program teaches young children in K–6 that if they see a gun, they must STOP! DON'T TOUCH! LEAVE THE AREA! TELL AN ADULT! The program is being taught in the schools all over the nation.

The National Rifle Association is, moreover, well qualified and has the necessary resources to provide expert education in this field. As the pioneer in the field of gun safety and training for private citizens for well over one hundred years, the NRA has been the recognized leader in training law enforcement firearms instructors for over fifty years. The association has over thirty thousand firearms instructors who conduct over ten thousand classes and teach over 1 million firearms owners annually. It has trained over 1.5 million police, 17 million hunters, and millions upon millions of other men, women, and children. Gun safety awareness taught in the schools will not only save countless lives of innocent children but will also make parents better aware of their responsibilities.

In October 1993, the National Safety Council gave its 1993 Outstanding Community Service First Place Award to the Eddie Eagle program and its creator, NRA Vice President Marion P. Hammer. The program has received national acclaim from educators, law enforcement officers, legislators, and organizations around the country. Its praises have been written into the U.S. *Congressional Record* and in formal resolutions adopted by some state legislative bodies.

But rather than help teach children to be safe, many argue that the way to prevent accidents is to punish parents after the accident occurs. These people contend that passing laws that would send parents to jail if their firearm is misused by a child will cause a decrease in such accidents. Actually, there are currently laws on the books in every state that deal with accidents caused by negligence.

Safety with guns is no different from safety with other products . . . pesticides and cleaning solutions under the sink . . . plastic bags lying in a closet . . . matches on the table. These are just some of the common household items that could lead to the tragic injury or even death of a child. Parents know of these dangers, so they teach their children not to touch pesticides, not to pick up plastic bags, and not to play with matches. Parents teach safety.

Groups like Handgun Control, Inc. continue to agitate over firearm accidents, even though such accidents are already on the wane. From 1967 to 1991, the number of accidental firearm deaths in the United States dropped from 2,896 to 1,400.[3] During the same period, the population, the number of gun owners, and the number of firearms owned increased substantially.

But despite the figures, some continue to sensationalize the trauma suffered by families involved in an accident in order to push their agenda of removing firearms from the home. Putting parents in jail would not reduce accidents; it would only further injure a family.

Parents are responsible for the conduct and safety of their children. But, like the police, parents cannot always be there. Today, with a firearm in an estimated one out of every two households in America, teaching children safety is the only way to prevent an accident from occurring. Education and responsible parenting are the keys to preventing these tragic accidents—not emotional rhetoric designed to drive a hidden agenda.

Surprisingly, the American Trauma Society president, Basil

A. Pruitt, Jr., MD, condemned the National Rifle Association's efforts to reduce firearm accidents by teaching young children to live safely around them. Summarily dismissing the Eddie Eagle educational program, Pruitt's solution was to urge the NRA "to take the definitive step in gun safety and work for effective gun control."[4]

Pruitt did not recognize that "effective gun control" is a contradiction in terms—no gun control has ever been effective in stopping accidents, or crime for that matter. Education and responsible parenting are the proven essentials in preventing accidents affecting children.

Everyone must surely recognize that a significant percentage of firearms accidents could be prevented if children were taught to eliminate situations in which accidents occur, or if adults were taught to avoid situations that could lead to such accidents. The medical profession, of all professions, should be aware of the value of education as a front-line preventive.

Drowning accidents, bicycle accidents, skate board accidents, automobile accidents, poisoning from drug (medication) accidents, and so on, result in far more deaths than firearms accidents. And, to put it bluntly, according to the National Safety Council, "medical misadventures" result in almost twice as many deaths as firearms accidents.[5]

Since there are far more firearms and firearms owners in America than physicians, it is clear that the record of firearms owners in preventing accidental deaths is far superior to that of the medical community in preventing "medical misadventure" deaths.

The overwhelming majority of physicians is made up of careful, professional, and responsible men and women, but as with gun owners, the small number who are irresponsible give a bad name to all. If some doctors misuse medications resulting in the death of patients, no one calls for banning the use of that medication by other doctors. The offending doctors are held individually responsible. Why does that logic escape those who would ban guns because a small number of people are irresponsible with firearms?

Dr. Pruitt attempted to compare the Eddie Eagle program with treating pneumonia with cough syrup. In doing so, he dismissed the value of preventive measures. But preventive measures—such as educating patients to take care of themselves through proper diet, rest, cleanliness, and common sense (to prevent pneumonia or other diseases)—is sound, standard medical advice. Educating young children to keep them from playing with firearms is also a sound, common sense approach.

Whatever the motives of the Dr. Pruitts, and whatever the stand of people on the firearms issue, *the stand we all must take must be that which best guarantees the safety and well-being of our children.*

CHAPTER 10

THE BRADY BILL II AGENDA

REGISTRATION, LICENSING, GUN BANS, AND TAXES

IMMEDIATELY AFTER PASSAGE of the Brady Bill, gun control proponents moved to continue their assault on the rights of law-abiding gun owners. Brady Bill II contains four more steps in the march to disarm the American people: firearms registration, licensing, gun bans, and taxes on firearms and ammunition.

President Bill Clinton wasted no time in signing the Brady Bill into law. Following his election as president, he promised Handgun Control, Inc. that the "Brady Bill" would pass and be signed into law before the end of his first year in office. He made good on that promise with time to spare.

Passage of the Brady Bill followed the most intensive lobbying and arm-twisting effort ever conducted by a president of the United States on a gun control bill since the passage of the 1968 Gun Control Act. The swift passage of the Brady Bill—the first step—and its impact on the filing of Brady Bill II speak volumes when seen in print.

November 10, 1993:   Brady Bill passed in U.S. House

November 11, 1993:   Brady Bill passed in U.S. Senate and sent to Conference Committee

November 22, 1993:   Conference Committee version of Brady Bill passed U.S. House

November 24, 1993:   Conference Committee version of Brady Bill passed U.S. Senate

November 30, 1993:   Brady Bill signed into law by President Bill Clinton

December 8, 1993:   Brady Bill II unveiled at press conference by House sponsor, U.S. Representative Charles Schumer and Handgun Control, Inc.

February 28, 1994:   Brady Bill I took effect

February 28, 1994:   Brady Bill II unveiled at press conference by Senate sponsor, U.S. Senator Howard Metzenbaum and Handgun Control, Inc.

President Clinton swiftly launched another blitz against America's firearms owners:

President Clinton said he views passage of the Brady Bill as only the beginning of a much broader effort by his administration to seek sweeping gun control measures . . . [*Los Angeles Times*, 12/5/93]

He [the president] ordered the Justice Department to begin studying gun licensing, registration and collection proposals. [*Washington Times* 12/12/93]

Passage of the Brady Bill unleashed a torrent of rhetoric from high-ranking government officials and gun ban lobbyists against the NRA, suggesting that some 65 million Americans were no better than criminals:

U.S. Representative Charles Schumer:

We're here to tell the NRA their nightmare is true! [NBC Nightly News, 11/30/93]

We're going to hammer guns on the anvil of relentless legislative strategy! We're going to beat guns into submission! [Press Conference held to announce the provisions of "Brady Bill II" 12/8/93]

Richard Aborn, Handgun Control, Inc. president:

[NRA] claimed that they vigorously fought [the Brady Bill] at every turn and every step ... because it was the nose of the camel [under the tent] ... Today we would like to tell you what the rest of the camel looks like. [Press Conference held to announce the provisions of "Brady Bill II" 12/8/93]

At HCI, we are proud of what we have accomplished—most significantly, enactment of the Brady Law—and have no need [now] to keep our agenda a secret. Our goal is simple—[pass Brady Bill II] ... We believe this can be accomplished ..." *Orlando Sentinel* 3/31/94]

U.S. Senator Joseph Biden:

[Banning guns] is an idea whose time has come. [Associated Press 11/18/93]

U.S. Senator Dianne Feinstein:

[Banning guns] addresses a fundamental right of all Americans, to feel safe. [Associated Press 11/18/93]

U.S. Representative Major Owens:

> My bill . . . establishes a 6-month grace period for the turning in of handguns. [*U.S. Congressional Record* 11/10/93]

U.S. Representative Mel Reynolds:

> If it were up to me we'd ban them all. [CNN "Crossfire" 12/9/93]

U.S. Attorney General Janet Reno:

> Gun registration is not enough. I've always proposed state licensing . . . with some federal standards. [Associated Press 12/10/93; ABC's "Good Morning America" 12/10/93]

James Brady, Handgun Control, Inc.:

> A little more than a week ago, President Clinton signed into law the foundation of America's national gun control policy. Today, we begin building on that foundation. [Press conference held to announce provisions of Brady Bill II 12/8/93]

The major provisions of Brady Bill II should give pause to every American who believes in civil rights, individual responsibility, and old-fashioned common sense.

NATIONAL FIREARMS REGISTRATION

Ultimately registration will let the government know who owns guns and what guns they own. History provides the outcome: confiscation. And a people disarmed is a people in danger.

In Germany, firearm registration helped lead to the holocaust. Each year we solemnly remember in sorrow the survivors and those lost in the holocaust, but the part gun registration and gun confiscation played in that horror is seldom mentioned. The German police state tactics left its citizens, especially Jews, defenseless against tyranny and the wanton slaughter of a whole segment of its population.

Of the highly acclaimed motion picture *Schindler's List* which tells the story of the survivors, Helena Silber said that "the ending depicted [in the film] at the Brinnlitz factory was, well, not quite right." In a March 18, 1994, article by *Washington Times* reporter Matt Neufeld, Helena Silber tells the rest of the story:

> The truth, she explains, was far more dramatic: Toward the end of the war, Oskar Schindler obtained guns for his workers. He wanted the Jews to be able to defend themselves if the Nazis decided to slaughter them.
>
> The author of the book *Schindler's List* says Mrs. Silber's account tallies with those of other survivors. Thomas Keneally says Schindler bribed the governor of the Moravian province for the arms. The workers then prepared for "a pitched battle."

Mrs. Silber wonders why the film's ending wasn't entirely accurate: "If he [Spielberg]—had gotten me, I would have told him."

Movie Director Steven Spielberg's omission of this essential part of history could not be because it was not known. Thomas Keneally wrote of the firearms acquisition in his book. He reported:

> During the winter, Oskar [Schindler] built up an independent arsenal . . . Most of the weapons, in any case, came from a flawless source, from *Obersturmbannfuher* Rasch, SS and police chief of Moravia. The small cache included carbines and automatic weapons, some pistols, some hand grenades . . .
>
> Once Oskar had the weapons, he appointed Uri Bejski, brother of the rubber-stamp maker, keeper of the arsenal. . . .
>
> Having selected a small body of prisoners for training, Uri took one at a time into Salpeter's storehouse to teach them the mechanisms of the *Gewehr* 41 W's [semi-automatic military-style rifles].

In producing the movie, perhaps someone along the line felt that this part of history was not "politically correct" given the force of today's anti-gun sentiment—particularly in light of the popularized misconception that semi-automatic firearms are "assault weapons" and unsuitable for self-defense.

From Mr. Keneally's account, there is no doubt that Jewish survivors of the holocaust were fully prepared to defend themselves with just such semi-automatic firearms. No part of those historical atrocities should be forgotten or rewritten or covered up for political reasons.

Many say that such abuse by government can never happen again. Yet we need look no further than a few short miles to the south at Cuba where firearms registration followed by confiscation put the Cuban citizens at the mercy of Fidel Castro—a leader they once celebrated as their liberator.

When Castro came to power and began confiscating firearms, Cubans who were reluctant to turn in their guns argued that they needed firearms. Castro responded, "Armas para que?" (Guns for what?)[1]

Deprived of firearms, Cubans lost their wealth, their property, their possessions, their freedom, and in too many cases their lives. Today they are a nation of poor, dispirited, and frightened people. The nation is in shambles, powerless at the hands of a modern-day dictator.

Liberal author and *Miami Herald* columnist Carl Hiassen recently returned to Cuba. His description of today's Cuba (*Tallahassee Democrat* 4/3/94) is grim:

> The last time I visited, 15 years ago, life in Cuba was hard but not hellish . . . The changes are jarring and sadden the heart . . . people in the city dine on dogs and cats . . . Cuba is in a time warp, rolling backwards.
>
> A computer engineer . . . explained why he doesn't think the people will rise up: "Thirty six years—[of] panic, panic, panic. I am panicked. My children are panicked. Panicked about going to jail." . . . In some places discontent is so palpable that foreigners wonder aloud why Fidel hasn't been overthrown. One

reason is simple—everybody in Cuba knows somebody in jail. People who speak out often get locked up.

Remember that Cubans have been coping . . . for three tough decades. Conditioned by both hardship and oppression, they survive by adapting.

As a result, thousands of Cubans have escaped to America and thousands have died trying to escape.

President Clinton's announced policy on gun ownership, as found in the *Los Angeles Times*, December 5, 1993, bears repeating:

President Clinton said he views passage of the Brady Bill as only the beginning of a much broader effort by his administration to seek sweeping gun control measures . . .

Another paper, the *Washington Times*, December 12, 1993, added that Clinton "ordered the Justice Department to begin studying gun licensing, registration and collection proposals."

Is Bill Clinton using the word "collection" as a soft word for confiscation—in much the same way as he uses the word "contribution" for taxes?

NATIONAL LICENSING OF HANDGUN OWNERS

Government licensing of gun owners as envisioned by the Clintonites would entail training and fingerprinting, a criminal record and mental history check, and license fees.

Their reason for licensing: to keep guns out of the hands of the "wrong" people. Yet any one of the criteria required for licensing could be used to deny a license to anyone.

Even with a spotless record, if you have no money you would fail to qualify—no license, no gun. Or if you can't pass the training course, or none is available—no license, no gun. If government officials don't want you to have a gun—for their own reasons—licensing is an ideal barrier.

If American history proves anything, it is that gun owners cannot trust politicians. Too often in American history, moderate-sounding gun control proposals, such as licensing, have led to a ban on possession of firearms. Listen to FBI Director Louis Freeh:

> The strongest gun legislation . . . I will enforce diligently and exhaustively. [U.S. Senate Confirmation Hearings 1993]

Gun licensing and other restrictions, for example, were used to suppress blacks before and after the Civil War. Licensing laws were designed to prevent those whom the government wished to disarm from being able to qualify for a license. In the case of blacks, it in effect banned free blacks from owning any type of firearm. In one instance in 1870, the Tennessee legislature banned possession of any handgun except the Colt .45— which ex-slaves could not afford.

Consider the words of Justice Buford in the 1941 Florida Supreme Court case of *Watson v. Stone* in respect to Florida's law requiring a license to possess a firearm:

> I know something of the history of this legislation. The original Act of 1893 . . . was passed for the purpose of disarming the negro laborers and to thereby reduce the unlawful homicides that were prevalent in turpentine and sawmill camps and to give the white citizens in sparsely settled areas a better feeling of security . . . and there has never been, within my knowledge, any effort to enforce the provisions of this statute as to white people, because it has been generally conceded to be in contravention of the Constitution and non-enforceable if contested.

State gun-licensing laws have been a vehicle for banning firearms possession for well over a century. And plans for national gun licensing today are just as dangerous. David Kopel, author of *The Samurai, The Mountie, and The Cowboy*, explains:

> In St. Louis, gun ownership permits have routinely been denied to homosexuals, nonvoters, and wives who lack their husbands' permission. Although New Jersey law requires that the

authorities act on gun license applications within 30 days, delays of 90 days are routine; some applications are delayed for years, for no valid reason.[2]

Civil Rights attorney Stephen Halbrook adds:

In some cases, it has taken years of protracted litigation to require [police] to issue firearms permits to which citizens are entitled. . . . In some states the courts have upheld police denials of firearms permits under the dogmas that handguns can never be effectively used by private citizens for self-defense. Physicians who carried narcotics in their bags in high crime areas at night were not entitled to permits because the New Jersey Supreme Court alleged, "their possession of handguns in the streets would . . . furnish hardly any measure of self-protection."[3]

Previous licensing laws have been designed to disarm a certain segment ("wrong people") or all of the population. Brady Bill II is no different. Clearly, given the far-reaching provisions of Brady Bill II, gun owners are all the "wrong" people.

NATIONAL BAN ON FIREARMS

A ban on any firearm is a vehicle for banning all firearms. The "Saturday Night Special" ban revives the 1970s' concept that was exposed years ago as a scam designed to ban all handguns.

Calling these guns "small, cheap handguns—the weapons of choice of criminals," gun banners claimed that "Saturday Night Specials" were handguns that "had no sporting use, no hunting use, were not suitable for self-defense, and that their only purpose is for killing people."[4] Such broad definitions could apply to almost all handguns.

Suppose the government were to declare that some common item in your home was contraband—that its mere possession was a felony. That's what a ban on "Saturday Night Specials" amounts to.

Take the situation that faced law-abiding gun owners in Cleveland, Ohio. In 1976 the Cleveland City Council enacted a law banning private ownership of some handguns—those with barrel lengths of under three inches and of calibers below .32-inch.

That law was thrown out by a municipal judge who declared that it discriminated against the poor, and further called the "Saturday Night Special" definition "an arbitrary distinction with no basis in fact or logic."[5]

Subsequently, Cleveland enacted a handgun registration law. Dutifully, Cleveland firearms owners obeyed, and of the firearms registered, over 5,500 handguns would have been covered under the defunct "Saturday Night Special" law.

But when an appeals court reversed the earlier decision and reinstated the "Saturday Night Special" law, all of those registered firearms were declared illegal contraband. The police sent notices to those who had registered their pistols and revolvers telling them their registration cards were revoked and that they must dispose of their illegal guns, surrender them to the police, or face gun confiscation.

Consider: Brady Bill II seeks to ban "assault weapons," a term designed to encompass semi-automatic rifles, shotguns, and handguns; and "Saturday Night Specials," a term that in effect encompasses all handguns. What's left?

U.S. Senator Howard Metzenbaum:

> Until we can ban all of them, then we might as well ban none. [U.S. Senate Hearings 1993]

Peter Franchot, Maryland House of Delegates:

> I have concluded that we should prohibit the sale, manufacture, and private ownership of handguns . . . I am pleased to find that 19 of my colleagues have joined me in introducing [a] bill . . . it is a complete ban on handguns . . . [*Montgomery Journal* 2/18/94]

GUN BAN EXPERIENCES IN AMERICAN HISTORY

In 1967, New York City required rifle owners to register their guns. City Council members at that time *promised that registration lists would not be used to confiscate the firearms of law-abiding citizens.* Roughly 1 million New Yorkers were obliged to register with police, as James Bovard reported in the *Wall Street Journal* on January 6, 1994.

The *New York Times* editorialized on September 26, 1967: "No sportsman should object to a city law that makes it mandatory to obtain a license from the Police Department and to register rifles . . ."

But in 1991 Mayor David Dinkins pushed a bill through the City Council banning possession of many semi-automatic rifles, claiming that they were "assault weapons." Tens of thousands of residents who had registered their guns in 1967 and scrupulously obeyed the law were stripped of their right to own these guns.

According to attorney Stephen Halbrook, police are now using the registration lists to crack down on gun owners. Police have sent out threatening letters, and in some cases knocked on doors, demanding that people surrender their guns. Halbrook noted that the New York ban "prohibits so many guns that they don't even know how many are prohibited" and that the law is so vague that city police "arbitrarily apply it to almost any gun owner."

The gun ban bill was enacted only a few weeks before the Crown Heights riot of 1991 in which New York police failed to protect Jewish residents being assaulted by mobs of angry blacks. Some of the victims of this riot later sued New York Mayor David Dinkins for the city's failure to defend them. In its official reply, as reported in the *New York Times*, June 28, 1993, the Dinkins administration asserted that "the plaintiffs simply had no constitutional or federal right to have the police respond to their calls for assistance or to receive police protection against potential harm caused by private parties."

It would be difficult to find a better statement from a government official to justify widespread private ownership of firearms. Yet, it came from an administration intent on confiscating its citizens' guns.

In 1976, the District of Columbia enacted one of the nation's strictest handgun registration and gun ban laws. All handguns currently owned had to be reregistered and no more handguns could be legally acquired by anyone. When the law was enacted, *politicians promised that gun registration lists would not be used to confiscate handguns from legal owners.* In 1977, a Superior Court upheld the handgun ban. On February 26, 1977, the *Washington Star* announced the decision:

GUN LAW UPHELD, BUT NO SEARCHES, YET

... police officials say they cannot begin "aggressive enforcement" of the law until "some administrative problems have been solved."

"It would be an inefficient use of manpower to send officers to all the homes of persons who had previously registered their weapons . . ." said police counsel Vernon Gill. "As of right now, there are no plans to go out looking for people," he said, adding, "but that could change after we get the administrative problems worked out."

In 1993, voters in Madison, Wisconsin, faced a handgun ban referendum brought by anti-gun politicians that proposed to ban mere possession. As reported on February 22, 1993, in the *Madison Edge*:

In Mayor Soglin's first press conference regarding the ban, someone raised the question of enforcement. Would a neighbor's call to police ("My neighbor's got a gun") be sufficient evidence to search that neighbor's home? Police Chief David Couper indicated that this was indeed the case.

This violates a citizen's civil liberties and privacy rights. As the police chief admitted, police would search homes if a person were "suspected" of having a firearm. A phone call by a disgruntled neighbor who didn't like the way you parked your car, or ex-sweetheart could make you "public enemy number one" in the eyes of police.

In the end, the citizens of Madison rose up and defeated the gun ban referendum. But such attempted distortions of the U.S. Constitution are indeed frightening.

In 1989, the California legislature banned the sale or transfer of "assault weapons" and required all owners to register their guns. The law's definition of "assault weapons" was confusing and arbitrary, as California Attorney General Dan Lungren later admitted. Indeed, some of the gun models specifically banned by the California legislature did not exist.

The vast majority of Californians did not register their guns. According to Michael McNulty, chairman of the private California Organization for Public Safety, as reported in the *Orange County Register*, August 16, 1993, "We estimate hundreds of citizens have been arrested and prosecuted for firearms not on the regulated list."

In numerous cases, the *Register* continued, police carrying out searches of people's homes have seized firearms they allege to be illegal "assault weapons" and refused to return the firearms even after receiving proof that the guns are not legally banned under California law.

In 1989, the Denver City Council forbade residents to own or sell so-called "assault weapons." (Residents could apply for police permission to continue possessing firearms obtained prior to the date of the ban.) The city even banned residents from using "assault weapons" to defend themselves in their own homes—as if government officials wished to put citizens at a disadvantage in repelling burglars or rapists. In February 1993, a local court struck down the law as unconstitutionally vague and as violating the state constitution.

In 1990, New Jersey banned ownership of "assault rifles." Governor Jim Florio declared: "There are some weapons that are just so dangerous that society has a right and the obligation even to take those weapons out of circulation."[6] But the ban was so extensive that even some models of BB guns were outlawed. Owners of the banned guns were required to surrender them to the police, sell them to a licensed dealer, or render the guns inoperable.

President Clinton, the Gannett News Service reported (October 8, 1993), considers the New Jersey law a model for the nation, declaring, "We need a national law to do what New Jersey has done here with assault weapons."

James Bovard, author of *Lost Rights: The Destruction of American Liberty*, wrote in a column in the *Wall Street Journal* on January 6, 1994:

> Assault weapons laws resemble hate speech laws. Hate speech laws usually begin by targeting a few words that almost no one approves. Once the system for controlling and punishing "hate speech" is put into place, there is little or nothing to stop it from expanding to punish more and more types of everyday speech. Similarly, once an assault weapons law is on the books, there is little to prevent politicians from vastly increasing the number of weapons banned under the law.
>
> The main effect of banning assault weapons is to give government an excuse to arrest and imprison millions of Americans while doing little or nothing to reduce crime. America has a limited number of police, and politicians must decide who the real public enemies are. If Mr. Clinton signs an assault weapons ban, it could signal the start of an attack on gun owners' constitutional rights that could far surpass all previous gun bans.

NATIONAL TAXES ON GUNS AND AMMUNITION

In 1819, Supreme Court Chief Justice John Marshall wrote that "the power to tax involves the power to destroy." (*McCulloch v. Maryland, 4 Wheat 316 (1819)*) That warning was well taken. In a *Washington Post* article on November 4, 1993, U.S. Senator Daniel Patrick Moynihan pledged: "[With a 10,000 percent tax] we could tax them out of existence."

The vast majority of gun and ammunition taxing devices are

not about raising revenue, they are about banning guns and ammunition. Designed to circumvent the Second Amendment through taxes, they are punitive in nature and prohibitive by intent.

Hillary Rodham Clinton:

> I'm personally all for [taxing guns to pay for health care coverage]. [*New York Times* 11/4/93]

U.S. Senator Bill Bradley:

> [With 25 percent more taxes on guns and ammunition] $600 million could be raised from these purveyors of violence. [Associated Press 10/6/93]

Regressive taxes have always had but one objective—to discourage or prohibit that which the tax sponsors find distasteful or troublesome. Any tax revenues derived from such schemes are an added bonus, incidental to the intended purpose.

In this case the gun banners aren't even attempting to hide their intentions. Their proposals are designed to curb the market for handguns and ammunition by pricing poor and middle-class buyers (the "wrong" people) out of the market.

Brady Bill II requires: national gun registration; national handgun licensing; a special license for a gun collection (or what they call a "gun arsenal" of twenty guns or more); the banning of semi-automatic firearms (so-called "assault weapons"); the banning of "Saturday Night Special" handguns; the banning of all "non-sporting" ammunition; a surtax of 30 percent on handguns; a surtax of 50 percent on handgun ammunition; and more.

There can be no doubt about the agenda. Brady Bill II proponents flaunt it—only the elite and the privileged can be trusted with arms.

CHAPTER 11

ARMING AGAINST CRIME

"Gun control advocates need to realize that passing laws that honest gun owners will not obey is a self-defeating strategy. Gun owners are not about to surrender their rights, and only the most foolish of politicians would risk the stability of the government by trying to use the force of the state to disarm the people."

—J. NEIL SCHULMAN, Los Angeles Times 6/8/92

WRITER NEIL SCHULMAN must have looked into a crystal ball to have reached the same conclusions as found in a public opinion survey conducted for the *National Law Journal* (NLJ) in March 1994.

Rorie Sherman, staff reporter for the *National Law Journal*, reported the results in the April 18, 1994, issue. Sherman wrote:

It is a time of unparalleled desperation about crime. But the mood is decidedly "I'll do it myself" and "Don't get in my way."

Today's citizens believe people must take more responsibility for their own protection. They reject government intrusion on basic civil rights, gun ownership and the media's displays of violence. And there is a pervasive willingness to forgive those who commit serious crimes motivated by the preservation of children or self. Yet for the lawless who lack compelling excuses, little mercy is shown.

Conducted by Penn + Schoen Associates, Inc., it is NLJ's second comprehensive survey of public attitudes toward crime in the past five years. Americans made it clear they are not willing to sit back and become victims nor allow government to tamper with their civil liberties:

- 75 percent agreed that police and the justice system can't protect them and said people have to take more responsibility for safeguarding themselves.
- As many as 85 percent said they are unwilling to forfeit basic civil liberties even if it could enhance personal safety.
- 62 percent said the need for guns is increasing, and a majority is *unwilling* to accept laws that restrict gun ownership greatly.
- 89 percent subscribe to the "mother lion defense" saying they would find it "compelling" if a mother tried to excuse a serious crime by saying she was trying to protect her children from an abusive father.
- More than 75 percent support "3 Strikes You're Out" proposals and want violent three time offenders behind bars for life. Respondents were unmoved by criticisms that older criminals would be kept behind bars, at taxpayer expense, though they *may* have been rendered relatively harmless by age. The message is: do the crime—do the time. Americans want violent criminals off the streets and out of their neighborhoods.

The bottom line: Americans are upset about crime and soundly reject government solutions which infringe on their rights and liberties. Clearly people recognize that legislative and administrative infringements of our liberties are designed to "convenience" government rather than to solve or curb violent crime.

When the public loses faith in the ability or willingness of the government to protect it, people rely more heavily on self-protection. This involves the purchase of firearms, protection devices, hiring security guards, building walls, and installing security systems. In 1993, $65 billion was spent on private security. All Americans want to be protected against crime— not just those who can afford it.

But the American Bar Association (ABA) isn't listening. In fact, these lawyers are working against strong crime fighting measures. On February 22, 1994, ABA testified before the U.S. House of Representatives Subcommittee on Crime and Criminal Justice that criminal justice policy is "inordinately tilted toward law enforcement and corrections."[1] A rather incredible statement—perhaps self-serving—when today prison is the sentencing alternative *least used* throughout America—and Americans are paying for it with their lives. Every day in America, hundreds of people are attacked by violent criminals who have been caught and convicted and returned to the streets on probation or early parole.

The ABA also testified against mandatory minimum sentences and "3 Strikes You're Out." But Americans want measures such as these, and the NLJ survey confirms it. The Washington Citizens for Justice and the National Rifle Association have been hard at work getting "3 Strikes" on the ballot and passed in Washington State, and working with the Three Strikes and You're Out Committee in California, and onto the books in that state. The measure was also included in a crime bill approved in the U.S. Senate and the House of Representatives.[2] ABA, however, testified that "this provision is unlikely to produce any real impact on reducing or preventing violent crime," because "criminal activity diminishes markedly by the time [violent criminals] reach their mid-thirties."[3]

Not only is the ABA at odds with public attitudes, it is out of touch with reality. In the fall of 1993, the pro-gun forces tried unsuccessfully to block the release of Oregon's Russell Obremski—a multiple killer nearly fifty years old. Soon after his release, Obremski was arrested for sodomizing a four-year-old little girl. Perhaps ABA will send an emissary to the child's family to explain how "criminal activity diminishes markedly" when life-long predators get older.

A July 1990 study by the U.S. Department of Justice, Bureau of Justice Statistics, of the 245,652 offenders serving time in state prisons in 1986 for crimes of violence, found that they had victimized an estimated 409,000 persons: about 79,300 victims killed, 51,100 victims assaulted, and 20,400 other types of violence. The criminals in prison in the year 1986 alone had killed nearly 50 percent more Americans than died in the Vietnam War.[4]

As we witness the carnage on our streets perpetrated by criminals released early by parole boards, we are forced to ask: Would members of parole boards make that gamble if they knew that their lives or the lives of their loved ones depended on that decision? Do they know what the rates of recidivism are for violent offenders?

The public has a right to ask tough questions of parole boards that release violent criminals before they have served 85 percent of their sentence. Where else would a failure rate of this magnitude—which sometimes results in the death, rape, or injury of the innocent—be tolerated?

Would the Federal Aviation Administration allow airplanes to fly with critical parts that failed 29 percent of the time? Would the Federal Drug Administration allow drugs on the market that either killed or caused crippling side effects 18 percent of the time?

Yet the ABA's soft-on-crime stance would put more criminals back on the streets, while attacking the fundamental right of self-defense, and, indeed, the Second Amendment itself.

William Ide III, president of the ABA, announced in a news release on April 15, 1994, that the ABA "will assist cities, counties and states in drafting and enacting ordinances and laws to regulate firearms, including legislation to ban the manufacture, sale and possession. . . ." Ide also claimed there "is no Second Amendment guarantee."

ABA is out of step with America. ABA rejects tough crime measures and calls for gun control while most Americans believe the concrete and steel of prisons are their best barricade against violent attackers. And if that fails, lawful gun ownership—not lawyers and litigation—is their best protection.

In the *Washington Post*, on July 9, 1989, Doug Bandow of the Cato Institute warned:

> Gun control has proved to be a grievous failure, a means of disarming honest citizens without limiting firepower available to those who prey on the law-abiding. Attempting to use the legal system to punish the weapon rather than the person misusing the weapon is similarly doomed to fail.

Anti-gun politicians fail to heed such warnings and further exacerbate the problem by wasting tax dollars and precious time pursuing nonsensical gun control measures, and all the while the toll of victims continues to mount.

The *National Law Journal* survey cited above sent a strong message to politicians and the White House:

- 53 percent of Americans are not satisfied with President Clinton's "crime-fighting" measures.
- 52 percent of American are not satisfied with the job Attorney General Janet Reno is doing.
- 62 percent of Americans said instead of more law enforcement, there is an increasing need for firearms for personal protection.

While 62 percent overall see the need for firearms for personal protection, 73 percent of blacks now hold that view. Blacks consistently have the highest victimization rates and do not believe that gun control measures are the solution to crime.

An even stronger message about civil liberties is reflected in the same NLJ survey:

> Despite intense concern about crime, losing basic civil liberties *will not be tolerated*—even if doing so might enhance safety. [Emphasis added.]
>
> A full 85 percent say they are unwilling to allow police to wiretap phones without prior court approval. Eighty-two percent say police should not be allowed a random search without probable cause.

Yet when it came to civil liberties in Chicago's public housing, President Bill Clinton acted most alarmingly in respect to the residents' Fourth Amendment privacy protections. The Chicago Housing Authority authorized random searches of apartments in Chicago's public housing, without warrants or probable cause, in a clear violation of the Constitution. In a class action suit brought to halt the searches, U.S. District Judge Wayne Anderson stopped the searches in February 1994, saying that random searches without probable cause are a "greater evil than the danger of criminal activity."[5]

President Clinton's response? He instructed Justice Department staff to find "a way around the Constitution"—a shocking directive for a United States president who has sworn to uphold the Constitution.

The president soon announced his administration's "way around the Constitution": add language to apartment leases that requires residents in public housing to waive their rights and grant permission for random searches of their homes. In other words, if the Constitution won't allow those rights to be taken away, the president would condone forcing the poor to give up their rights. The message of the NLJ survey—which condemned trampling on civil liberties—apparently did not reach the White House.

Eroding civil liberties by door to door searches to confiscate guns in public housing sets a dangerous precedent.

Karl Day, a West Point graduate and Vietnam veteran, writing for the *Washington Times* on February 2, 1994, spoke for most Americans who reject door-to-door searches as "crime fighting" tactics when he said:

> . . . All we have to do is tear up the Bill of Rights, shred the Constitution, call out the National Guard and, starting with high-crime areas (if this isn't perceived to be racist), commence house to house searches, seizing all guns and other contraband. Roving police and National Guard patrols could set up random roadblocks, stop and search vehicles, seize guns and arrest those who possess them. Citizens could be stopped at random and frisked for weapons.
>
> Sound like the America you'd like to live in? It certainly isn't the America I fought for. . . .

Joseph McNamara, former police chief of San Jose, California, although well known throughout America as a gun-hater, waded into the gun-search controversy in defense of the Constitution's protections against search and seizure. In the *Los Angeles Times* on April 17, 1994, he wrote:

> . . . President Bill Clinton recently asked Atty. Gen. Janet Reno to find ways to circumvent a federal judge's injunction forbidding random police searches of apartments in a federal housing development in Chicago. Clinton could have assured tenants that the federal government would do all it could do to provide whatever level of policing was needed to stop the violence in the complex. Instead, the President pandered to police and public impatience with rising crime. He urged the department responsible for prosecuting officers who violate people's constitutional rights to assist police in evading the Constitution . . .
>
> There is no need for any dilution of individual rights that took centuries to achieve. The murderers striking the most terror in the hearts of people during this century have not been serial killers like Ted Bundy. They have been governments that

have killed millions of their citizens in the name of social order. The authors of the Bill of Rights knew the danger and drafted a document for our protection. We should not let panic about crime erode it.

Judging from responses to questions specifically about guns in the NLJ survey, it is clear that the American people are sometimes slow to realize what is really going on—or are willing to give others the benefit of the doubt—but they are not stupid. The survey shows that since passage of the Brady Bill, support for the waiting period gun legislation has already dropped to 58 percent from the 80 percent support before passage. Indeed, support for restricting gun sales has now dropped to 22 percent.

Reacting to the survey results, the National District Attorneys Association president, William O'Malley, said:

> The interpretation that somebody puts on those statistics is important.
> I don't think it is vigilantism or hostility to police, prosecutors or the courts. It's more a recognition that the system is powerless without community support and participation.[6]

O'Malley's interpretation of the NLJ data is skewed. When he suggests a lack of public hostility toward the criminal justice system and instead sees public recognition of the need for community support and participation, he downplays the message Americans are sending. People are angry and frustrated with the criminal justice system. Unless by "participation" he means people that intend to protect themselves, he has misread the message.

The NLJ survey data don't need interpreting or "spin doctoring"—the responses are straightforward and unambiguous.

For years Americans have been attempting to participate in criminal justice reform. And their message has been crystal clear: get tough on criminals, quit gratuitous plea bargaining, make our streets safe by keeping criminals locked up for their full sentences, and stop probation and parole of violent criminals.

The message has for too long fallen on deaf ears. Citizens—and victims, in particular—have been treated as meddlesome and have been shooed away as one would a small child underfoot.

People are saying, enough is enough! The criminal justice system has shifted its focus from protecting the rights of victims to protecting the rights of criminals. Law-abiding citizens are tired of being prosecuted and persecuted for defending themselves.

No victim of crime should be required to surrender his life, health, safety, personal dignity, or property to a criminal, nor should a victim be required to retreat in the face of attack.

The Castle Doctrine is an ancient common law doctrine with origins going back at least to Roman law. It proclaims that one's home is a castle and hence an inhabitant may use all manner of force, including deadly force, to protect it and its inhabitants from attack. Further, the Constitution guarantees basic rights to all persons, including the right to defend life and protect property. Citizens have a right to expect safety within their own homes or vehicles.

The criminal justice system must be refocused. It must protect victims by keeping criminals behind bars and restore the absolute rights of law-abiding people to protect themselves, their families, and their property from unlawful intruders and violent attackers without fear of prosecution or civil action.

A person who unlawfully enters or attempts to enter another person's home, dwelling, residence, or occupied vehicle should be presumed to be entering or attempting to enter with the intent to commit an unlawful act involving force or violence. Thus, any manner of force may be employed in self-defense. There should be absolutely no duty to retreat from any place where a law-abiding person has a right to be.

Citizens support "Castle Doctrine" initiatives and other

proposals to correct the failures of lawmakers and the criminal justice system.

A citizens' movement to put a "3 Strikes" initiative on the ballot in Washington State failed in 1992—until the National Rifle Association and the Washington Citizens for Justice stepped in to help. On Election Day 1993, the people didn't wait for the sluggish government to take back their streets. The people of Washington State gave up on their own legislature and overwhelmingly passed, by a 76–24 percent margin, their own Initiative 593—"3 Strikes and You're Out"—which delivers life in prison to criminals convicted of a third serious felony. No probation, no parole—for life. The result—a people's victory, a defeat for soft-on-crime politics.

It is, quite simply, a national disgrace that citizens anywhere should need a ballot measure to prevent killers, rapists, and child molesters from getting out of jail after they've been convicted of these serious crimes.

Although the Washington victory may seem a small step, it helped, because following that victory, "3 Strikes" laws have taken off. On the election's heels, various organizations pledged their resources to enact a similar law in California, including the collection of some 600,000 signatures of registered voters to place the crime-fighting measure on the state's November 1994 ballot. Thousands upon thousands of dollars were raised to promote the measure, and countless California activists did their part. In the end the California legislature was forced to take "3-Strikes" seriously and pass legislation mandating the reform.

In Texas the people voted an overwhelmingly 89 percent to 11 percent to deny bail to career criminals and sex offenders, and voted by 62 percent to 38 percent to put up $1 billion to increase prison capacity substantially. They knew in their hearts what researchers have proven—states that increase imprisonment drive down violent crime. The result—a people's victory, a defeat of soft-on-crime politics.

On November 2, 1993, the real leadership in America—the people—spoke to the need for criminal justice reform.

Wherever there was an anti-crime platform, the results showed a stunning loss for criminals.

In many states, the American people have voted for real solutions—tougher prison sentences and the abolition of parole in Virginia and Arizona, double prison sentences in Texas, the passage of victims' rights amendments in Illinois, Missouri, Kansas, Colorado, and New Mexico—and demanded a crackdown on gang crime in Arizona, Colorado, Florida, and Utah.

As the *Wall Street Journal* editorialized November 4, 1993, under the head "Criminal Control Beats Gun Control":

> If indeed crime is one of the deciding electoral issues of our era, the adherents of gun control won't be deciding much of anything until they figure out a way to also talk in public, credibly, about controlling the criminals.

Americans are using the power of their votes to defend their very lives. They know that each year sixty thousand criminals are convicted of serious crimes and never see prison. And those who do are released after serving an average of a third of their sentences.

What is difficult to comprehend is why so many politicians do not stand before the American people and demand that criminals with guns be apprehended.

We don't have a gun problem in America, we have an enforcement problem. Tough laws are already on the books to remove criminals from society, but they should be used. Existing federal and state laws must be applied to criminals who use guns, drug users, drug dealers, and other law breakers.

Under the Gun Control Act of 1968 (GCA '68), as amended in 1986, it is presently a federal felony punishable by a five-year prison term and a $250,000 fine for a convicted felon to be in possession of an "assault weapon." That law covers all felons—whether convicted by a state, county, municipal, or federal court.

It covers any firearm that anyone could possibly define as an "assault weapon." It covers guns with large magazine capacities, pistol grips, and flash suppressors. It even covers single shot .22 rifles.

In addition, other prohibitions with the same or greater penalties include use of firearm in any crime, selling of a firearm by a convicted felon, alteration of any firearm to a fully automatic firearm, and the use of a firearm during a drug trade. And remember, all of these criminal activities should result in long, hard jail time for criminals, or drug users and drug dealers with "assault weapons," or with any kind of firearm—shotgun, rifle, pistol, revolver—single shot to "machinegun." Why aren't these laws being used?

Every victim of every violent crime in which a gun is used ought to demand an answer to that question.

Congressman Steve Schiff of New Mexico recently asked the Justice Department how many criminals were prosecuted under various of the provisions just cited. He was told that in the last three years the law had been used in only 530 cases.

There are hundreds of thousands of armed criminals out there who fall under the prohibited categories in current federal law. There are thousands of federal agents who could be enforcing that law. They are not.

If federal law enforcement agencies did their jobs with respect to guns and convicted violent felons—using only the GCA '68, as reformed—gun control would not be an issue and we would be a long way toward solving the violent crime problem. We would be getting criminals off the street and into jail.

The FBI or BATF could go today to any city in America and make wholesale federal prosecutions of convicted felons whom local police have already arrested for whatever crime in which they possessed any gun.

Think about that. Every convicted criminal in America who picks up a gun could now be in a federal prison. *Should* be in prison. That's the law! But other than these few existing statutes which would remove armed criminals from the midst of the innocent, all other "gun control" measures are a cruel hoax, a diversion, and a threat. In all of the "gun control" proposals now pending before Congress, the target is not criminals, but ordinary people.

Since it is already illegal for criminals to purchase and possess even one gun, why limit the number of guns or types of guns honest people can own? The answer: arresting violent criminals is dangerous, but arresting nice, peaceable citizens is safe.

To foist "gun control" laws on decent citizens is comparable to Congress passing a law to eradicate cancer by forcing every healthy person to undergo chemotherapy or radiation. It might cure cancer, but it might also kill most of us in the process.

Gun ban laws have accomplished one thing—massive civil disobedience by peaceful, formerly law-abiding citizens. There are millions of good, honest citizens in every state who own guns that some in Congress would ban. And those millions of citizens are not going to give up their private property. And even if they did, their loss would not reduce violent crime.

Those few elite who drone on about gun bans are being drowned out by the angry voices of voters who are rebelling against America's catch-and-release criminal justice system and beginning to flex their muscles at the ballot box.

Politicians should take note of what the people are trying to tell them. Politicians who don't listen to what their constituents are saying about crime control can expect another message on election day.

CHAPTER 12

CRIME AND PUNISHMENT IN AMERICA

THE STATE OF OUR DISORDER

IN TEXAS, THEY now call him the "Monster"; in 1989, the Texas parole board called him a "Good Risk" for return to the community.

Kenneth McDuff had been sentenced to a total of fifty-two years in prison for a series of burglaries in 1964—committed after he raped a woman, cut her throat, and left her for dead. After serving less than ten months of his sentence, he was released in December 1965. Texans would pay dearly—with their lives in some cases—for this act of leniency, and not only for this one.

On August 6, 1966, McDuff was in Everman, Texas, just

south of Fort Worth. He and Roy Dale Green were "cruising" through town when McDuff spotted sixteen-year-old Edna Sullivan with her boyfriend Robert Brand, seventeen, and Robert's cousin, fifteen-year-old Mark Dunnam, near a local baseball field.

McDuff stopped his car and, in violation of federal gun control laws, armed himself with a .38 caliber pistol. At gunpoint he forced Edna and her two friends into the trunk of the car and locked them in.

McDuff drove to a remote area outside of town, stopping in an open field. He ordered Green, who had followed in McDuff's car, to put Edna in his trunk. The two boys, on their knees, began begging for their lives—McDuff shot them both, repeatedly, in the face and head.

McDuff and Green left the scene of the murders with Edna in the trunk of the second car. They stopped alongside a dirt road, McDuff took her out of the trunk, and both McDuff and Green raped her repeatedly. Edna was then forced to lie on the ground and, while Green held her down, McDuff killed her by crushing her neck with a broomstick that he laid across her throat. Her body was then abandoned by the side of the road.

Green confessed to the killings when they became public. And McDuff was tried, convicted, and sentenced to death. But in 1972, the Supreme Court of the United States said, in effect, that every death penalty in the country was unconstitutional, and McDuff's sentence was commuted to life in prison. Under the law then applicable in the state of Texas, this meant that McDuff would be eligible for release on parole by 1976—ten years after his vicious murders.

Incredibly, despite his record and the horror of his crimes, the Texas parole board voted to release McDuff on parole in 1989. He was set free. And, once again, he began to kill.

Authorities now believe McDuff may have raped and murdered as many as six more women before he was apprehended. Six lives lost, six families shattered by a criminal predator who had been caught and convicted, and then, in effect, aided and abetted by a justice system that had collapsed. For it could be said that the Texas parole board was McDuff's accomplice in every one of his heinous crimes.

But this is just one instance. All across America violent repeat offenders are regularly released back to the streets for incomprehensible reasons: the leniency of parole boards, the courts' sympathy for violent criminals with "underprivileged" childhoods, and court-mandated early release due to prison "overcrowding."

The crime statistics do not reflect the pain and suffering of the victims but their sheer numbers have become so shocking, and the crimes have been repeated so often, that we are becoming numb. If present reported crime rates continue, five out of six American twelve-year-olds will become the victims of a violent crime—murder, rape, robbery, or aggravated assault—during their lifetimes.

Picture a sixth-grade classroom. Go up and down the rows of children, look at their young and eager faces. And recoil at the thought: five out of every six of them murdered, raped, robbed, or seriously injured; their lives not only denied a child's innate innocence, but also the peaceful order that was the promise of America.

In 1994, one American will lose his or her life to violent crime every 21 minutes. One woman will be raped every 5 minutes. One of our citizens will be robbed every 46 seconds, assaulted every 29 seconds, or have his or her home invaded by a burglar every 5 seconds. Day in and day out, a torrent of crime has changed the way we live, the way we think of one another, and the way we look at our country and our future.

Even so, the numbers do not tell the real story of crime in America. They do not tell of the pain of the victims, the story of shattered lives and fractured order. Behind each of the numbers live real human beings. It is through their stories, chilling stories, of what happened to them and their assailants, stories of why and how, that we can truly learn the scope of our disorder. Stories of criminals and their victims teach a lesson that we dare not ignore.

On March, 17, 1969, Russell Obremski entered the Oregon

State Penitentiary for the murders of Laverna Lowe and Betty Anne Ritchie. Laverna Lowe was eight months pregnant when Obremski killed her. At the time, he was on parole after having served one year of a twenty-year prison sentence in Washington for sexual assault and carnal knowledge of a child.

Although his prison record was replete with convictions for continued drug use and unlawful sexual conduct, and although during one of his parole hearings he threatened the daughter of one of his victims, the Oregon parole board released him in late 1993.

Within weeks of his release he was arrested and is now charged with sodomizing a four-year-old girl. Obremski's accomplice was the Oregon parole board just as surely as if its members had joined in stalking his victim.

In 1988, Henry Louis Wallace was convicted of burglary in the state of Washington. His sentence was suspended and he was given probation, which he broke by fleeing. He remained a fugitive and traveled to South Carolina where, in March of 1990, he was accused of attempting to rape a sixteen-year-old girl at gunpoint. Eight days after his arrest, he was released and put into a "pre-trial intervention" program, which was supposedly reserved for first-time, nondangerous offenders.

In 1991, Wallace was sent to prison for burglary convictions, but he was once again released by the system after serving only four months. In February 1992, although he was a repeat offender with at least one prison term, Wallace was freed on his own recognizance after being arrested for the rape, again at gunpoint, of a seventeen-year-old girl.

Wallace was no doubt emboldened by his first-hand knowledge of the collapse of our criminal justice system. At present, he stands charged with the murder of eleven women.

These cases are not unusual, but rather typical of what is happening in every state of our country. Every American knows the truth about our revolving door justice system and knows that every day it places him or her in harm's way. Acts of excessive leniency have become self-inflicted wounds, or more aptly, wounds inflicted on others.

As Americans, we cannot but look on this system with dismay and disbelief. How could any parole board release dangerous repeat felons and allow them to return to our communities? How could judges grant probation to perpetrators of violent crimes and put them back in our neighborhoods? How could our laws fail to mandate that violent and repeat offenders be sent to prison and remain there?

The answers are complex. The state of our disorder springs from weak laws and weak leaders. To right the situation, we must demand straight answers about the failures in the justice system and tough-minded solutions that will restore order to the streets of our country.

No problem could be more pressing for the American people. Politicians can debate the merits of health care reform, education, transportation, or welfare, but unless lawmakers restore order and free the American citizen from criminal attack little else will matter.

Nothing erodes the spirit of the American people more than the constant fear that at any moment their home may be invaded or that they may be attacked or killed. The best schools are of little value to the child who walks to school in fear of the juvenile gangs in his or her neighborhood. The resources of the best hospitals and health care system are squandered on the repair of the damage inflicted by chronic offenders who daily stalk new victims. The best transportation systems become rivers of death when car-jackers or drive-by shooters can roam our streets with virtual impunity. The best neighborhoods and the most vibrant local businesses deteriorate and are ruined when crime drives neighbors and customers behind locked doors. Yet this sorry picture describes the situation in community after community across our country.

Somewhere along the way our political leaders have lost sight of the fact that government's most important responsibility is to protect the lives, liberties, and property of its citizens. It was to provide for the common defense and ensure domestic tranquility that our republic was originally founded.

But today, the protection of the law-abiding and the innocent figure little in the halls of "justice," which seem far more concerned with protecting criminal defendants. Not that those protections are trivial. Indeed, protection against an abusive government is critical to the well-being of a free people. But the imbalance today between the rights of the law-abiding and the rights of the accused and convicted is enormous.

Nowhere is this imbalance more clearly seen than in the mistreatment of the victims of crime. While defendants' rights are protected by both the federal and state constitutions of this country, victims' rights are not—except in the case of fourteen states that recently enacted constitutional rights for crimes victims.

Victims have no right to be informed of the proceedings involving their case, no right to be heard at the most critical stages, indeed no right even to be present in the courtroom during the trial of their cases. For victims it is a cruel and oppressive reality that often leaves them embittered and with a sense of abandonment by the very system that was supposed to protect them. This failure to protect victims is real—it is not something for constitutional scholars to debate in the abstract.

It is more than an abstraction when the parents of a murdered child are told that they must wait outside the courtroom while others testify about the murder. It is more than an abstraction when a battered and raped woman is told she has no right to tell the judge what she thinks the sentence for the crime ought to be. It is more than an abstraction when the victim of a brutal assault finds out by reading the newspapers that his attacker has been released to the streets—and he, the victim, has not been given the opportunity to speak regarding the release.

How, the question begs, could we have come to this?

During the 1960s, the American criminal justice policy was driven by the notion that somehow society and social conditions were the "root causes" of crime, and that individuals were not responsible for their own actions. Experts proclaimed that if we dealt with poverty, poor education, unemployment, or lack of adequate housing—by eliminating the social conditions that "caused" crime—crime could be controlled. When the concept of individual responsibility and accountability was jettisoned, punishment lost its moral moorings.

With heady enthusiasm, America embarked on the war on poverty, spending more and more of our resources on social programs and social engineering, and less and less on imprisonment. The ranks of those on probation began to swell. And crime soared. From 1960–1969 violent crime rates increased by over 200 percent. Now, $4.5 trillion of welfare programs later, families have been split, dollars squandered, education reduced to a state of dysfunction, and we live with crime levels that threaten the very existence of our republic.

Moreover, crime dramatically lowers property values in the inner-city. Studies show that for every 1 percent increase in the crime rate, rents and home values drop 2 to 3 percent. For businesses trying to survive in the toughest markets, uncontrolled crime virtually guarantees failure.

Crime and the fear of crime drive investment decisions even more than high taxes or labor costs. Indeed, as does no other contributing factor, crime causes poverty. Surely the duty of our government is to restore order to these communities. In doing so, minorities and the poor would benefit the most.

While our justice system lies in a state of collapse, incapable of discharging its most fundamental duty, some press for passage of laws that would strip us of firearms and the means to protect ourselves and our families. We cannot fix our justice system by giving even more advantages to armed criminals. We cannot restore justice to the innocent and the law-abiding by taking more of their God-given rights away from them. We can only restore justice and order and preserve freedom by addressing the known failures in our system.

Despite all the disheartening evidence, there is nothing inevitable or irreversible about our current criminal justice collapse. We are a free people with the power and the will to rebuild the infrastructure of order in this country, but only if we understand that bad policy choices caused the problem and wise choices can correct it. And in the process we need not, indeed we must not, give up the precious freedoms that have distinguished this society from every other in the history of mankind.

While the crime numbers continue to mount, the U.S. Congress and state legislatures are awash in debate over gun laws, gun proposals to restrict the rights of law-abiding citizens that will not reduce crime—cannot reduce crime—but will only ensure more victims.

This nation is currently being held hostage by crime, gripped with fear and burdened with the economic impact of crime, yet politicians, backed by a relentless media, spend their time promoting useless and dangerous gun control measures.

Guns laws—gun bans, waiting periods, registration, licensing, gun and ammunition taxes, and a litany of restrictive measures—only divert the attention of America from true crime solutions. The inescapable fact is: criminals don't obey laws; criminals range the street because of a failed criminal justice system.

The history of effort, energy, and resources squandered on attempts to impose gun restrictions is a tragic epitaph for the victims of crime, victims of parole boards, victims of early release—victims of the total disorder of today's criminal justice system.

CHAPTER 13

THE CRIMINAL JUSTICE SYSTEM

In 1967, Mitchell Blazak, a heavy drug user, murdered a man he suspected of being a police informant. He beat him savagely with a tire iron, took his wallet, and left him for dead. Blazak was convicted of assault with intent to kill and robbery. The conviction was set aside on appeal, and he was reconvicted in a second trial.

Blazak was sentenced to eight years in prison. After two years and eight months, he was eligible for parole and released.

Parole board members later admitted they had not read Blazak's psychiatric reports, which described him as a violent psychopath. One report noted that he could murder a human as easily as most people would step on a blade of grass.

In December 1973, Blazak walked into a tavern and demanded the till. When the owner refused to hand over his money, Blazak threatened to kill him. The owner again refused and Blazak murdered him. He then opened fire on customers, killing one and wounding another.

Blazak and an accomplice were arrested for the crime; the accomplice confessed and testified against him. Blazak was found guilty and sentenced to death.

In 1977, although initially affirming the conviction, the state supreme court ordered a resentencing in light of a changed law. The trial court once again sentenced Blazak to death.

Then, in 1982, the state supreme court rejected a second appeal, holding that Blazak qualified for the death penalty by reason of his past attempt at murder and his decision to kill for monetary gain. The U.S. Supreme Court declined to hear another appeal.

One surely would expect that to end the case. The sentence had been examined twice by the trial court, twice by the state supreme court, and once by the U.S. Supreme Court. After ten years of litigation, none had upheld his objections. It should have been over.

Blazak's attorneys, however, filed five state habeas corpus petitions with consequent appeals. The trial court gave these careful consideration; one petition alone was given hearings that spanned several months. After all five state petitions failed, Blazak filed three federal habeas corpus petitions.

By the time the federal court ruled on his third petition, Blazak's victims had been in their graves *twenty years*.

But this time the killer struck pay dirt. Incredibly, the federal court found—his attorneys had never argued this point at trial—that the state courts, on their own, should have been alert to the possibility that he was mentally incompetent to stand trial and should have ordered a psychiatric examination before hearing the case.

The federal court set aside Blazak's murder conviction and ordered yet another new trial.

Knowing the difficulty of proving a case after twenty years, the state appealed. At last report, the federal judge was assessing whether to order the state to release Blazak pending the appeal.

The criminal justice system is broken. Not only are victims and families of victims brutalized by the continuing process described above, society itself becomes a victim. Millions of tax dollars are consumed—wasted—and the message to criminals is that the criminal justice system can be manipulated to virtually any extreme.

Many Americans blame defense attorneys for the problem: they invoke technicalities, seek out loopholes, and argue that because criminals were abused as children they should go free.

But though many are angered by these attorneys, particularly in cases where the defendant is obviously guilty of an appalling crime, a defense attorney has the ethical duty to defend his client to the limits of the law. Still, at times the law seems to be far too accommodating.

If the defense attorney takes advantage of a legal loophole, the proper approach is to ask why that loophole exists, not why it was invoked. If the argument is flimsy, yet succeeds, the proper approach is to ask why the judge found it so persuasive, and why that judge still sits on the bench.

In the case of Mitchell Blazak, the question is not why his attorneys sought to keep him from being executed—that was their duty. The real questions are vastly more important. Why did a dangerous psychopath who had already attempted murder receive a sentence of only eight years? Why was parole available when only a third of his sentence had been served? Why did the Board of Pardons and Paroles release him?

These are not loopholes. These are system failures brought about by legislatures that don't provide tough punishment standards and adequate resources to house violent offenders for the duration of their sentences.

And why, having already had two direct appeals to both the state and federal supreme courts, was Blazak allowed to bring five state and three federal habeas corpus petitions, to secure twenty years of stays on his execution, and finally to overturn his conviction based on an argument his attorney had never made to the trial court?

Clearly, there is little "justice" in today's criminal justice system—on that point, there is little disagreement.

At the state level, prosecutors boast of a conviction rate that runs around 90 percent. Without question, many of these convictions are the result of plea bargains, some of which are mandated by logistic limitations: not enough courtrooms, prosecutors, and public defenders to try all charges filed. Ruling out plea-bargaining without expanding the justice system would only worsen the problem. But while plea-bargaining can be an effective prosecution tool in some circumstances, it should not be an excuse to avoid investigations to build cases. It has become too common and undermines the system.

U.S. Attorney General Janet Reno has often been criticized for her plea-bargaining record while a state attorney in Florida. The *Miami Herald* reported (10/20/85) that a 1985 study revealed that *97 percent of criminal cases in Dade County, Reno's jurisdiction*, were resolved through plea-bargaining. The *Herald* reported, "Judges blame plea bargains for the seemingly lenient treatment of repeat offenders and sex offenders."

And Janet Reno's response? "Plea bargains are a fact of life in a major urban area."

On March 1, 1993, the *Miami Review*, reported that in 1991 Reno's office only brought 2 percent of all felony defendants to trial.

People want prosecutors, not plea bargainers who put violent perpetrators in jail for a few months rather than build a case to take to court. A defendant cannot *force* a prosecutor to bargain if the prosecutor is willing to go to trail. In light of the evidence before the prosecutor, a plea bargain is either wise or unwise. If wise, it can be a quick way to get an offender off the street. But if it is unwise, it is time to replace the prosecutor.

If the criminal justice system functions well in determining guilt, it utterly fails in the next step—doing something significant to those found guilty.

The sentences handed down are minimal. One recent study found that the median sentence was seven years for rape, five years for robbery, and three years for burglary. But those sentences are mere window-dressing to obscure the time actually served—they overstate the actual penalty and make a sentence sound far more impressive than it is. "Twenty years to life with ten suspended" often translates into back on the streets in twenty-four months or less.

In most states, the offender is sentenced to a wide range of time—five to twenty years, or ten years to life, are fairly typical. In practice, the maximum term is almost meaningless. Calculated against this is "good time," where the convict gets two days credit for every one day he actually serves as payment for not getting caught committing an offense behind bars!

If the maximum sentence is window-dressing, the minimum often has little more meaning—it is a rare convict who serves even the minimum. Parole is often available at one-third of the minimum sentence, and this is the rule rather than the exception.

Since the convict is generally given credit for "time served" (meaning that time spent waiting for trial and conviction is deducted from the sentence), he can be sentenced to years and in fact be free within days. In theory, a convict on parole or probation is monitored and can be imprisoned if he so much as associates with known criminals. But in practice, the paroled convict is free to do as he pleases.

Parole officers have little way of monitoring the day-to-day life of released convicts, and are often fearful of provoking a violent parolee. Parole revocation proceedings are often as complex as a criminal trial. The released offender thus knows that nothing less than being caught at, and convicted of, another felony will end his release. He has little to lose by returning to crime.

Consequently we are left with a system where the public is given the assurance of impressive sentences and convicts are given the assurance that the sentences will never be carried out. The results are bizarre:

- Mitchell Blazak was walking the streets and killing his victims before he completed the appeal from his first conviction for attempted murder of the police informant. The parole board did not bother to read the five psychiatric reports that described him as a violent psychopath.

- James Mackel of Baltimore was sentenced to fifteen years in prison for robbery with a deadly weapon, but was paroled after four years—even though he had past convictions for theft, counterfeiting, and assault with intent to kill. Less than a month later, he robbed a seventy-one-year-old man at gunpoint, threatened to murder an eight-year-old witness, and wounded an FBI agent who pursued him.
- Peter Donohue of New York was sentenced by a federal court to twenty years for bank robbery, and later sentenced to seven years for attempted escape. He was given "work release" after eight years, despite the attempted escape and the fact that he had past convictions in five states. Two months later he murdered one policeman and wounded another.
- Thomas Wiesnhaut was convicted of assaulting a young woman and beating her nearly to death. He was sentenced to twenty years in prison. Prison psychiatrists diagnosed him as psychotic and homicidal, particularly toward women, and likely to repeat his act if ever released. Without reviewing the psychiatric reports, the parole board gave him early release. He went on to rape, murder, and mutilate three more women before he was caught.

These are not isolated cases. It is estimated that in New York City alone, some thirteen thousand convicted killers are on parole on any given day. A quarter of the criminals who kill police are on probation or parole. In any given year, fifteen or more police officers will pay with their lives for the criminal justice system's leniency toward convicted felons.

James Wootton, president of the Safe Streets Alliance in Washington, D.C., prepared an analysis of recidivism among violent criminals. He cited a three-year follow-up study conducted by the Bureau of Justice Statistics of 108,850 state prisoners released in 1983 from institutions in eleven states. It found that 60 percent of violent offenders were rearrested for a felony or serious misdemeanor and that 42 percent of all violent offenders released were reincarcerated. Altogether, the study revealed that these felons had been arrested for 14,467 homicides, 7,073 kidnappings, 23,174 rapes or sexual assaults, 101,226 robberies, and 107,130 assaults.

Ultimately, the issue of parole reform in most cases boils down to housing. Many states have chronic prison overcrowding. In the face of federal court orders designed to improve prison conditions, corrections officials daily find themselves granting convicted dangerous felons early release from prison in order to make room for prisoners newly entering the state's correction facilities. But this short-sighted policy has obvious results: the revolving-door justice encourages criminals, discourages law enforcement, and erodes public confidence in the criminal justice system.

The federal government should work cooperatively with the states to construct and operate regional prisons designed to accommodate the worst offenders in our society: the violent and chronic predators who commit well over one hundred crimes a year when allowed to roam free. These regional facilities would allow for economies of scale and would permit existing facilities to provide needed space for other offenders.

Many argue that we cannot afford to build more prisons. Failure to do so, however, will be far more costly in the long run. More importantly, it will result in government failing in its first and most fundamental obligation to its citizens. Studies have placed the cost of the unincarcerated career criminal at over $300,000, far more than the cost of locking him or her up.

With the dramatic downsizing experienced by the nation's military, dozens of bases are in the process of being closed. They could be converted to regional incarceration facilities.

Regional facilities could also be the impetus for more fundamental changes in the state and local criminal justice systems. In order for a state to make use of these regional facilities, it must bring its criminal justice system up to certain minimum standards, all of which should be designed to curb unreasonably early parole and raise the stakes for criminals.

Then there is the pretrial detention, which has proved to be an effective tool. In Kansas City, it was one of the most effective weapons in dismantling the "Jamaican Posse," a gang trying to control that community's drug trade. When gang members were arrested and failed to reappear on the streets, the posse became known as the "Black Hole" posse. The group soon disappeared as a significant criminal enterprise. Similar results were seen in Philadelphia, where the Violent Traffickers Project had significant success in targeted high-crime areas.

Finally, reform of the sentencing system is imperative and should be straightforward:

First, we need a system of "truth in sentencing," where the penalty assessed is actually imposed, and shows the exact point at which the convict will, if at all, first be eligible for any type of release.

Second, in the case of violent or repetitive felonies, there should be fixed *minimum* sentences, from which *no* release is permitted.

Third, the commission of a felony while on release, whether parole, probation, bail, or any form of early or conditional release, should be a separate and serious offense with no parole allowed.

Finally, parole decisions and files should be made public. In too many states, parole board positions are patronage plums and those who hold them are tempted to ladle out parole to all applicants. If a decision is made to release a convict, both the decision and the background data should be made public knowledge, and those who made the decision should be accountable for it.

Thus far we have considered the impact of the criminal justice system on the offender. Equally important, we must minimize the burdens on the honest citizens—victims, witnesses, and jurors—involved in the system.

Of all the people who have contact with the criminal justice system, none are harder hit than victims. How are they treated? That should be obvious from the surveys of crime victims which show that *only 38 percent of crimes are reported to the police.* Barely half of rape, robbery, and burglary victims bother to report the crime and over 70 percent of theft victims do not call the police.[1]

Although the victim's report is pivotal to an investigation, the criminal justice system treats the victim as excess baggage, or an interloper into a technical process. Whether he or she is informed of any stage of the process is left utterly to chance. This must end.

Crime victims should, like criminals, be able to demand certain rights from the criminal justice system. No court should sentence a serious offender without testimony of the victim, or at minimum a written report of the victim's experience. The victim should, in turn, be entitled to be notified of the sentence imposed, of his or her right to testify, and (should the offender later be considered for parole) of the possibility that the offender may be released and thus be given an opportunity to appear or otherwise contest the offender's early release. When an offender is given probation or parole, the court should be obligated to set out a sum which represents restitution to the victim for the losses caused, and make release conditioned upon making all efforts to repay that amount.

It is time the justice system view the rights of victims, as well as those of criminals, as within its protection.

It is time we take control of our criminal justice system and put it back on track. The only way to restore it is to stick with sound policies for a long time. The message must be delivered clearly and strongly every day, not just by words but by behavior.

Those who maintain that punishment has failed as an answer because we keep imprisoning more and more people miss the point. Regardless of how one views the Vietnam War, it is generally agreed that the United States fared badly there because, instead of committing massive numbers of troops initially to overwhelm the Viet Cong, we kept adding a few more troops and a few more troops and a few more troops—and could never get on top of the situation. We can apply the same lesson to imprisonment. If we don't send the right message and send it clearly and strongly every day, we will continue to fight a losing battle—and we will indeed soon have to pave over the nation with prisons.

CHAPTER 14

JUVENILE JUSTICE

Dateline New York: Fifteen-year-old Shaul Linyear approaches a man, places a gun to his head, and slowly cocks the hammer. A policeman witnesses the assault and tackles him before he can execute the victim. A juvenile judge releases Linyear into the custody of his mother. Two months later, Linyear robs Ricardo Nunez-Reyes and executes him. As a juvenile, Linyear had not even been fingerprinted or photographed in connection with the first offense. Prosecutors find out about it only when someone recognizes Linyear's name and telephones them.

NO AREA OF the criminal justice system is as much in need of reform as its treatment of serious juvenile offenders.

The escalation of juvenile crime tells the story. Juvenile arrests have increased by 300 percent over the past twenty-five years, increasingly for violent offenses. In 1980, 9 percent of arrested murderers were juveniles, but by 1990, this had burgeoned to 14 percent. Today, juvenile criminals account for about one-sixth of murders and rapes, and one-quarter of robberies, burglaries, and thefts.

These offenders, who make up but a tiny fraction of the population, each year account for around two thousand arrests for murder, four thousand for forcible rape, twenty thousand for robbery, and nearly half a million for property crimes.

Two national juvenile gangs, dedicated to murder and drug dealing, are found in forty-five of our states. Under their leadership, joyriding and vandalism are giving way to gang violence and contract hits. Victims die for wearing clothes of a wrong color, making a gesture associated with the rival gang, or simply looking a gang member too intently in the eye. The killers express no remorse, nor do they have reason to. They know that as juveniles they can, quite literally, get away with murder.

As with the adult population, juvenile criminality is concentrated in a small segment of society, and serious criminality in a still smaller segment. A Maryland study singled out chronic juvenile offenders—those with at least three arrests—and found they numbered less than 1 percent of teens and only about 6 percent of juvenile offenders.[1] A Chicago analysis drew a bead on a group of 317 juveniles. This handful—average age sixteen—had already been arrested an average of thirteen times apiece. Charges included fourteen murders, twenty-three rapes, five hundred robberies and assaults, and a thousand burglaries and thefts.[2] And these figures reflect only arrests. In all probability, the offenses actually committed ran into the tens of thousands. For their most recent offense, the justice system "cracked down." The result: an average of ten months in a juvenile hall!

This approach to juvenile justice bears tremendous costs:

Chicago: "J.M.," arrested for burglary, gets a "station adjustment"—translated as a lecture by police. He is later arrested twice for theft. Same result. At thirteen, he is arrested for burglary, and a second time for robbery. More "station adjustments." The following year six more arrests and six more adjustments. He then tears the necklace from a woman's neck and is finally scheduled for a juvenile court hearing. He is released. On release, he smashes the window of a woman's car and snatches the purse from her side, receives probation for the first robbery, and thirty days in an institution for the second. Before he reports to the institution, he stops off to commit yet another robbery.

Washington, D.C.: Teenager Elton Smith laughs as he talks of having put a gun to a cabdriver's head, and speaks proudly of how he calmly robbed a bank. Police suspect him of shooting a tourist in the head in a robbery the month before. His mother explains her worry that something might happen to him, but adds that she never asks where he gets the money that he gives her.

Pima County, Arizona: A defense attorney representing an eighteen-year-old argues that he should not be sent to jail for his first adult felony: as a juvenile, she points out, he had been arrested and released so often for the same charge that he had never learned that it was unacceptable behavior. He's not alone. In an area where juveniles account for half of all burglary arrests and a fifth of those for rape, police filed 11,485 juvenile charges in a recent year. The result? A total of 160 orders for confinement, mostly for periods of a few days, and twenty-three remands for trial as adults.

How did we get into this mess? The path to this particular inferno was, as is so often the case, paved with the best of intentions.

Up through the last century, juvenile offenders—if old enough to have the required criminal intent—were simply tried as adults. If found guilty, they were usually sent to separate juvenile reformatories so as to protect them from exposure to adult convicts.

Late in the last century, reformers argued for a different approach—for a system in which juveniles charged with crime would be rehabilitated by court-sponsored programs and care. In 1899, the Illinois Juvenile Court Act established the first separate court system for juveniles—limited by its terms to those under sixteen. The proceedings were classed as noncriminal; the hearing was informal; the judge, in the words of one reformer, was not to ask whether a crime had been committed but rather, "what is the best thing to do for this lad?"[3] Offenders might be given probation, or where their home environment might encourage crime, be placed in an appropriate juvenile institution.

The Illinois approach became a model for the nation. Within twenty years, most states had adopted a similar system. Most guaranteed that a juvenile offender would not be incarcerated past a certain age, and ensured that any records of criminality by minors would be destroyed upon reaching maturity—at first to twenty-one years of age and later to eighteen in most states.

Left to a judge's discretion, most systems also had provisions that minors could be charged as adults, but only when a long line of serious offenses showed that the offender was completely beyond "rehabilitation." As a practical matter, only a few juvenile offenders were ever transferred to adult court. In fact, barring a long string of felonies capped by a headline-grabbing murder, a juvenile had no great risk of an adult trial.

This traditional system functioned well for a time. Juvenile crime was largely limited to property offenses—petty thefts and vandalism—not of so great a volume as to clog the system. Then, in 1966, the U.S. Supreme Court held that a judge who allowed a juvenile rapist/robber to be tried as an adult must do so after a formal hearing at which the "lad" had the right to an attorney.[4] The Court said that a juvenile offender had the right to proper notice of charges, to an attorney, to confront opposing witnesses, and not to have his statements used against him unless he had been given "Miranda" warnings of his right to silence. In later decisions, the Court found that juvenile charges must be proven beyond a reasonable doubt.

The juvenile system thus became the best of all possible worlds for offenders. A seventeen-year-old rapist was entitled to most of the protections given an adult criminal, down to the right to have his confession excluded if he had not been given the Miranda warnings before he admitted the violation. Yet if found guilty he faced only the treatment given a wayward child—often a lecture and release, at worst a few months in juvenile hall, with his records then destroyed to give him a "fresh start." Juvenile adjudications could no longer be processed informally: trying youthful offenders required staffs of appointed defense attorneys, formal hearings, and appeals.

The juvenile system was also hit by the demographics of crime. The rise in criminality associated with the 1960s combined with the minor sanctions given juveniles produced an explosion of juvenile crime. For every one juvenile entering the system in 1965, *three* entered it in 1990. As with the adult system, the criminal justice system entered a self-perpetuating cycle: more criminals meant more load on the system, and the odds of being caught, convicted, and punished went down, and as they did so, more persons turned to crime.

The end result: a system in which juvenile offenders are "rehabilitated" by being taught that persons caught committing a felony are given a warning. Even those found guilty of rape or armed robbery receive probation or sixty days' confinement. That lesson is taken to heart. One detailed study, undertaken in Chicago, indicated that even modest confinement—less than a year—was enough to reduce serious juvenile offenders' later arrests by nearly 60 percent.[5] A follow-up study gave more detail.[6] The key to reducing later arrests was control. An intensely supervised, tightly restrained individual was less likely to return to crime even after the restraints were released; he had learned the price. Offenders with fewer restrictions and a lower burden returned to their predatory ways. The offenders were violent, but not stupid. They had understood the juvenile system's earlier message—"do as you will"—and they understood a new message—"the game is over."

Once serious juvenile offenses were limited to joyriding or siphoning gas, but today offenses involve gang rape, crack dealing, and drive-by shootings. We must preserve the useful core of the juvenile justice system, and apply it to the offenses for which it was intended. But we must also modify it to protect society against serious violent crime and budding career criminals.

A new juvenile code must retain the ability to settle first-time nonviolent offenses quietly, but it must also deal firmly with those who commit especially serious violent crimes and those who repeat property crime—the serious offenders and the career offenders.

For nonviolent, noncareer offenders, the present system is adequate. Many of these are in fact "scared straight," or will naturally abandon their ways as adulthood approaches. If that is accomplished, their records should be sealed and their errors forgotten. Most juvenile offenders fall into this category.

A long-term study of criminality, undertaken by Marvin Wolfgang in Philadelphia, tracked a hard core of over six hundred juveniles, who racked up five or more arrests apiece, and several thousand arrested a single time as juveniles who thereafter "went straight."[7] When the two groups reached adulthood, most of the serious adult crime and virtually all of the homicides were committed by the former hard core juvenile offenders; the majority of those who "went straight" as juveniles, remained law-abiding as adults. For the latter group, the current approach is adequate, and in fact it may be advisable to extend its coverage to allow juvenile treatment of a first, nonviolent offense if the person *commits* it any time before he turns eighteen, even if he is not charged until after he comes of age.

Serious violent offenders, including those who commit serious offenses such as first and second degree murder, kidnapping, forcible rape, and robbery with a deadly weapon or which result in serious bodily harm should *automatically* be bound over for adult trial. A person who is old enough to put a knife to a woman's throat and rape her, or beat a robbery victim within an inch of his or her life, is no erring child. Whether he was born seventeen or eighteen years ago makes no difference to the victim, nor to the next person he will victimize. Police and prosecutors should be authorized to file charges as if the offender were an adult.

Studies have shown that juveniles who commit crimes of an increasingly violent nature are among the most dangerous of offenders, the ones whose careers are most likely to be capped with murder. We must stop them early, or live with the fact that a victim will pay the price later.

Measures should be taken to protect the rights of victims within the juvenile system. Where a juvenile is allowed probation, or given informal release, he should be required as a condition to make restitution to the victim. Many states have enacted laws that make parents liable to repay the victims of a child's violence. Provision should be made to allow the juvenile court to assess restitution, within limits, against the parents as well as the juveniles. Restitution orders will aid the victim and encourage responsibility by both juveniles and parents.

Every juvenile proceeding should automatically include an order, at the very outset, against harassing or intimidating witnesses and victims, an order whose enforcement will be of the highest priority. Victims of a juvenile's crime should be entitled to be informed of the proceedings, allowed to testify during hearings, and allowed to be informed of the outcome.

For serious and career offenders, juvenile justice records should be retained past the eighteenth birthday, and destroyed only if the former juvenile "stays clean" for his first adult years. Identifying data—name, fingerprints, photograph—from the records must be available to police and courts. Where there are mandatory sentencing laws for adult offenders with past records, the laws should be amended so that findings of guilt for the most serious juvenile offenses can be treated as if they were past adult criminal convictions.

These reforms will furnish a much-needed stiffening of the juvenile justice system. The question is not so much leniency versus harshness, but rather who will receive harshness and who leniency—the offenders, or their future victims.

A juvenile justice system, as such, is irreplaceable. The teen years are a time of raging hormones and testing of limits; the childhood of many a respectable grayhair reads like the index to a criminal code. But the need for leniency toward youthful breaches of the public order does not require similar treatment for murder and rape, or the release of career offenders. Nor does it require that serious offenders be given a "birthday present" of an end to juvenile court sanctions or control.

In 1899, reformers created a juvenile justice suited to their time. Today, a century later, it is time for us to recognize that it is not suited to ours.

CHAPTER 15

PRISONS

CRUEL AND UNUSUAL PUNISHMENT?

ACCORDING TO HIS rap sheet, Douglas DeChaine was a predator. From 1975 through 1977, he was arrested for four separate attempted rapes. In June of 1977 he was charged with the ambush and rape of a fifteen-year-old and within the next three months he was charged with four more rapes.

In February 1978, DeChaine was finally sentenced to prison for one to twenty years on each of five counts of rape. Six years later he was released to a halfway house in Minnesota, but within six months of his release he was charged with another attempted rape. DeChaine was sentenced to a further six years, but because he joined a "sex-offender therapy" program his sentence was again cut short.

In June 1989, over the objections of his parole officer, the parole authorities in Minnesota released Douglas DeChaine once again. And innocent people of Minnesota paid the price for the board's decision.

Soon after his release, Tonya Smith was murdered. Her driver's license was found in DeChaine's pickup truck. One month later Louise Johnson disappeared. Her body was found in a shallow grave, in a cemetery where DeChaine once had worked. She had been last seen in the parking lot of a grocery store where DeChaine had also worked and her purse was found in a trash bin where he used to live.

One month later, a saleswoman was bound, gagged, and raped. She managed to escape her attacker, summoned the police, and a search was on for DeChaine. Days later he put an end to the horror that Minnesota authorities had failed to stop. He suffocated himself.

A powerful well-funded lobby—the anti-prison lobby—is selling deception to the American people. The lobby tells us that locking up criminals does not control crime, that our laws are too harsh, that our prison conditions are draconian, and that there is no evidence that prisons work to reduce crime.

The anti-prison lobby wants to sell the nation on "alternatives" to incarceration. Across this country they tell us that probation and "home arrest" should be used more often, and that we need more treatment programs, more jobs programs, more therapy, and more counseling for convicted criminals . . . and that these programs can better protect the law-abiding and the innocent.

Consciously or unconsciously, they are misleading the American people and we are paying for it with the blood of innocent victims.

Back to the case of Douglas DeChaine.

One year after DeChaine's rape-murder rampage, an article in *Corrections Today* declared Minnesota a "success" in treating sex offenders in community residences.[1] The state had sixty-five such "homes" in the Minneapolis area alone. The program was brought to Minnesota through the "Community Corrections Act" and was promoted by the anti-prison lobby. It was sold to the people of Minnesota with the promise that putting more offenders on the streets would not increase the risks to law-abiding citizens.

But after these "reforms" took effect, women and children in Minnesota suffered record levels of sexual violence. In November 10, 1991, the *Minneapolis Star-Tribune* reported that the "much praised treatment programs don't work. . . . In fact, their main impact has been to keep many sex criminals out of prison."

After studying the records of 767 rapists and child molesters convicted in the 1980s, the *Star-Tribune* reported that the average rapist had been charged with more than three sex crimes—the average child molester more than four. Even more significantly, the offenders who received treatment were rearrested more often than those who received no treatment.

Such is the record of treatment and "alternatives" around the country. Yet despite this shocking record we are constantly being lectured by the anti-prison lobby that we are too tough, tougher now than ever in our history, and that prisons don't work. The facts speak otherwise.

In 1960, 738 people were in prison for every one thousand violent crimes. By 1980, after the apologists had had their way for two decades, the number had plunged to 227.[2] Our criminal justice system was firmly in the grip of those who believed in the limitless possibilities of "rehabilitation" and who opposed punishment. This collapse of the concept of punishment, specifically imprisonment, was accompanied by astonishing increases in crime. From 1960–1969 the violent crime rate in America increased by over 200 percent, in the decade following by over 225 percent.[3] At the same time, of course, we were spending record levels in the "war on poverty."

During the decade of the 1980s, we started to climb out of this punishment trough. By 1992, 423 people were in prison for every one thousand violent crimes, clearly a dramatic turnaround but nowhere near the 1960 level.[4]

Moreover, it is simply not true that America is now more punitive than at any time in our history. Nor is it true that we are more punitive than any other Western society. The true measure of how punitive a society is may best be judged by the consequences of a criminal conviction. In the United States, 49 percent of those convicted of robbery are imprisoned; in Canada, the figure is 52 percent; and in England, it's 48 percent.[5] In other words, we send people to prison after conviction for a felony at roughly the same rate as our two closest allies. While it is true that we have higher per capita prison populations, that is because we have more crime. During the 1980s, while we were increasing our imprisonment rates, we were simply closing the previous gap.

The results of getting tougher during the 1980s were dramatic to say the least. For the first time in two decades, crime rates actually began to fall. From 1980–1992, the ten states that had the highest increase in their prison populations relative to total FBI index crime (including murder, rape, robbery, aggravated assault, burglary, theft, motor vehicle theft, and arson) on average experienced a decline in their crime rates of more than 20 percent. The ten states with decreases or the smallest increases in their imprisonment rates averaged almost a 9 percent increase in their crime rates.[6]

The lessons from individual states bear out these conclusions. In a 1992 study, the U.S. Justice Department found that in Michigan, when funding for prison construction dried up in the early 1980s, the state was forced to institute an early release program and became one of two states whose prison population declined from 1981–1984.[7] Between 1981 and 1986, the rate of violent crime rose 25 percent while at the same time national crime rates were declining. In 1986, however, when Michigan embarked on a major prison-building effort and increased its imprisonment rate, the state's violent crime rate began to fall. By 1989, it had dropped 12 percent.

Increasing the certainty of punishment for crimes, that is, of having criminals imprisoned after conviction, yields even more powerful crime control effects. Dr. Michael Block, professor of Economics and Law at the University of Arizona and a former member of the United States Sentencing Commission, has shown that for every 10 percent increase in the certainty of punishment for those convicted of a violent crime, the violent crime rate can be expected to fall by 7 percent.[8]

These crime control effects are profound and unmatched by any other proposed policy, including every treatment alternative. If the number of violent criminals sent to prison were to increase by as few as nine thousand each year, almost 140,000 violent crimes would be prevented annually.

The best kept secret of the 1980s is simply this: Getting Tough Works. Sadly the anti-prison lobby closes its eyes to the hard evidence and instead clings desperately to its worn-out dogma that we punish too much and that we cannot afford to "build our way out" of our endemic crime crisis.

Today, unfortunately, those forces seem to be regaining the ground they lost in the 1980s. This time they have emerged as born-again fiscal conservatives, arguing that we can no longer burden the taxpayers with the high costs of building and running prisons. But aren't prisons a wise investment in the infrastructure of order in this country?

The National Center for Policy Analysis reported in June 1991:[9]

Although the cost of building and maintaining prisons is high, the cost of not creating more prisons appears to be much higher. A study by the National Institute of Justice concluded that the typical career offender turned loose in society will engage in a one-person crime wave causing damage more than 17 times as costly as imprisonment.

- Sending someone to prison for one year costs taxpayers about $25,000.
- A Rand Corporation survey of 2,190 professional criminals found that the average career criminal commits 187 to 287 crimes a year, each costing society an average of $2,300.
- So keeping a career criminal out of prison costs, on the average, $430,000 a year—$405,000 more than the cost of imprisonment.

The evidence from the 1980s is clear. We must build enough prison capacity to lock up every violent and repeat offender, and to keep them, at least the most violent offenders, locked up for substantially more time.

It has been estimated, again by Professor Block, that in order to imprison all murderers, rapists, robbers, and those convicted of aggravated assault involving the use of a firearm or causing serious physical injury, and every repeat offender not currently sent to prison, would require 250,000 additional prison beds by the year 2000.[10] With this level of imprisonment we would still not match the 1960s' level, but the effects on crime control would be enormous.

An estimated 2 million violent crimes could be prevented over the next ten years, and by the year 2004 this number could prevent close to 700,000 violent crimes each year. The annual victim losses saved through this crime prevention strategy would approach $30 billion.

The savings to victims and to the taxpayers would be even more profound if sanity were restored to the way we build and operate prisons in this country. Costs for these critical government functions have been driven to excess by requirements from the federal courts that go far beyond the conditions demanded by the Eighth Amendment to the Constitution.

The Constitution does not mandate comfortable prisons. And yet, we find federal judges in this country—in total disregard of the Constitution, the Supreme Court, taxpayers, and victims—ordering prison officials to provide cable TV, footballs, and frisbees to inmates.

These federal judges have gone so far as to dictate the paint color on inmates' cell walls, the room size, the library size, the recreation field size, and the kitchen size in prisons all across America. They have even stopped serving meatloaf in a prison when the inmates complained. These orders have obviously taken their toll.

Adjusted for inflation, the cost per prisoner is 179 percent higher today than it was in 1960. Prisoners' living standards have grown 40 percent faster than median income over the past thirty years, even though the general consensus in this country believes that providing better living conditions inside the prison wall than outside undercuts the very purpose of punishment. As Judge Richard Posner observed, "the infliction of disutility . . . is one of the objectives of criminal punishment; only if the only objective of punishment were incapacitation could it be argued that living conditions should be as comfortable in prison as outside."[11]

This stranglehold that federal judges now have on state prison officials must be broken. As a starting point, we should adopt the proposition that a prisoner should not live any better than an honest able-bodied poor person subsisting at the nation's poverty level.

Making living standards in prison too comfortable undercuts the deterrent effect of imprisonment and the ability of the states to build and operate prisons. Reducing the cost of imprisonment will not only save dollars, it will save lives. Prisons are the key to increasing the personal safety of the American people but, like everything else in the market, the more they cost the fewer we will have.

Part of the answer lies with the Congress of the United States. First, the U.S. Congress should set a national standard for prison conditions so that federal courts will have a guide to contemporary standards of decency. These standards should be set so that prison administrations spend no more per inmate, per year—excluding security costs—than the poverty line. For food, shelter, clothing, and programming, the state should not spend more than the amount the federal government sets as the subsistence level for the honest poor.

Second, Congress should restrict the ability of a single federal district court judge to second-guess the combined judgments of a state's governor, legislature, and corrections department. Changes in federal laws that require judges to pay more attention to state decisions should be made. It should take a three-judge panel, moreover, to declare prison conditions unconstitutional, and states should then have the opportunity to correct the condition before any attorneys' fees are awarded to the inmates' lawyers. A federal court's power should not extend beyond what is necessary to prevent abusive conditions. Frisbees and cable TV? No.

Third, America must embark now on a course to build enough prison capacity to house the violent and repeat offenders we have caught and convicted. They must be housed in facilities to which they will not want to return, and for long enough to ensure the safety of the law-abiding. Prisons stop crime.

America's prisons must cease to provide luxury accommodations for criminals such as:

- exercise rooms that rival health spas—beyond the financial reach of average Americans
- law libraries that not only rival our colleges but provide criminals with access to the tools needed to become "jailhouse lawyers" who then embark on legal shenanigans that cost hundreds of thousands of tax-payer dollars
- day rooms with TV sets, VCRs, video movies, and pool tables—recreational equipment that inner-cities desperately need for programs to keep underprivileged juveniles off the streets and away from crime.

Add to that list the amenities that prisoners brag about in those prison publications where they rank their prison facilities as one would luxury hotels. One such inmate publication carried a feature called "AN INSIDER'S GUIDE TO AMERICA'S TOP TEN JAILS," compiled and written by three inmates. According to the "insiders" the top rated jail is:

Fairbanks Correctional Center, Fairbanks, Alaska: *Capacity:* 194. *Inmates per cell:* dormitory-style bunks and single cells. *TV:* total cable. *Visits:* regular contact visits. *Meals:* eclectic and plentiful. All social events and religious services are co-ed. Inmates wear Levis 501 jeans. The indoor-outdoor recreational facilities are fully equipped. People are still talking about the time they served the Captain's Plate: Alaskan king crab, shrimp and fried scallops.[12]

Florida's Hernando County jail in Brooksville came in tenth:

Capacity: 252. *Inmates per cell:* two to eight. *TV:* basic cable, video movies on weekend. *Visits:* contact visits. *Meals:* hot, above average. Florida orange juice served at breakfast and a commissary that supplies toiletries, cakes and candy make this air-conditioned facility Florida's finest.

The eight jails between one and ten feature such outrages as:

- "holiday feasts (Kalua pig) prepared"
- "aerobic classes"
- "unlimited free phone calls and daily newspaper deliveries allow for placing bets with friends on the outside. Cash winnings may be dropped off or moneygrams deposited in noninterest-bearing accounts."
- "jails doctors and surgeons are the same ones who treat presidents and heads of state at Mayo Clinic. And their prison services are free."
- "Stylish pink wool blankets cover cryptlike beds. Inmates wear high-visibility orange coveralls in this space-age island complex. Women are known to flash their breasts at cons they know on the opposite bank of Cedar River."
- "Meals of chicken, black-eyed peas and dumplings are served here. Or you may order pizza from Pizza Magic—they take *anybody's* check."
- "Inmates dress in robes and slippers, and lounge on down pillows and watch movies."

Millions of inner-city and low-income citizens, struggling to survive, live in squalor compared to prison accommodations. What of the anti-prison lobby's mournful lament about "cruel and unusual punishment"? For some of the victims of these lavishly kept criminals, life itself has become cruel and unusual punishment.

Some corrections officials will argue that the amenities are paid for out of prisoners' "canteen" funds—yet another miscarriage of justice! That money should be used to compensate victims—not reward criminals. Our prison system has become a national disgrace.

CHAPTER 16

DEATH PENALTY

A FEW YEARS ago, noted columnist William F. Buckley took exception to a comment appearing in the British journal, *The Economist*. The magazine noted March 24, 1990, that "one of the most striking differences between the United States and other advanced industrial countries is America's enthusiasm for execution." Buckley quipped that "if America had that great an enthusiasm for execution, America must be most fearfully frustrated."

In reality, Americans are frustrated—and fearful. Frustrated, not from lack of executions, but from the government's inability to enforce capital punishment. And fearful of the government's inability to protect its citizens. Buckley pointed out that at the time, 1990, only 124 executions had taken place in the years since the Supreme Court reauthorized the use of capital punishment. During that same period, nearly 265,000 murders had been committed.

Buckley observed correctly that rather than an "enthusiasm" to see criminals die, society has mobilized its resources under provocation. More than 77 percent of Americans have come to favor the death penalty today (compared to 50 percent thirty years ago) because they are scared, and they are fed up with being scared. Moreover, according to research conducted by Penn+Schoen Associates, Inc. on March 19–20, 1994, for *The National Law Journal*, 75 percent of Americans believe the death penalty may be appropriate for those under twenty years of age—up from 52 percent approval recorded in 1989. Americans favor the use of the death penalty for particularly monstrous crimes. It is time for government to do its part and reform its implementation of this most necessary punishment.

Unfortunately, the modern history of the death penalty in the United States is pitted with indecisiveness and delay. About three hundred prisoners are condemned to die every year, but fewer than twenty are executed. Endless procedural maneuvers and dilatory tactics by Death Row inmates, or special interest advocates on inmates' behalf, have slowed implementation of capital punishment to a snail's pace.

For years, U.S. Supreme Court Chief Justice William Rehnquist has been urging the legal community to reduce the number of applications a condemned prisoner can make to the federal courts. These at present are unlimited, and they have crowded the Death Row population to more than 2,300 in the several states that sanction capital punishment.

Justice Rehnquist's point put simply is this: If a state legislature wants capital punishment for certain kinds of crimes, and the Supreme Court has authorized it, let them get on with it. If a state legislature does not want the sanction, let *it* repeal those laws. Whatever course a particular state chooses to follow, it is not the courts' role to uphold the laws while, simultaneously, frustrating them.

The basic function served by the death penalty is the *permanent* removal from society of extremely violent offenders, those who cannot be controlled even in an institutional setting. These are not people who commit "crimes of passion," but people who execute fellow human beings with cool calculation and without remorse or hesitation. These people are a permanent danger to society and should be dealt with accordingly.

Our criminal justice system is designed around the common sense notion that the more certain the punishment, the less likely the crime. Moreover, the more severe the crime, the greater the retribution.

The death penalty—properly assessed and implemented—serves both of these just goals. Indeed, a study by Stephen K. Layson appearing in a 1985 edition of the *Southern Economics Journal* estimated that each execution in the United States deters approximately eighteen murders.

In the well-known 1961 California case of *People v. Love* (366 P.2d 33, 41–42), police files and other sources of convicts' statements indicated that their decisions to use toy guns during felonies rather than real firearms, and not to kill hostages, were motivated by fear of the death penalty.

Not only does the death penalty serve permanently to incapacitate the most violent criminal offenders, it allows society to exact just retribution. More importantly, it conveys to the victims' family and others that society takes their loss seriously.

In 1992, former Attorney General William P. Barr issued twenty-four recommendations for improving the criminal justice system to the states. Concerning capital punishment, Attorney General Barr cited the following compelling Senate Judiciary Committee testimony:

> Murder does not simply differ in magnitude from extortion or burglary or property destruction offenses; it differs in kind. Its punishment ought to also differ in kind. It must acknowledge the inviolability and dignity of innocent human life. It must, in short, be proportionate.[1]

Americans support capital punishment, but when confronted with a specific case—a particular life—resolve often softens. Real people, such as judges and juries, grow fearful of making a mistake. They need to be assured that the condemned prisoner deserves his punishment.

Professor Christie Davies of the University of Reading states that repeatedly violent nonmurderers are a far greater threat to the public than the one-time murderer who has suddenly exploded under stress, e.g., found her spouse in bed with another woman. Davies suggests that once a habitually violent offender finally commits murder, there can be no objection to executing the prisoner on the chance of killing a totally innocent person. Professor Davies concludes: "Executing such a person for murder would serve the purpose of deterring others, and it would also satisfy the requirement of just retribution—in this case, not for a single homicidal crime but for a lifetime's thuggery."[2]

The U.S. Supreme Court has, over the past twenty years, narrowly structured the grounds on which a death sentence may be given.

First, the crime charged must be first degree murder or its equivalent—not just a killing, but a premeditated, malicious one.

Second, if the person convicted did not actually perform the killing himself (that is, he is charged with murder because he was an accomplice or was one conspirator, while another made the killing), he must be found to have intended or foreseen that a death might occur.

Third, the murder must in some way be found to be an *exceptional* first-degree murder, according to categories fixed by law. In most states, this means it involved torture, a killing for hire, a mass murder, a killing of a law enforcement officer, or killing in a manner exceptionally cruel and heinous.

Finally, the convicted murderer must be allowed to argue *any* conceivable grounds in mitigation—that is, while the grounds to give him the death penalty must be narrow and fixed, he must be permitted to use any argument he pleases against it. The end result of all this legal channelling is that, in any given year, only the few dozen worst of the nation's eighteen thousand murderers ever see death row.[3]

As mentioned previously, the U.S. Supreme Court has required that states impose the death penalty only on narrow categories of especially aggravated first degree murderers.

What categories, if any, qualify is a matter for the people of each state to determine. Where those categories have been defined, and upheld as constitutional, there is no reason for each sentencing to be followed by fifteen or twenty years of litigation.

Former Attorney General Barr's twenty-four Recommendations to Strengthen Criminal Justice urged states to make the death penalty available in at least three situations:

1. Killing a Law Enforcement Officer

Every day thousands of law enforcement officers leave their families for work not knowing whether they will be coming home again. The dedication and commitment—both by the officers and their families—required to be a good cop obligates society to provide them the best protection available. Consideration should be given to making murder of a police officer (or his or her family, if in retribution for carrying out his duties) a federal capital offense. The punishment should be certain and swift. Criminals should know that killing a law enforcement officer is never worth the price.

This reform may encounter criticism that it "federalizes" what is properly a state crime. The trouble with this criticism is that many of the people making it have been in favor of federalizing local matters when it suits their purposes. Gun laws and waiting periods are obvious examples, as well as matters that have made sufficient headlines, such as carjackings.

Look at the question for yourself. There is no reason why trying a car-jacker, or a person who waits six days instead of seven to sell a firearm, is more worthy of federal consideration than punishing the murderer of a police officer.

2. Killing in the Course of Serious Felonies

Rapists, armed robbers, and other felons who commit murder in the course of these serious crimes should also face death upon conviction. Criminals must also know that there is a grave penalty for eliminating witnesses to their crime. More-over, witnesses of these crimes are entitled to added security in the event the criminal murders his victim.

3. Killing While in Prison

Attorney General Barr notes that from 1982 to 1987, five federal prison officials were killed by inmates. Inmates in-volved in at least three of these killings were already serving life sentences for murder. In states that do not permit the death penalty, corrections officers are placed at much greater risk than their colleagues in states that do.

Prisoners serving long sentences may feel that they have little to lose by killing a corrections officer or another inmate. The prospect of a likely death sentence would certainly alter their thinking. The loss of privileges or temporary isolation do not penalize in proportion to the crime of murder.

Reform in implementing the death penalty is badly needed. As matters stand, endless delays frustrate capital punishment laws, and accordingly society. Fortunately, steps can be taken that will provide convicted capital murderers fair and reason-able opportunities to appeal without subjecting society to un-due delay.

1. Reform Habeas Corpus

Most delays stem from appeals based on writs of habeas corpus, which permit prisoners to challenge how they were arrested and convicted. The current system allows prisoners to attack their convictions by repeatedly filing federal habeas corpus petitions, which are legal papers that require federal judges to review their cases after they have lost all of their direct appeals and their state-level habeas corpus class. These filings result in years of delay and consume enormous amounts of time, energy, and money of the already overbur-dened legal system.

We should expect the criminal justice system to give these a speedy review, make sure that there were no errors in the process, and either affirm or reverse the death sentence. This is precisely what does *not* happen.

The average case takes a minimum of fifteen years from sentencing to execution or final reversal of the sentence. Some cases are still pending twenty to twenty-five years after the murder occurred.

The object of this exercise of appeal after appeal after appeal is simple. In each court, the convict usually obtains a stay of execution, and there is always the chance that *one* of these many courts will find a reason to reverse the death sentence.

To end this travail will require rethinking the existing procedures. Death penalty cases are already exceptions to a few appellate rules—in some states, a death penalty case goes straight to the state supreme court, while all other sentencings go first to an intermediate court of appeals. More changes are necessary.

Presently, the direct appeal only deals with pure legal issues as presented on the trial record; the appellate courts do not take additional evidence. The result is that after the direct appeal is finished, the convict files a separate action, in the trial court again, to raise all issues which would not be covered in the trial record (arguments that his attorney was incompetent, that the overall death penalty system is flawed, and so on), and then the decision on those issues is separately appealed.

Today, even liberal Democrats such as Senate Judiciary Chairman Joseph Biden support reining in the habeas corpus writ actions, proposing time limits within which habeas corpus claims may be raised.

2. Bind Juries to Their Decisions

It is difficult to imagine the terrible responsibility of recommending the execution of a criminal defendant. State legislatures ought to ease the jury member's burden by binding juries to their conclusions concerning aggravating and mitigating factors. Where the former outweigh the latter, a jury should be required to impose a sentence of death.

3. Allow Victim Impact Evidence

Juries rarely see a murder victim outside the circumstances of his or her death. Sometimes they see photographs of murdered bodies and crime scenes, but not of picnics and graduation ceremonies. When the time comes for a sentencing hearing, the murderer is allowed to parade his family and friends in front of the jury to create a sympathetic atmosphere in order to lighten the sentence. The victim and his or her family, meanwhile, are forgotten.

Victim impact evidence should be allowed to show the consequences of the murderer's crime on those left behind at the death of the victim. The jury should see the victim and the victim's family as unique individuals whose loss is relevant to the punishment.

Too often the criminal is presented as the victim by special interest advocates who organize protests and prayer vigils. But who protests for the victim? Who prays for the person whose life was snuffed out by a killer? The family. Our society needs to respect and honor their loss and pain. The state should afford survivors the opportunity to present evidence that conveys their loss to the jury.

CONCLUSION

Car-jackings and drive-by shootings are commonplace today. Ten years ago they were unheard of. Americans in central cities and suburban communities alike are afraid to leave their homes at night. Children can no longer ride their bicycles to the neighborhood store or to a playmate's house. Families cannot go to the park in safety. Our communities are under siege.

The criminal justice system in the United States has cracked. Innocent Americans are dying at the hands of criminals who are set free by a system that seems to accord criminals more rights than victims.

Criminals do not respect the justice system. They do not fear retribution from society and therefore have no incentive to be law-abiding citizens. Violent criminals are particularly insolent. In short, citizens are fearful while criminals are fearless. Government must stop this spiral toward chaos.

CHAPTER 17

CRIME AND MORALITY

WITH A STREAM of gruesome murders receiving massive media attention, violent crime has jumped to the forefront of American politics. Strangely, the visceral response of some politicians, such as President Bill Clinton, is to punish law-abiding citizens by criminalizing the ownership of firearms. Stranger yet is the tendency of some to blame the victim, and more often, society at large.

Although few people actually endorse crime, some are willing to excuse it, saying that criminals are themselves victims of large social forces: poverty, lack of parental guidance, poor education. All are cited as reasons for treating criminals more leniently and focusing attention on social programs rather than punishment. Personal responsibility is seen as only a minor facet of the problem.

Yet an increased emphasis on individual moral responsibility is the *key* to controlling crime. Government, particularly at the local level, can and should do more to catch and punish wrongdoers and to deter would-be criminals more effectively. Better social policies might decrease the likelihood of some people to commit crimes. But we will markedly reduce crime rates only by reinstituting respect for morals in society as well as punishing individuals for their crimes.

Today, unfortunately, violent crime rates demonstrate that an increasing number of people no longer accept anyone's rules of conduct but their own. Clearly, we must reevaluate, and dramatically improve, our efforts to develop and maintain a moral framework for our society.

As more people violate society's rules, it becomes increasingly tempting for apologists "inside the Beltway" to blame society. Some suggest the rules themselves must be unfair, or that society must be forcing people to break them. Some excuse those who commit the most depraved acts by pointing out that they have grown up under harsh and even tragic circumstances. Social factors obviously do play a role in crime, since young minority males from poor, broken homes are much more likely than others to commit violent crimes. But being poor or not having a pair of $100 tennis shoes should never excuse one person for attacking or killing another person.

As horrid as someone's childhood may be—and many, many people have suffered scarring experiences—no hardship can eliminate the moral responsibility of individuals for their own actions. And no hardship can justify acts of violence for material goods such as expensive shoes or clothing—or violence for the sake of violence.

Having been abused as a child does not make a person rape or assault another. For centuries children were treated as little more than property, yet there was no consequent crime wave. Similarly, poverty does not force someone to kill or steal. Indeed, while poverty may be the favorite excuse for crime, it has little impact on crime rates. There was no dramatic upsurge in crime during the Great Depression or other American economic downturns.

Earlier this century, when a far larger percentage of people were impoverished, lower-income neighborhoods were quite safe. Even today, most poor people do not commit crimes. Why? Because they are deterred by the force of law and the

threat of punishment, of course, but more importantly because the vast majority understands that to kill, rape, or rob
would be morally wrong.

Crime should be understood most fundamentally as a moral
problem. Those who murder, rape, and steal are committing
evil acts. And the evil seems to be growing. Increasingly violent crimes are premeditated, callous, and committed for no
purpose other than to harm others. In fact, some older criminals profess shock at the seemingly irrational brutality of today's younger killers.

Murder has always been an ugly part of American society, of
course, but now murder has become sport, and there is no
remorse. A Capitol Hill aide is murdered because the alleged
killer wanted to murder a white; foreign tourists are executed
even though the criminals abandon their robbery attempts.
Basketball star Michael Jordan's father and others are killed
for their cars, despite their lack of resistance. Inner-city gang
members murder one another over being "dissed" and slaughter helpless innocents caught in bloody cross-fires.

These well-publicized killings barely scratch the surface of
the vast problem facing us. Annually, there are almost 34
million "victimizations," as the government puts it, dramatic
evidence that crime reflects a moral problem of stunning di-
mensions.

Consider the following observations from the Clinton Justice Department's report, *Highlights from 20 Years of Surveying Crime Victims*:

> Overall crime rates have been stable or declining in recent
> years; however, violent crime has increased for some groups.
> Violent crime rates for teenagers increased in recent years,
> while rates for other age groups remained stable or declined.
> The violent crime rate for blacks in 1992 is the highest ever
> recorded.
>
> From 1973 to 1991, 36.6 million people were injured as a
> result of violent crime including over 6 million people who
> received serious injuries.

One in four households in the United States is victimized by one or more crimes each year.

In 1991, an estimated $19.1 billion was lost directly from personal and household crime.[1]

Nor is crime an equal opportunity scourge. Although violence affects everyone, it disproportionately harms the poor. Middle-class suburbanites can wall themselves off from the problems of the inner-city. Wealthy city-dwellers can create enclaves of relative safety. But the urban poor are largely helpless.

To ignore the wave of terror now engulfing innocent individuals and entire neighborhoods—or act as if it is somehow inevitable given larger social factors—is to hand over to destruction the most vulnerable members of our population—the poor.

Murders of foreign tourists may receive disproportionate media attention, but the *primary victims of crime are minorities*. Explains the Justice Department, "Black households, Hispanic households, and urban households were the most likely to experience crime."[2]

In 1992, almost half of all murder victims were African-Americans; in fact, blacks are twice as likely than others to be victimized by a violent crime. Someone earning less than $7,500 a year is three times as likely to suffer from a violent crime as someone earning more than $50,000. The poorest families are twice as likely to suffer a burglary. The highest victimization rates of all are for black teens, both males and females. And the problem is getting worse—the number of violent crimes affecting blacks jumped 42 percent from 1980 to 1992.[3]

The problem is particularly painful to address because the primary victimizers of minority communities are minorities. Yet most blacks, Hispanics, and others are law-abiding citizens: only a relatively few African-Americans, for instance, are terrorizing their own community: roughly 1.7 percent of black males account for *45 percent of all arrests*.[4] Thus, blacks and other minorities have the most at stake in efforts to control crime. And, increasingly, African-American leaders and members of the civil rights establishment have begun to discuss the problem.

Washington Post columnist Courtland Milloy wrote of the case of William Simpson, driven by white racists out of an all-white housing project in east Texas back into his old neighborhood, where he was promptly murdered by two African-American robbers. Wrote Milloy, "Here was a classic race relations case for our times, complete with white bogeymen who divert attention from the fundamental problem in black America: us, black people."[5]

Eric Holder, Jr., the U.S. attorney for D.C., recently argued, "There has been for too long a conspiracy of silence in the black community—a reluctance to discuss our manifest problems, a desire to avoid painful truths. . . . we are the ones who pull the triggers, and we are the ones who sell and use the drugs. We must talk about these things and confront these truths."[6]

Similarly, Jesse Jackson observed, "There is nothing more painful to me at this stage in my life than to walk down the street and hear footsteps and start thinking about robbery—then look around and see someone white and feel relieved."[7]

What is to be done? At a recent conference co-sponsored by Jackson's Rainbow Coalition and the National Black Caucus of Local Elected Officials, Baltimore Mayor Kurt Schmoke said, "We do need to send a signal throughout our communities that certain types of activities will not be tolerated, that people will be held accountable, and that if there is evil manifested by actions taken by individuals who choose to prey upon our residents that evil will be responded to quickly and correctly."[8]

Robert Woodson, president of the National Center for Neighborhood Enterprise, noted that "black people can't change racism," but that "what we can do is change our minds. We can return to what has worked for us: the primacy of moral consistency. We can once again establish codes of conduct for those we would elevate to leadership."[9]

As these leading African-Americans realize, crime must fundamentally be treated as a moral issue. And it must be addressed in this way by all Americans. Black-on-black violence in large cities may be most harmful, because it is destroying communities and decimating younger generations. But whites, too, kill, rape, and steal. And while a larger percentage of white crime might be "white-collar," that in no way diminishes the moral failings behind the actions. Theft remains theft, even if no gun is pulled. To romanticize criminals, whether brutal predators or silver-tongued con-men, is not only foolish, but immoral.

The reconstruction of morality in America will not be a simple task. Responsibility lies first with the family and then with the many institutions that help shape and implement society's moral values. The most important, and most obvious, task is to promote a sense of the value of life: individuals are not to be killed, harmed, or robbed because it is morally wrong. Only slightly less critical is the need to support the family as an institution, and to emphasize the importance of work in molding character and escaping poverty.

The disintegration of the family has taken a frightening turn. As former Education Secretary William Bennett pointed out, since 1960 illegitimacy rates have jumped 400 percent, while those for violent crime have risen 560 percent. Over the last thirty years the black illegitimacy rate has jumped from 25 percent to 68 percent generally, and 80 percent in the inner-city.[10] Particularly grievous is the problem of children having children.

Between just 1986 and 1991, birth rates for teens between fifteen and nineteen years of age rose by 24 percent. In 1960, there were five times as many babies born to married teens as to unmarried teens; in 1991, there were more than twice as many born to unmarried teens.[11] This lack of family formation, joined with a rise in family breakup, has also had severe economic and social consequences, especially when combined with a lowered will to work. As of 1990, the official poverty rate for two-parent households with one full-time worker was just 2 percent. For all two-parent households, it was 5.6 percent. For female-headed households, it was 32.2 percent, almost one in three. For single women who don't work, the rate was 67 percent.[12]

Families and community organizations need to teach morality, a moral code of conduct. All need to preach against crime, irrespective of the hardship the family is undergoing or the societal affliction a person has suffered. All need to work to address destructive social problems, such as promiscuity, illegitimacy, and divorce. All need to emphasize the overriding responsibility of parents, particularly absent fathers, to provide safe, stable, and secure homes for their children. And all need to point out the importance of work to improve self-respect and living standards. The role of churches is particularly necessary since only they can speak of the ultimate consequences of immorality.

The government, too, has a duty in this area, but different from that of private institutions. There is little that the state can do directly to improve the moral tone of society: public officials possess no special qualification to lecture others about morality. The best that we can hope for—indeed, should expect—is that political leaders exercise high standards in their personal and public lives, thereby acting as good role models.

The most important responsibility of the state is to stop hindering private efforts to rebuild American society. Having a surgeon general act as a condom queen hinders the efforts of parents to teach their children sexual morality. In one outstanding instance, when asked about the moral appropriateness of having a child out of wedlock, Surgeon General Joycelyn Elders responded, "Everyone has different moral standards. . . . You can't impose your standards on someone else."[13] But if you cannot make a moral case against children having children, what value is your professed moral code? Another detrimental influence is the public schools, which have put a virtual stop on teaching morality and values, let alone the mere mention of religion.

And bear in mind that the welfare state has financed the destruction of both family and work. In effect, the government is now directly subsidizing immorality. The rise in the crime rate over the last three decades largely tracks the rise in government welfare spending.

First, the problem of the family breakup—even the lack of forming a family—has grown far more serious as government anti-poverty programs have expanded. And that change has inevitably spawned more poverty. In 1959, women headed 28 percent of poor families with children; in 1991 it was 60 percent.[14]

Welfare clearly bears much of the blame for this phenomenon. Dr. June O'Neill of Baruch College figures that a 50 percent increase in welfare benefits upped illegitimate births by 43 percent.[15] Other research found that higher benefits reduced the marriage rate for single mothers. Young women, that is, may in effect "marry" welfare to set up their own households and have babies, no matter whether the fathers ever contribute to the children's upbringing. This is not to say that inner-city women are having children for the money; it is to say that federal funds enable them to escape the normal economic, social, and moral pressures against illegitimacy.

These social trends are advancing elsewhere in society, too; veteran welfare researcher Charles Murray points out that the illegitimacy rate for whites is now 22 percent.[16] Observes University of Pennsylvania Professor Elijah Anderson, "[I]n cold economic terms, a baby can be an asset, which is without doubt an important factor behind exploitative sex and out-of-wedlock babies."[17]

The result is a self-reinforcing, ever more destructive cycle. Children have children, whom they must raise without a father in the home, and who will, in turn, have children without marrying. Argues Charles Murray, "[I]llegitimacy is the single most important social problem of our time—more important than crime, drugs, poverty, illiteracy, welfare, or homelessness because it drives everything else."[18]

Today's poor are also far less likely to work than in the past. In the 1950s, reports Bob Rector of the Heritage Foundation, nearly one-third of poor families were headed by a full-time worker. In 1990, half as many, 15 percent, were headed by full-time workers. Fully *half* of nonelderly adults considered to be poor did no work. One of the most important reasons: Eligibility for payments disappears if a woman works or marries a man who works regularly.[19]

Thus, welfare ensures that many women in particular will never work, at least for most of their child-bearing years. A detailed study of the impact of welfare in San Diego and Seattle during the 1970s, for instance, found that for every extra $1 in benefits, recipients cut their earnings by $.80.[20] And the failure to work ensures permanent dependency. More than half of the 4.4 million families now receiving AFDC benefits will be on the rolls for at least a decade. Children in families on AFDC are three times as likely to end up on welfare as adults.[21] Observes the Heritage Foundation's Rector, "This inter-generational dependency is a clear indication that the welfare system is failing in its goal to lift the poor from poverty to self-sufficiency."[22]

Of course, welfare is not the only cause of inner-city social and economic collapse. Government also uses measures such as occupational licensing, minimum wage, the Davis-Bacon Act, and business regulation to foreclose employment opportunities for inner-city residents, who tend to have poorer educations and less experience. Urban public schools are notoriously unresponsive to parents and utterly incapable of educating even those children who desperately want to learn. Housing policies—exclusionary zoning regulations, counterproductive rent control, antiquated building codes—ensure that ghetto residents will be concentrated in poor and unsafe housing. All of these problems need to be addressed by reforming and removing existing, misguided government interventions.

But above all it is morality that is the root problem of many social problems, including crime. Government welfare today is an enabler, a subsidy that accelerates the larger moral breakdown in society. Most poor people would prefer to be off welfare; most single-mothers would prefer to be married to a working spouse. Even today many, many poor people, for reason of moral principle, seek to stay off welfare and avoid illegitimate births. But more and more people no longer hold these principles.

Teaching about the values of family and work is necessary but not enough: Ending welfare subsidies for immorality is also necessary to society to reconstruct the larger moral framework in our all-important campaign to reduce crime.

A government that cannot protect the people is failing in its most essential task. Officials who cannot stop people from murdering tens of thousands of their fellow citizens are not likely, among other things, to meet the health care needs of tens of millions of patients.

Crime is the direct outgrowth of a growing moral breakdown in society. Indeed, the consequences of this phenomenon are truly catastrophic. Children from broken homes are more likely to do poorly in school, use drugs, require psychiatric attention, and commit crimes than those in equally low-income homes where a father is present. And the sort of crimes that they are likely to commit grow increasingly vicious as their moral understanding of the value of human beings disintegrates.

Unfortunately, there are no panaceas: The solution to the problem of crime is complex and multifaceted. But an important part of that answer is the recreation of the moral framework that once guided the conduct of the vast majority of people. In the end, people will stop shooting other people only when they acknowledge that it is wrong to do so and when they fear punishment for such crimes. It's the responsibility of the private sector to do a better job of setting moral standards, and the duty of the government to stop getting in the way.

Gun laws will not provide solutions to problems that arise from a decay in morality. Self-respect, respect for others or the property of others cannot be legislated—it can only be taught.

CHAPTER 18

IS AMERICA TOO FREE?

AN INTERNATIONAL PERSPECTIVE

GUN CONTROL ADVOCATES are quick to cite crime statistics from selected foreign countries and compare them to crime statistics in the United States to justify gun bans and other forms of gun control. That is, they blame crime in our country on our right to keep and bear arms.

But these crime comparisons by gun banners are not based on scientific studies, but rather on politics; they can be supported neither by reason nor qualified data.

Heinous crime statistics relevant to the Second Amendment, which guarantees the right to keep and bear arms, concern the slaughter of 6 million Jews in the holocaust.

In the closing scenes of the highly decorated film *Schindler's List*, some 1,200 Jewish survivors of the Nazi holocaust presented Oskar Schindler with a simple gold band inscribed, "Whosoever saves one life, it is as though he has saved the world" in remembrance of his heroic deeds that had saved their lives.

Near the end of the war Schindler further risked his life obtaining firearms to arm Jewish prisoners in his factory. He armed and trained them against the day the Nazi guards would get the order to execute them. Armed by Schindler, the Jews were no longer powerless against certain death.

That simple but powerful act of arming perfectly exemplifies our Founding Fathers beliefs when they wrote the U.S. Constitution's guarantee on the right of the individual to keep and bear arms.

If we believe that the holocaust in Nazi Germany—not to mention other examples of other state-sponsored genocide— "can't happen here," it is not because we Americans are morally superior to the rest of the world. It is because, among other reasons, we are guaranteed the right to keep and bear arms— the ultimate safeguard against despotism and genocide.

Gun control proponents, intent on disarming the American people, ignore history that reveals the greatest crimes against humanity occur when ruthless governments disarm and then kill powerless civilians.

In Germany, Jewish extermination began with the Nazi Weapon Law of 1938, signed by Adolph Hitler, that required police permission for ownership of a handgun. All firearms had to be registered. Germans who enjoyed using bolt-action rifles for target practice were told to join the Wehrmacht if they wished to shoot "military" rifles. The Nazis also enacted the "Regulations against Jews' possession of weapons" within the days of *Kristallnacht*—the "night of broken glass"—when stormtroopers attacked synagogues and Jews throughout Germany. In documentaries that show Nazi troops rounding up masses of Jews destined for death camps, there is no instance of any of these innocent people possessing a gun which might have been used in self-defense.

Firearms registration lists, moreover, were used to identify gun owners. When the SS arrived, more than the gun would disappear—the owner would never to be seen again. These policies were promulgated in every country conquered by Hitler, and with the same results.

Jews were able to resist being slaughtered only when they had guns.

Dr. David I. Caplan chronicled a lesser known moment in history in his 1988 article entitled "The Warsaw Ghetto; 10 Handguns Against Tyranny" that appeared in the February 1988 issue of the *American Rifleman*. In it Dr. Caplan writes:

> When the Jews in the Warsaw ghetto in 1942 realized that "the meek submission to the slaughter did not lessen the Holocaust, but increased it," they decided upon a plan of armed resistance. However, at first they had no arms, and the only arms that the Poles outside the ghetto would supply the Jewish resistance fighters were pistols and revolvers.
>
> In January of 1943, the first armed resistance by the Jewish fighting organization was carried out with only "10 pistols" [no doubt "Saturday Night Specials"]. For three months thereafter, Nazi soldiers did not dare venture into the ghetto. During that three-month period, the Nazis under Heinrich Himmler decided they would have to burn down the ghetto house-by-house in order to conquer it. They proceeded to do so, although not without considerable difficulty in the face of armed Jewish resistances fighters.

Dr. Caplan reports that one of the survivor-leaders of the Jewish ghetto uprising in Warsaw saw the action as a turning point, saying:

> Many had thought that the 18th of January was the beginning of the final liquidation of the ghetto. However the shock of encountering resistance evidently forced the Germans to discontinue their work in order to make more thorough preparations. At the time we had only 10 pistols. Had the Germans known the truth, they would have probably continued the raids.
>
> Jewish resistance would have been nipped in the bud as a

minor, insignificant episode. By interrupting the extermination action on the 21st of January the Germans allowed us to better organize and arm ourselves.[1]

Clearly, the Warsaw ghetto stands in history as a shining example of the dangers of gun control. As Dr. Caplan put it:

That is what is wrong with gun control legislation involving the registration or licensing of arms. For the records of arms registration [would] tempt a would-be dictator in America into thinking that he can disarm the people swiftly before they can act to restore the Constitution through appropriate militia action, and that he could disarm the people so quickly and thoroughly that he could maintain power without the need for any house-by-house burnings of our cities or suburbs.

Elliott C. Rothenberg, an attorney and former national law director of the B'nai B'rith's Anti-Defamation League, made profound points in his article, "Jewish History Refutes Gun Control Activists," that appeared in the same February 1988 issue of the *American Rifleman*. In reference to the revolt at the Warsaw ghetto, he reported that Nazi propaganda chief Joseph Goebbels wrote in his diary on May 1, 1943: "This just shows what you can expect from Jews if they lay hands on weapons."

In his discussion of the Israeli victory in the 1967 Six-Day War, Rothenberg said that Israel's astounding triumph was due to one of the most brilliant military campaigns in history. The reason was self-explanatory, according to Rothenberg:

Israel has avoided extinction for the past 40 years because its people have attained sufficient skill in the use of firearms and other weapons to overcome the superiority in population size, land area and oil wealth of the enemies surrounding it.

Goebbels was spared the pain of having to see the supreme accomplishment of Jews who "lay hands on weapons," but the call for disarming Jews has not vanished with the Nazi movement. The baton of leadership has passed to—the American Jewish Community.

For years, much of the established Jewish leadership in the U.S. has been reflexively banging the drum for gun control.

Indeed, had they shared their American brethren's enthusiasm for government control of access to guns, no Israel would have survived in 1967.

In the last years of their occupation, the British authorities in what was then called Palestine prohibited the Jewish population from acquiring weapons . . . Only Jewish residents' refusal to obey the British attempt to impose gun control prevented a second Holocaust in the same decade.

The different fates of European and Israeli Jews in the past half century demonstrate the folly of a disarmed citizenry entrusting its rights and welfare to the supposed benevolence of its government. None should be more cognizant of this than the Jewish organizations so enamored of gun control.

State-sponsored genocide was not limited to Germany. Just a few years earlier, Stalin murdered between 10 and 20 million peasants in order to force collectivization on the Russian countryside. More recently, the Khmer Rouge committed genocide against vast millions of unarmed peasants and intellectuals. And today, Bosnia is undergoing "ethnic cleansing."

Let us now examine the crime statistics of other countries that have been used to justify harsher gun laws in the United States. As starters, these comparisons ignore the complex causes of crime—criminal justice systems and population disparities. They do not take account of the failure today of government to deal effectively with violent and recidivist criminals.

Of special note is Switzerland, which has a *higher* rate of firearms possession than the United States. It was the only European country that the Germans were afraid to invade in both world wars, knowing as they did that every man was armed. The armed Swiss have never been victimized by anybody.

It is said that a German general observing Swiss maneuvers

just before World War I asked a Swiss militiaman what the Swiss would do if the German armies invaded. The militia-man said, "We will all take one shot and then go home."

The Swiss have maintained their freedom for seven hundred years. In our history, the Second Amendment reflects the in-fluence they had on America's Founding Fathers.

Today's William Tell has in his home a fully automatic rifle rather that a crossbow. The rifle is supplied free of charge by the government, which, to borrow from Madison, is not afraid to trust the people with arms. Every Swiss male citizen is required to keep this rifle and ammunition at home, to partici-pate in group training, and to enter shooting matches.

The citizen is not a soldier, because Switzerland has no standing army. Rather the citizen is a member of the militia—the body of citizens trained to arms. At a certain age, the rifle is kept as private property. Swiss citizens are entitled to pur-chase and own all the firearms and ammunition they wish. Target shooting is the national sport, and the whole commu-nity participates in regular shooting festivals.

In 1990, there were only thirty-four firearm-related homi-cides in Switzerland. Three times more persons were killed while mountain climbing. Murders tend to be committed by foreigners rather than Swiss.

This is not to suggest that the Swiss system would work in the United States, but it does show that there is no causal effect between firearms possession and crime. Indeed, just the opposite seems to be the case: a thoroughly armed people is relatively crime free; it is the ultimate deterrent to crime.

Consider a case on the other side of the globe, Japan, where there is no right to keep and bear arms. Weapons control in Japan existed centuries ago as a tool to ensure the absolute rule of various emperors and war lords. In order to exploit the labor of the serfs, all were forbidden to possess a sword except for the samurai warriors who served the rulers. The social order was feudalistic and repressive. The average person had no rights and only one obligation: absolute obedience to the authori-tarian regime.

Japanese militarism was a scourge to the world in this century. While most Americans no longer bear hatred against the Japanese for Pearl Harbor, Koreans and Chinese, whose populations were massacred in astonishing numbers—after first being disarmed—have not forgotten.

While Japanese militarism ended in 1945, the government exercises vast control over its citizen's everyday lives. There is no more right to privacy of the home in Japan than there is to own a firearm. Few Americans would wish to live under such laws, which originated in political absolutism and continue to reflect the government's control over a defenseless people.

Of the governments which made available homicide data for the 1990 *Demographic Yearbook* published by the United Nations, Columbia had the highest murder and non-negligent homicide rate in the world—forty-nine per 100,000 population each year. Next came El Salvador with forty, then Mexico with twenty. The United States came seventh with nine such homicides per 100,000 people.

One could explain away Columbia, with its drug wars, and El Salvador, with its civil war. But how does one account for Mexico's murder rate which more than doubled that of the United States? Mexico has extremely strict firearms control laws making it virtually impossible for an honest citizen to own a gun. Advocates of similar laws for the United States never seem to make the connection. Instead, they like to discuss Canada.

Canada strictly controls handguns and recently banned numerous semi-automatic rifles. Since Canada has a lower homicide rate than the United States, gun ban proponents point to these firearms laws as the reason for the discrepancy. They compare homicide rates of Seattle, Washington (eleven per 100,000 population), and Vancouver, British Columbia (seven per 100,000 population). But they are hardly comparable when you consider other historical and cultural factors.

First, gun ownership in Seattle is four times that of Vancouver, so if guns are responsible for crime, as the anti-gun crowd would have you believe, surely the homicide rate in Seattle should be 300 percent higher than that of Vancouver rather than a mere 60 percent.

Dr. Brandon Centerwall reported in the *American Journal of Epidemiology*, December 1, 1991, that the homicide rates among non-Hispanic whites in Seattle and Vancouver were almost identical at just over six per 100,000, and that blacks and Hispanics could not be meaningfully compared because so few live in Vancouver.

Moreover, in the March 1994 *Journal of the Medical Association of Georgia*, Dr. Edgar A. Suter took anti-gun physician, A. L. Kellermann, to task for his faulty conclusions concerning Seattle and Vancouver crime statistics. Kellermann published "study" results of his examination of Seattle and Vancouver shooting deaths in the *New England Journal of Medicine* in 1988.

"Kellermann and his co-authors have persisted in their discredited methodology," said Suter. Dr. Suter pointed out that Kellermann attempted to show that strict gun control laws in Canada have reduced violence in Vancouver. In order to draw this conclusion, he simply ignored the 26 percent increase in Vancouver's homicide rate *after* a gun ban had been enacted.

Kellermann also ignored pertinent demographic distinctions. When the study was conducted Seattle was 12.1 percent black and Hispanic to Vancouver's 0.8 percent. The minorities in Seattle had astronomical homicide rates—36.6 per 100,000 for blacks and 26.9 for Hispanics.

Dr. Suter reports that excepting blacks and Hispanics, Seattle's homicide rate was actually *lower* than Vancouver's.

Dr. Centerwall further demonstrated that several Canadian provinces along the border with the United States have higher homicide rates than the adjacent states of the United States. For instance, New Brunswick and Quebec have higher criminal homicide rates than Maine, New Hampshire, and Vermont—states with virtually no controls over the ownership and carrying of firearms by law-abiding citizens.

Ontario has a homicide rate of only two per 100,000 while New York's rate is eleven. Does this prove the prohibitionist argument? When New York City, with its rate of twenty-three, is excluded, New York State is left with a rate of only 3.4. And how does New York City differ? It has the Sullivan law, America's strictest gun control law since the antebellum slave code was enacted in 1911. In New York City, it is almost impossible for an honest person to own a handgun, and most rifles, even .22 caliber target rifles, are deemed "assault weapons" and banned.

Across the Atlantic, England's low crime rate is invariably highlighted by gun control proponents. Switzerland, which entirely disproves the "guns cause crime" thesis, is of course ignored.

According to *International Crime Rates*, U.S. Bureau of Justice Statistics (1988), England/Wales and Switzerland had exactly the same homicide rate: 1.1 per 100,000. Yet, as previously noted, every Swiss male is required to keep a fully automatic rifle in his home and firearms of all kinds are freely sold and possessed. What then is the causal relation between firearms ownership and homicide, when disarmed England has exactly the same homicide rate as armed Switzerland?

The robbery rate in England (forty-five per 100,000) is almost double that in Switzerland (twenty-four). Why are there six times more burglaries in England (1,640) than in Switzerland (277)?

The United States has even fewer burglaries than England. An armed household is obviously a far stronger deterrent to robbery and burglary than a telephone call to the police. U.S. citizens like to say, "Call for a cop, and call for a pizza. See which comes first." The Department of Justice reports that in 1991, for all crimes of violence, only 28 percent of calls to the police were responded to within five minutes.[2]

Many believe that failure of American citizens to take responsibility for their own safety in the face of rising crime and decreasing police response is responsible for the high crime rates in this country. Consider the words of Jeffrey Snyder in his essay, "A Nation of Cowards," in *The Public Interest* quarterly/Fall 1993:

> Crime is rampant because the law-abiding, each of us, condone it, excuse it, permit it, submit to it. We permit and encourage it because we do not fight back immediately, then and there, where it happens . . . The defect is there, in our character. We are a nation of cowards and shirkers.

Later, in response to questioning by columnist George Will, in the November 18, 1993, issue of *Newsweek*, Snyder responded:

> Regarding your observation about our society's level of aggressiveness and disregard for rules, you may wish to consider Robert Heinlein's famous dictum that "An armed society is a polite society." Knowing that one's fellow citizens are armed, greater care is naturally taken not to give offense.[3]

Crime statistic arguments of the gun control proponents are superficial, because gun control is not about crime control—it is about controlling law-abiding people. And that is exactly what the Second Amendment was written to prevent. Indeed, gun ban advocates reveal an intolerance toward gun owners that they would find condemnable in any other context, such as in the civil rights battles.

Countries that have enacted harsh gun laws have done so for political control, not out of a fervor to reduce crime. In years past, England's monarchs disarmed republican thinkers and serfs in order to preserve feudalism and power.

In the American colonies, British troops tried to disarm the militiamen at Lexington and Concord as well as every inhabitant of Boston, and it sparked the American Revolution.

After the U.S. Constitution was proposed in 1787, James Madison wrote in the *Federalist Papers* that the federal government would not be "afraid to trust the people with arms," unlike the monarchs of Europe, who disarmed their subjects. The Founding Fathers knew that the purpose of gun control was not to reduce crime, but to enable governments to rule unhampered over powerless citizens.

Gun control came to England after World War I, a time of discontent when the ruling elite mistook the demands of workers for a potential "Red Revolution." As David Kopel shows in *The Samurai, the Mountie, and the Cowboy* (1992), England's first modern gun control law, enacted in 1920, had nothing to do with crime but everything to do with making it harder for honest working men and women to own firearms.

So things stood until Hitler's blitzkrieg reminded the English that firearms ensured liberty. They begged for arms not just from the American government but also from American sportsmen. Many issues of the *American Rifleman* magazine during the war included pleas by the British for American rifles, shotguns, pistols, and revolvers so that English citizens could defend themselves.

Today firearms ownership in England is limited to shotguns used by the landed aristocracy. Even target rifles are banned. That was made possible because the English have no written Constitution and Bill of Rights; Parliament is as free to ban firearms as it is to authorize arbitrary searches and seizures in the homes of honest citizens.

Americans believe in their Bill of Rights which protects the individual. Despite the rise of big government, Americans recoil at the thought of a police state. Any plan to ban firearms, including the police-state tactics necessary to enforce it, would be rejected out of hand by the American people.

Thomas Jefferson saw America as a beacon of liberty that would inspire peoples all over the world to throw off their shackles and come live in a nation that trusted its people with arms and guaranteed other civil rights. A just and peaceful society can be assured only if we protect fundamental rights, not curtail them, as history fully attests.

Any "international comparison" focusing on gun control laws that fails to consider the lessons of history and the reality of crime is nothing more than an attempt to justify an action that could lead to what history has taught us to fear—tyranny.

CHAPTER 19

BATF ABUSES

TRAMPLING ON CIVIL LIBERTIES

"If I were to select a jack-booted group of fascists who were perhaps as large a danger to American society as I could pick today, I would pick BATF. They are a shame and a disgrace to our country."

—U.S. Congressman JOHN D. DINGELL, 1980

THE BUREAU OF Alcohol, Tobacco and Firearms, commonly referred to as BATF, has been blasted as a "rogue agency" that persecutes ordinary citizens—people who have never been a party to crime.

A February 1982 report of the U.S. Senate Judiciary Committee hearings documented that BATF was engaged almost entirely in harassing innocent citizens. Illegal BATF actions, the report says, such as entrapment and secret lawmaking via undisclosed administrative interpretations of gun laws, "amply documented in hearings before this Subcommittee, leave

177

little doubt that the bureau has disregarded rights guaranteed by the Constitution and laws of the United States."[1]

The report of the committee further concluded that "expert evidence was submitted establishing that approximately 75 percent of BATF gun prosecutions were aimed at ordinary citizens who had neither criminal intent nor knowledge, but were enticed by agents into unknowing technical violations."

Such criticisms have given rise to BATF's unsavory reputation; in short, they behave like street thugs. Charged with enforcing federal gun control laws, federal agents persecute and entrap citizens who have done nothing wrong and would never contemplate doing anything wrong.

BATF's tactics can make for a deadly game, attested to by the horrifying national headlines that highlighted the cases of Randy Weaver and David Koresh.

If agents decide to target a person who has done nothing wrong, they manufacture a case, as documented in the above Senate Judiciary Committee hearings. Again, from U.S. Congressman John Dingell:

> The goal of the agency appears to be less the prosecution of criminals and persons unlawfully engaged in the illegal use of firearms than in the manufacturing of a statistical record of persons who have committed some technical violation of the 1968 Gun Control Act.[2]

Outrage over these abuses rose to such heights that President Ronald Reagan considered abolishing BATF and moving its enforcement activities to another agency.

Of those 1982 congressional hearings, syndicated columnist Paul Craig Roberts wrote on June 3, 1993, for the Scripps Howard News Service:

> BATF is a bureaucracy that has outlived its mission. Prohibition ended a half century ago. Eliot Ness is no longer needed to chase down gangsters and their untaxed profits from bootlegging. Today no one smuggles tobacco. Treasury agents no longer have anything to do but harass innocent gun owners . . .

The committee [Senate Judiciary Committee] concluded that BATF was a rogue operation that trampled all over the Second, Fourth, and Fifth Amendments. Following the congressional hearings, the Treasury Department was so embarrassed by the documented abuses that it drew up plans to abolish the agency. However, it was unable to do so, because neither the Customs Bureau nor the Secret Service would accept the transfer of the discredited BATF agents into their organizations.

Today, BATF's constituency consists entirely of Sarah Brady of Handgun Control and the anti-gun *Washington Post*. It was BATF's effort to create a gun scare in order to broaden this narrow constituency that led to the deaths of 100 people in Waco.

If Bill Clinton wants to cut the federal budget, he can begin with BATF.

Though soundly rebuked in 1982 for its abusive actions towards firearms collectors and dealers, BATF's nasty entrapments continue today. BATF abuse has reached new lows, as evidenced by the cases of Randy Weaver and the siege of the Branch Davidian Compound near Waco, Texas.

Author Jim Oliver's factual presentation of the Randy Weaver case should instill horror and outrage in every American.[3] It is presented below in its entirety:

THE RANDY WEAVER CASE

"Seeing his dog, Striker, shot to death by masked intruders clad in camouflage, Sammy Weaver, 14, fired back in fear for his life. The 4' 11" tall youngster was hit in the arm, then shot in the back as he turned to run for home. He died instantly, killed by an *agent of the federal government*.

"Cradling her 10-month-old daughter in her arms, Vicki Weaver stood in the doorway of her home, mourning her slain son, unaware that she herself had only seconds to live. In an instant a bullet tore into Vicki Weaver's face, blew through her jaw, and severed her carotid artery. The bullet was fired from 200 yds. away by an *agent of the federal government*.

"What had the Weaver family done to bring FBI snipers and submachine-gun-toting U.S. Marshals to the woods around their cabin on Ruby Ridge in northern Idaho? Why did the government act as though the Weavers had forfeited the protections guaranteed all Americans by the United States Constitution? Who made the decisions that led to their unjustified deaths and also to the death of deputy U.S. Marshal William Degan?

"For the six men working near Weaver's plywood cabin on Ruby Ridge, August 21, 1992, was just another day on a job that had been going on more than 16 months. Their employer, the U.S. government, was spending $13,000 a week, and there had been no end in sight to the work.

"The cabin, though really a shack, was home to 44-year-old former Green Beret Randy Weaver and his family: wife, Vicki; son, Sammy; and daughters, Sara, Rachel, and Elisheba. It was also home to their young friend, Kevin Harris. They were subsistence hunters, and tended a garden, putting up vegetables. A generator produced occasional electricity. They had no TV, only a radio.

"This day there were some new men on the job site not far from the cabin; one, 42-year-old William Degan, had been brought to northern Idaho on special orders. He was to help plan a successful conclusion to the job.

"The men in the woods were dressed in their work clothes—camouflage commando outfits complete with masks. They carried the tools of their trade—two-way radios rigged for quiet operation, night vision equipment, semi-automatic handguns, fully automatic military rifles, and at least one silenced HK submachine gun. One of the men was a medic, prepared to care for any casualties.

"The Weaver family had dogs. Somebody threw a rock to test their reaction. A golden retriever barked near the cabin and came running their way. A mission somebody in the Marshal Service had dubbed 'Operation Northern Exposure' was about to end.

"The 'operation' had included use of jet reconnaissance

overflights with aerial photographic analysis by the Defense Mapping Agency, and placement of high-resolution video equipment recording activity by the Weaver family from sites 1½ miles away—160 hours worth of tape used.

"For nearly a year and a half, federal agents had roamed the area, picking locations for surveillance and for snipers. Degan belonged to the Special Operations Group, the marshals' national SWAT team. The six on-site this day were deputy U.S. marshals.

"The target of all of this—and of a federal law enforcement and prosecution effort that would eventually total approximately $3 million—was Randy Weaver. What kind of criminal was he to demand this kind of attention? Was he a major drug dealer? Serial killer? Was he a terrorist bomber?

"No. On October 24, 1989, Weaver sold two shotguns whose barrels arguably measured ¼″ less than the 18″ length determined arbitrarily by Congress to be legal. The H&R single-barrel 12-ga. and Remington pump were sold to a good friend who instructed Weaver to shorten the barrels. The good friend was an undercover informant working for the Bureau of Alcohol Tobacco and Firearms (BATF), who later told reporters he was in it mainly for the excitement.

"Eight months after he sold the shotguns, Weaver was approached by two BATF agents with an offer—spy on the Aryan Nations, a white supremacist hate group headquartered in northern Idaho, or go to jail. Weaver refused to become a government informer, and—six months later—he was indicted on the shotgun charge.

"On January 17, 1991, as Weaver and his wife were driving to town for supplies, they encountered a pickup truck-camper with its hood up, a man and woman seeming to be in trouble. The Weavers stopped to offer their help. A horde of federal agents piled out of the camper. A pistol was pressed against Weaver's neck. Vicki Weaver was thrown to the slushy ground.

"Weaver was arraigned before a federal magistrate, who later admitted he cited the wrong law. Out on bond, Weaver went back to his cabin. According to friends who testified in court, he and his wife vowed not to have any more dealings with the courts of the federal government. They would just stay on their mountain.

"A hearing was set on the shotgun matter for Federal Court in Moscow, Idaho. The government notified Weaver by letter that he was to appear March 20, 1991. The actual hearing was held February 20—one month earlier. The error in dates was enough to give rise to a memo within the Marshal Service saying the case would be a washout. (Weaver did not show for the wrong date, either.) U.S. Attorney Ron Howen went to the grand jury anyway, and Weaver was indicted for failure to appear.

"But why had the BATF picked Randy Weaver to set up as an informer? He was a man devoted to his family, a man with no criminal record, a veteran who served his country with honor. It was Weaver's beliefs that made him an ideal target. His unorthodox religious and political views were far outside mainstream America. He was a white separatist. And, Randy Weaver was little, a nobody.

"Over the next 16 months, the feds painted Weaver as racist, as anti-semitic, as a criminal. But they had to entrap him into his only crime, altering two guns. The media were unquestioning. In print and on TV and radio, Weaver's home—the plywood shack he built himself—became a 'mountain fortress,' and then 'a bunker,' and 'a stronghold protected by a cache of 15 weapons and ammunition capable of piercing armored personnel carriers.'

"The common shotguns Weaver sold became the chosen 'weapon of drug dealers and terrorists' or 'gangster weapons' that 'have no sporting use.' The media always added the universal out . . . 'agents said.' But there were no gangsters. There were no terrorists or drug dealers, just Weaver, the gun buyer and the government.

"It was all a lie. Hate-hype. People believed it, maybe even the agents who planted the hate-hype began to believe it. It all ceased to matter on August 21, when Striker barked and sniffed out the agents spying on the cabin—lives changed, lives ended.

"Nobody, except the people who were there, knows exactly what happened next. There were several versions of the story. But some facts jibe. Randy Weaver's little boy, Sammy—a kid whose voice hadn't yet changed—and Kevin Harris followed Striker. Harris and Weaver later said they thought the dog was chasing a deer. Harris carried a bolt-action hunting rifle. The boy also had a gun.

"Without warning a federal agent fired a burst into Striker, killing him. (It came out in court later that there had been a plan to take the dog 'out of the equation.') The boy, frightened, shot back, and when one of the agents fired another burst, Sammy lay dead.

"Kevin Harris shot deputy William Degan in the chest. He died a few moments later. The shooting ended relatively quickly. The agents would claim Harris fired first. Harris claimed he fired after the boy was shot. Agents told the media their men had been pinned down for eight hours. It was a lie.

"The dog was dead. The boy was dead. Deputy Degan was dead. Two American families had tragically lost loved-ones. During the night hours, Randy Weaver and Kevin Harris brought the little boy's body to a shed near the cabin and washed it.

"Deputy Degan's shooting brought in the FBI. Soon, the Weaver's property was ringed by a huge force of FBI, BATF, U.S. marshals, Idaho state police, and local law enforcement and Idaho National Guard.

"Among the federal law enforcement commanders was Richard Rogers, the head of the FBI's hostage rescue team, which includes its snipers. On the flight out, he took an extraordinary step—he decided to alter radically the prescribed rules of engagement of FBI sharpshooters.

"Normally, agents can only shoot when they are facing death or grievous harm. But the 11 snipers that were positioned around the Weaver cabin were given new orders:

" 'If *any adult* in the compound is observed with a weapon after the surrender announcement is made, deadly force can and *should be employed* to neutralize the individual.' This meant Randy Weaver's wife would be fair game. It went on:

" 'If any *adult male* is observed with a weapon *prior to the announcement*, deadly force can and should be employed if the shot can be taken without endangering the children. (Emphasis added.)

"In words reminiscent of hollow justifications used in Waco, Texas, federal spokesmen kept telling the media of their concern for the children. In fact, Gene Glenn, the agent in charge of the siege, told the *New York Times* he considered the kids to be hostages. Yet they'd already killed one child.

"The negotiators were not in place, and no effort had been made to contact the Weavers, when Randy Weaver, Kevin Harris—armed—and 16-year-old Sara Weaver left the cabin and moved to the shed where Sam's body lay.

"As the three reached the shed, an FBI sniper some 200 yds. away aimed at Weaver. He told the court he was aiming for the spine, just below the neck. He missed; shot Weaver in the back of the arm, the bullet exiting through the armpit.

"Sara later told *Spokesman Review* staff writer Jess Walter in a copyrighted story:

" 'I ran up to my dad and tried to shield him and pushed him toward the house. If they were going to shoot someone, I was going to make them shoot a kid.' "

"At the cabin, Vicki Weaver was waiting at the door, holding her infant daughter, Elisheba. The sniper fired again. His bullet hit Vicki Weaver. She was dead before the baby hit the floor, miraculously unhurt. Harris was hit by bullet fragments and bone from Vicki's skull. He was bleeding badly. Randy Weaver, daughters Sara, and 10-year-old Rachel all saw the violent death.

"Later, sniper Lon Horiuchi stated in court that killing Vicki Weaver had been a mistake; that he was aiming for Kevin Harris. Defense attorney Spence asked him, 'You wanted to kill him, didn't you?' He answered, 'Yes, sir.'

"Sara Weaver recounted the night following her mother's death. Again from reporter Jess Walter's story:

" 'Elisheba cried during the night. She was saying, "Mama, mama, mama." . . . Dad was crying and saying, "I know baby. I know baby. Your Mama's gone. . . .' "

"She told Walter that on Sunday, they tried to yell at federal agents and get their attention, to tell them that her mother was dead. She said they got no response. Instead they would hear FBI negotiators.

" 'They'd come on real late at night and say, "Come out and talk to us, Mrs. Weaver. How's the baby, Mrs. Weaver," in a real smart-alecky voice. Or they'd say, "Good morning, Randall. How'd you sleep? We're having pancakes. What are you having?' "

"The FBI later claimed it had no idea that its sniper had shot Vicki Weaver. Yet, a *New York Times* stringer quoted FBI sources as saying they were 'using a listening device that allow[ed] them to hear conversations, and even the baby's cries in the cabin.' Another lie?

"On Thursday, August 27, radio newsman Paul Harvey used his noon broadcast to reach the Weavers, who he'd learned were regular listeners. Urging Randy Weaver to surrender, Harvey said, prophetically, 'Randy, you'll have a much better chance with a jury of understanding homefolks than you could ever have with any kind of shoot-out with 200 frustrated lawmen.'

"As part of their efforts to make contact with the Weavers, the FBI sent a robot with a telephone to the cabin. But the robot also had a shotgun pointed at the door, so the Weavers feared that reaching for the phone could result in death or injury.

"Somewhere in all of this, the FBI discovered the body of Sammy. They told the news media they didn't know he'd been killed.

"The siege began to unravel six days after Vicki Weaver had been killed. Her body remained in the kitchen of the cabin all that time. Sara crawled around her to get food and water for her family. It was during this time that Randy Weaver and Kevin Harris dictated their version of their story to Sara. In this letter, Weaver accused his government of murdering his wife.

"The news media, based on information from the feds, repeatedly reported that Vicki had been killed in 'an exchange of fire' or in a 'gun battle.' More spin control.

"The only shots were two—from the government's sniper.

"Kevin Harris was the first person to come out. Sunday, August 30, badly wounded. He was rushed to a Spokane hospital where he was treated and charged with murder. A magistrate told him he was facing the death penalty.

"The rest of the family came out on the next day. The surrender was negotiated—not by the FBI—but by Bo Gritz, former Green Beret hero.

"All the lies and federal spin control over the story were about to end. The case was going to go to court.

"The 36-day trial took place in the U.S. District Court in Boise, with Judge Edward Lodge presiding. The jury of eight women and four men heard the government put on 56 witnesses. The defense rested without calling a single witness, confident that the government had destroyed its own case. They were right.

"The jury deliberated for nearly three weeks, and found Harris not guilty of murder or any other charges leveled against him. They found Weaver not guilty of eight federal felony counts. The judge had earlier thrown out two other counts.

"Weaver was found guilty of two counts: failing to appear in court and violating his bail conditions. He was declared not guilty of the gun charge—the seed of all of this misery.

"It was a bizarre trial, full of contradictions, with government witnesses countering each other's stories as to the events of August 21, and countering the events leading up to Vicki Weaver's death the next day.

"The question of who fired first—Harris or the Marshals— was key to the jury deciding on the murder charge against Harris. In the end they believed Kevin Harris acted in self-defense. Earlier, the death penalty had been ruled out. The law the prosecution cited had been struck down by the U.S. Supreme Court two decades before.

"The government spent days going over the Weavers' religious views, trying to establish they were racist and demonstrate a long-lived conspiracy to violently confront the government. The jury didn't believe it.

"Marshal Service witnesses told about a series of pre-siege scenarios to root Weaver out of his cabin. But when pressed by the defense, they said they never considered simply knocking on the door and arresting him.

"During the trial, the government admitted that the FBI had tampered with the evidence; that the crime scene photos given the defense were phony reenactments. Physical evidence had been removed and replaced. The prosecutor knew this and had failed to tell the defense.

"The prosecution also withheld documents that might have helped the defense. When ordered by the judge to produce them immediately, the FBI sent the material from Washington, D.C., via *Fourth Class mail*, which took two weeks to cross the country. For prosecutorial misconduct, the judge ordered the government to pay part of the defense attorneys' fees, an action almost unheard of in a criminal case. Prosecutor Howen also was forced to apologize in open court. At the end of the trial, he collapsed in the middle of a statement, telling the judge, 'I can't go on.'

Gerry Spence [Weaver's defense attorney] told the jury, 'This is a murder case, but the people who committed the murder have not been charged. The people who committed the murder are not here in court.'

"After the trial, Spence told the *New York Times*, 'A jury today has said that you can't kill somebody just because you wear badges, then cover up those homicides by prosecuting the innocent.

" 'What are we going to do now about the deaths of Vicki Weaver, a mother who was killed with a baby in her arms, and Sammy Weaver, a boy who was shot in the back?'

Spence has asked the Boundary County, Idaho, prosecutor to bring charges against various federal agents. Should that happen, lingering questions about the Weaver case finally may be answered. Should that happen another jury undoubtedly will serve notice to those who have forgotten that the United States government is supposed to serve its citizens, not entrap them, not defame them, not falsify evidence against them and absolutely not kill their children."

On January 6, 1994, a *Washington Times* editorial revisited the case of Randy Weaver:

> Another piece of unfinished business is what appeared to be a vendetta against Randy Weaver of Idaho. It has been suggested that Mr. Weaver was entrapped by Justice Department agents. In a later incident, agents of the same department trespassed onto Mr. Weaver's property and shot and killed his son and wife. This needs to be explained to the American people.

The trial of Randy Weaver and the court transcripts tell a story that needs to be fully disclosed to the American people. Randy Weaver was treated badly by the government; federal agents lied to him. He didn't want to be an undercover informant—a snitch—for the government and he didn't want to be entrapped. He only wanted to be left alone.

But BATF was determined. And so they entrapped Randy Weaver.

Wyoming attorney Gerry Spence has fought and won some of the most important civil and criminal cases of our time. His clients are "little people," sometimes called the forgotten people of America. Gerry Spence represented Randy Weaver and in his summation to the jury he explained exactly what entrapment really means and how the government tried to "get" Randy Weaver:

> [T]he prosecution has to prove that he had a propensity to commit the crime before you induced him to do it. In other words, it's sort of like a virgin sole [sic], if you have a virgin sole

[sic], that is you haven't done these crimes before and the government induces you to commit the crime, you've been entrapped. In other words, that makes a criminal out of you. The law tries to be fair. We've got enough criminals in this world, without having our government agents out making criminals of our citizens . . .

If you've had no propensity to commit crimes in your life and the government goes out and induces you to commit a crime, it's entrapment.

. . . Randy Weaver was not a criminal. He had no propensity to commit crimes . . . this is a man who never had even a traffic accident. Never even had a traffic ticket. Never been charged with a crime of any kind, and honorably served his country. Had no history of any kind of any criminal record . . .

Now, who do you think approached who in the deal? It's very clear who approached who in the deal . . .

I want to talk to [you] about . . . punishment. Randy Weaver would willingly go to the penitentiary for the rest of his life if he could have his boy back. Randy Weaver would go to the penitentiary for the rest of his life and willingly walk into it and say lock me up forever if he could have Vicki back. Hasn't he been punished enough? Doesn't this terror and this horror have to end sometime? Shouldn't it end with you and shouldn't it end without having to compromise? Shouldn't this jury have the courage to stand up and say no, they overexercised their power? I ask you to do that.

I want to tell you a story. I want to tell you a story of the times, it's one of my favorite stories. It's a story about an old man and a smart alec little boy. The smart alec boy had decided he was going to show the old man up, show him what a fool he was. The smart alec boy caught a little bird on the porch and his plan was to go up to the old man and say, old man, what have I got in my hand? What have I got in my hand? And he figured the old man would say, well, you've got a bird. And the smart alec boy's plan was to say, well, old man, is the bird alive or is it dead? And if the old man said, the bird is dead, then the smart alec boy would open his hands and the little bird would fly off into the forest. Or if the old man said, the bird is alive, then the smart alec boy would crush it and crush it, crush it, crush it.

And say, see, it's dead. So he went up to the old man, the kid did, and he said, old man, what do I have in my hand? And the old man said, you have a bird my son. He said, old man, is the bird alive or is it dead? The old man said, the bird is in your hands my son. And justice, truth, and the future, but not only of this country, but this family is in your hands.

Gerry Spence's closing summation to the jury speaks right to the heart of what this case was all about—entrapment by smart-alec federal agents of BATF, determined to make a fool—a criminal—out of Randy Weaver. In the end, two innocent people and a law enforcement officer were dead. Randy Weaver's life was shattered by federal agents who prefer to entrap innocent citizens to taking real criminals off the street.

Congressman John Dingell put it well: "They are a shame and a disgrace to our country."

THE WACO CASE

Violence at the hands of BATF would occur again and in greater magnitude. The agency's new target: David Koresh and the Branch Davidians.

On February 28, 1993, approximately six months after the first shot was fired at Ruby Ridge, the first shot was fired at the Mount Carmel Center near Waco, Texas. It housed the religious followers of David Koresh, a sect known as the Branch Davidians.

With search and arrest warrants, based on an affidavit by the Bureau of Alcohol, Tobacco and Firearms agent Davy Aguilera, in their possession, seventy-six to one hundred BATF agents stormed the farm house, known as the Branch Davidian Compound.

It has still not been factually determined who fired the first shot, but when the agents stormed the compound, the shooting began. When the assault ended that day, four BATF agents were killed and fourteen to twenty-eight others were injured.

A fifty-one day stand-off followed, led by the Federal Bureau of Investigation (FBI).

To TV viewers, the scene resembled a war zone in a foreign country, not America. An isolated farm house surrounded by men, some in strange black "terrorist-looking" outfits, some in camouflage. Military tanks and helicopters hovered in the area. Loud music and other unpleasant noises—psychological warfare tactics—bombarded the compound.

And what kind of terrorists had federal law enforcement agents trapped inside the encircled compound? A religious cult of men, women, and children, who grew their own food, taught their own children, and pretty much stayed to themselves.

The BATF affidavit claimed that David Koresh and the Branch Davidians had firearms—including semi-automatic rifles—which federal agents called an "arsenal." And there were "accusations" of child abuse.

The search warrant was part of an investigation of "possible" federal firearms violations—technical violations. No one had been shot, or threatened, and no violent crimes with guns had occurred or been reported.

Agents would later admit they never even considered walking up to the door and knocking to serve the warrant. It was a "hot dog," TV-style operation from the start—complete with TV cameras and media reporters. They charged the farm house like Nazi storm troopers, and the shooting started.

Did they expect less? There was no element of surprise. Koresh had been tipped off that they were coming—and the federal agents knew it. Koresh, in his own home with his religious following of men, women, and children—minding their own business—was tipped off that over seventy-five federal agents were going to storm his compound.

The government agents in charge knew there were firearms in the compound—the "alleged" type of firearms is what the charade was all about. Did they expect to charge the farm house and not a shot be fired?

What occurred is reminiscent of the stand-off at the Warsaw

ghetto. The Jews, whose religious views were unpopular with the Nazis, were trapped inside the ghetto and had *ten hand-guns*. When the Nazi soldiers tried to take the Jews from the ghetto, shooting started, the soldiers fell back, and the siege began. In the end, the Nazis burned down the ghetto to end the tiring siege.

In a letter to the *Wall Street Journal*, on March 15, 1993, John D. Dingell III brought the transgressions of BATF into historical perspective. He wrote:

On Feb. 27, black-uniformed men of the Bureau of Alcohol, Tobacco and Firearms wearing "coal scuttle" helmets and carrying German-made machine pistols attacked the Branch Davidian compound in Waco, Texas. Fifty years earlier, in January 1943, black-uniformed SS men wearing "coal scuttle" helmets and carrying German-made machine pistols attacked the Jewish compound in Warsaw, Poland.

The BATF men were searching for illegal weapons reported by a paid informant to be in the Branch Davidian Compound. The SS men were searching for illegal weapons reported by a paid informant to be in the Warsaw ghetto.

Reports from Texas indicate the Branch Davidians kept to themselves and harmed no one outside their compound prior to the BATF assault. History tells us the Jews kept to themselves and harmed no one outside the Warsaw ghetto prior to the SS assault.

The U.S. broadcast news media tell us that the Branch Davidians practice contemptible sexual rituals involving young children, so they are an evil religious cult. Nazi news media told the German populace that the Jews practiced contemptible sexual rituals involving children, so they were an evil religion.

The BATF invited the U.S. news media to document the BATF assault to show the American public how dangerous the Branch Davidians are. The SS had propagandists document its assault to show the German public how dangerous the Jews were.

Four BATF men were killed and 16 wounded in the initial assault on the Branch Davidian compound. Eleven SS men were killed and an unrecorded number wounded in the initial assault on the Warsaw ghetto.

After the initial assault, the BATF men magnanimously arranged a truce so children could be evacuated from the Branch Davidian Compound (and they could tend to their casualties). After their initial assault, the SS men magnanimously arranged a truce so children could be evacuated from the Warsaw ghetto compound (and they could tend to their casualties).

The BATF called up military units with armored vehicles to finish off the Branch Davidian compound after encountering fierce resistance against the initial assault. The SS called up military units with armored vehicles to finish off the Warsaw ghetto after encountering fierce resistance against the initial assault.

Fifty years have passed, but little has changed.

On April 19, 1993, having grown impatient—Attorney General Janet Reno claimed her agents were "fatigued"—the FBI began their assault, ramming holes into the walls of the structure to pump in CS gas, purportedly over concern for the twenty-five children remaining in the compound.

Eventually, fire broke out killing most of the seventy-five persons still in the compound. In the end, the children who had been in the compound for the fifty-one day siege lay dead—all because of an effort to protect them from alleged child abuse.

Civil libertarians were outraged by the government's actions in Waco, as, indeed, they should have been. The children in the Branch Davidian Compound were subjected to the ultimate abuse—death at the hands of federal agents.

Regardless of how you feel about the religious views of David Koresh and the Branch Davidians, regardless of how you feel about where they lived, regardless of how you feel about their lifestyle, regardless of how you feel about firearms, these men, women, and children were living in the United States of America and their civil liberties were trampled as though no Constitution and Bill of Rights had ever existed.

Attorney General Janet Reno made the decision to use tanks and gas to assault the compound—a decision she has yet to explain or justify. She accepted the responsibility for her decision, as well she should. She made the decision and she was, in fact, responsible for the travesty.

Until she gave permission to use tanks and gas, there was no escalation—and the children were alive. Some tried to make her a heroine for taking responsibility when, in fact, she could not escape it. But when Reno took responsibility she appeared to be saying, don't blame me, I stood up like a man and took charge. And the House Judiciary accepted her statement without even a reprimand.

Columnist William Safire, however, wasn't buying the cover-up. On October 14, 1993, in the *New York Times*, he wrote:

> If you were the Attorney General and had something terribly embarrassing to hide, to whom would you turn to oh-so-gently investigate your conduct?
>
> Janet Reno had that problem in the wake of her blunder at Waco, Tex., after she ordered the storming of a fanatic's compound that resulted in 85 deaths, including 25 children.
>
> We now know that she misled the public after the attack (and probably the President before the attack) by arguing that the children were being "abused" inside. She now admits that was her "misunderstanding" of something somebody—she forgets who—told her. A footnote buried in Justice's own report illuminates her nonfeasance: After calling for a written analysis with evidence of the situation within the compound, Ms. Reno "did not read the prepared statement carefully, nor did she read the supporting documentation."
>
> At the time she was putting out the false excuse of child abuse to justify her misjudgment, Reno was the darling of the media for seeming to accept responsibility bravely. . . .

Along with Safire, many others in the media refused to grant absolution to Reno. This whitewash was just too much for many to swallow. On May 10, 1993, Paul Craig Roberts wrote in the *Star Tribune*:

Can anyone imagine the House Judiciary Committee falling over itself to praise Hitler or one of his henchmen for personally taking blame for the Holocaust?

Something like that happened the other day when Attorney General Janet Reno defended her decision that led to the deaths of 24 children and 62 adults in Waco, Texas.

"You've raised the responsibility and accountability of public service to an incredibly high level in a way we've never seen before," effused Rep. Pat Schroeder, D-Colo. Republican Jim Ramstad from Minnesota couldn't wait to chime in: "You're a lot more than a breath of fresh air."

This is really sick. How come the policemen who beat Rodney King didn't get off for taking responsibility? They admitted that they beat King, and said that they had to in order to subdue him. How does that differ from what Reno is saying? . . .

Generally when someone steps forward to take credit for killing innocent people, it's a foreign terrorist organization in the Middle East—not the attorney general of the United States of America!

Reams have been written about the Waco atrocities, and the wanton abuse of civil liberties in this outrageous case have offended and alarmed many people.

A *New York Times* op-ed piece on April 17, 1994, by Richard A. Shweder, professor of Human Development at the University of Chicago, makes some essential points:

Today, after much Congressional celebration, an evasive Justice Department report and an inconclusive criminal trial the events and images at Waco are so absurd that the temptation is to tell the story as a satire. "This is not an assault," said the voice of a Government official at the scene as an M–60 tank tore off the wall of the Branch Davidians' home and shot tear gas in their faces . . .

Of course, the Branch Davidians were not the easiest people to love or understand. They seemed strange, weird. They celebrated Passover, practiced "strict Christian discipline," believed in the literal truth of the Bible, maintained separate sleeping quarters for men and women, permitted polygamy and acquired an arsenal of guns in anticipation of the end of the world. But for the most part they minded their own business, which was to have as little to do with the outside world as possible.

To the bureaucratic state and its regulatory agents, this can be very annoying. And of course the leader, David Koresh, was a "madman" whom the F.B.I. came to despise and view as a coward because he broke a promise and decided not to dash out of his home and commit suicide on national television.

So no one stepped forward to be the Davidians' friend. The Bureau of Alcohol, Tobacco and Firearms spent months planning and rehearsing the largest "law enforcement" operation of its 200-year history. This turned out to be a major military operation, worthy of a police state, carried out against the domestic residence of an unpopular and readily stigmatized religious community. The American Civil Liberties Union does not like guns, and it's very busy, so it didn't get involved. The religious leaders of our country do not like "cults," and the women's movement does not like patriarchal living arrangements, so they didn't much care. And no one wanted to seem sympathetic to "child abuse" or unsympathetic to the F.B.I.

Throughout the 51-day standoff, an uncharacteristic silence fell over the editorial pages of many leading newspapers. In seven weeks of jeering, taunting and lunacy in which the Government floated imprecise reports of child abuse, amassed an army to liberate children from their parents and engaged in a theological debate over the meaning of the Book of Revelations, witty and acerbic columnists just bit their tongues . . .

Most of the important questions about Waco may never be answered. Why did the agents first storm the compound? What evidence of child abuse compelled Ms. Reno to order an end to the waiting game? Did the Davidians really have illegal weapons or just lots and lots of weapons, legally acquired, like many other individuals and communities in Texas?

Yet one thing is clear. Waco is not the story of how 81 men, women and children gallantly killed themselves to avoid capture by the Government. That may be a noble goal, but at Waco most (although not all) of them died against their will. They suffocated. They were incinerated. They were surprised. They ran from room to room. The roof fell on their heads. . . .

Many believe that what really propelled BATF to take action in Waco was money. Grandstanding to look good at budget time is not unheard of. In fact, in the March 1994 issue of *Spy* magazine, author Carol Vinzant wrote:

In the jargon of at least one BATF office, the Waco raid was what is known as a ZBO ("Zee Big One"), a press-drawing stunt that when shown to Congress at budget time justifies more funding. One of the largest deployments in bureau history, the attack on the Branch Davidians compound was, in the eyes of some of the agents, the ultimate ZBO. . . .

Clearly, BATF was there to put on a show: the media knew about the raid and were there to get it all on record. It doesn't take seventy-five to one hundred men to serve a search warrant. Agents were wearing their black ninja outfits, well dressed for "show time."

BATF has been manufacturing criminals for decades, creating phoney gun law violations to justify its existence. In a column called "Blame gun control for Waco disaster," on April 22, 1993, columnist Paul Craig Roberts wrote in the *Houston Chronicle*:

If Rodney King's civil rights were violated in Los Angeles, what happened in Waco?

If a billy club is excessive force, what is a tank?

If four Los Angeles police officers—their adrenalin flowing from exertions to subdue a resisting, large, strong man—used bad judgment in applying force, what kind of judgment was exercised by President Clinton, Attorney General Janet Reno and the FBI in the relative calm of their Washington offices?

The Branch Davidians are not a preferred minority, but their civil rights were nevertheless violated . . . Fully armed with all the facts, the federal government set out to bring the tragedy to pass. Numerous opportunities were ignored to serve Koresh with the warrant on his trips to town or to detain and question him about the government's suspicion that he possessed illegal firearms. Instead, 100 armed agents of the BATF unexpectedly assaulted the compound.

The agents dressed themselves in black assault uniforms and brought the TV cameras along to record their exploits, but their assault was repelled by the Branch Davidians, with loss of lives and injuries on both sides. Then the FBI showed up with armored vehicles . . .

True to form, many liberals have rushed forward to blame the Waco disaster on the Second Amendment, which permits Americans to own guns.

To the contrary, it happened precisely because of federal laws regulating gun ownership.

The Branch Davidians hadn't assaulted anyone. They lived peacefully within the Community. Except for the federal gun laws, they would all still be alive.

It wasn't the state of Texas that provoked the confrontation.

It is the gun control propaganda that has let the BATF off the reservation and encouraged the T-men to throw their weight around.

From the standpoint of the Sarah Bradys of this world, to own an unregistered gun is a matter of serious import; it ought to be illegal.

The liberals' premise that gun ownership should be illegal or in the least heavily regulated, has created the atmosphere in which the ATF, like an unthinking bully, feels compelled to increasingly and brazenly show its presence. That is what produced the deaths of more than 80 children, women and men.

An embarrassed attorney general lamely blames her "fatigued agents" and "reports" that babies were being beaten and children molested. After the event, she pleads the Clintons' concern with children to justify setting in motion a plan that gets all the children killed. Some solution. . . .

Author Carol Vinzant also interviewed a former BATF agent, Kay Kubicki, who said the agency picks socially marginal targets as one of its tactics. She revealed that for over a decade BATF agents have had an obsession with the Hare Krishnas.[4]

The Hare Krishnas have annoyed people in airports for years, but are generally thought of as harmless. Kubicki told Vinzant:

> Somebody put a bug in their [BAFT] ear about the temple. I find them annoying but not violent. I was just in disbelief. There was always talk, especially in the eighties, about the Hare Krishnas. They thought they were like the Waco thing: they were storing guns in the big temple that's in West Virginia . . . Here I'm working on people in narcotics and these people are worried about individuals who shave their heads!
>
> Kubicki suspects that if the Branch Davidian raid had been a success, the Hare Krishnas would have been next . . .
>
> According to Kubicki, the bureau attracts sincere crime fighters as well as bureaucrats and testosterone-driven cowboys. . . . The team that worked together in Waco for the first time was an assemblage of Special Response Teams [SRTs] from around the country. The AFT forms SRTs by "hand-picking these superhormone guys," Kubicki said. It was this formula that, in part, led to the disaster. A disaster that, she predicted, is likely to be repeated. . . .

We must all ask ourselves some serious questions about the government's conduct at Waco. Does holding unpopular religious views justify the government's conduct at Waco? Does owning a collection of firearms justify the government's conduct at Waco? Does "alleged" child abuse justify the government's conduct at Waco?

Don't civil liberties matter when a rogue government agency decides to play "Rambo" with the lives of innocent people whom they ridicule and target? People, after all, are supposed to be innocent until proven guilty—by a court—not BATF. And neither Randy Weaver nor David Koresh was ever found guilty in a court of law of any allegations charged by BATF.

In the David Koresh case, BATF used alleged possession of firearms "arsenals" as the catalyst for its abuses and atrocities.

Bear that in mind when you read or hear U.S. Treasury Secretary Lloyd Bentsen call for new laws restricting firearms dealers, and read or hear about arbitrary administrative bans on various shotguns. Add to that the language of Brady Bill II, which will create "arsenal" licenses for gun collectors and average citizens who own more firearms than the government wants them to own.

If owning multiple firearms is of itself sufficient reason to justify the conduct and actions of BATF and the FBI at Randy Weaver's home and at Waco—and the Randy Weaver and Waco cases are just the beginning—we are clearly on a road to government oppression.

CHAPTER 20

MEDIA BIAS

THE "THOUGHT POLICE" IN AMERICA

"There is no reason for anyone in this country, for anyone except a police officer or a military person, to buy, to own, to have, to use, a handgun. The only way to control handgun use in this country is to prohibit the guns. And the only way to do that is to change the Constitution."
—NBC News president, MICHAEL GARTNER, *USA Today*, 1/16/92

NOT EVERY JOURNALIST or news reporter is so blatantly biased as media mogul Michael Gartner. Indeed many reporters strive for balance and accuracy. Yet the people who sign the paychecks wield an inordinate amount of control over news professionals who do not have final say on their own reporting—whether it's major TV networks, radio, large daily newspapers, or wide-circulation magazines.

The major news media are biased. We all know it. There isn't a public opinion poll that disputes it.

Bias in itself is not the problem. We're all biased. We are all entitled to our opinions and philosophies and we have First Amendment rights that allow us to make our voices heard.

The problem arises when bias controls public communications, and the media act as if the First Amendment only applies to them. Professionalism is destroyed when facts and truths are distorted, filtered, ignored, or suppressed because they don't support the preconceived prejudices of those who rule the main media outlets in this country.

The media have an overriding duty to act responsibly and honestly with the public they serve. Their function is to report the news factually, not create the news or selectively report what they want the public to know. Lacing bias into the context of news reports is nothing less than a dangerous attempt to mold public opinion to their political viewpoint—and that's wrong. It's a misuse of power and an abuse of the First Amendment.

Opinion pages or electronic editorials are the appropriate places for "mind bending." These forums provide an opportunity for management to lobby and influence the opinions of others. There is no camouflage: we're conditioned to accept or reject different points of view. We do not expect objectivity there. But the news should be different.

Monopolistic media outlets trap readers, listeners, or viewers because the news giants have virtually no competition. In consequence, the national news media monopolize the marketplace of opinion and ideas.

Consider what you might do if you wanted to buy an automobile and the dealership you visited only had orange vehicles. Orange being the owner's favorite color, he thinks everybody should drive orange vehicles. So his salesman will try to convince you that orange is the safest color to drive, orange vehicles are involved in fewer accidents, manufacturers will soon only produce orange, orange is cheaper, some insurance companies will give you a discount for orange, orange will make you popular with your friends, and finally that everybody likes orange so if you don't buy an orange car, you'll be out of step with mainstream American. If you're gullible, you might buy an orange car, but if you don't believe the sales pitch and don't want an orange car you can walk out the door and go to another dealership where you can find a color you *do* like.

But the opportunity to "walk out the door" and find un-slanted news coverage, or coverage more in line with your views, does not exist in some areas.

Rush Limbaugh has provided an alternative perspective to the current news and events output, and those people fortunate enough to hear him have eagerly welcomed him. Radio audiences and TV viewers—given the choice—have flocked to hear or watch his program, like nomads to an oasis of cool water in a vast desert wasteland. Rush Limbaugh's popularity is not an aberration; it's a signal that American is waking up. His irreverent way of confronting manipulative politicians and exposing phoney issues is helping to rouse this nation back to its senses; it is sparking a renewed respect for our basic values and our patriotism.

In his book, *The Way Things Ought to Be*, Limbaugh discusses today's media:

> [T]he profound anger and distrust of our political institutions felt by so many Americans now includes The Media as well. When people say they feel betrayed and sold out by the old-line political institutions of the country, they include The Media in the mix. The Media are now considered just another part of the arrogant, condescending, elite, and out-of-touch political structure which has ignored the people and their concerns and interests. People are beginning to view the media not as a watchdog against governmental abuse of power but as an institution which is itself engaging in the abuse of power.[1]

Talk Radio is now finding wide audiences across America as millions of frustrated people seek a thorough discussion of news and events; indeed, a rebellion is brewing against media "institutions." Nationally syndicated talk-show hosts Rush

Limbaugh and G. Gordon Liddy, and locals such as Ken Hamlin of Denver, David Gold and Mark Davis of Dallas, and Sean Hannity of Atlanta are offering alternatives to the scripted pap of the networks—and people are hungry for them.

When it comes to federal gun laws, media bigwigs consider themselves public policymakers much like the dealer of the orange vehicles. As "thought police" they wield enormous power by controlling the debate. Worse yet, they set themselves above the average citizen feeding him or her a steady diet of distortion aimed at making everyone conform to their viewpoint.

Take the steady drum beat of the nightly crime news. In its March 21, 1994, issue, *Newsweek* magazine asks: "Is there a crime wave or merely a wave of crime news?" According to *Newsweek*:

> A recent survey by the Center for Media and Public Affairs shows that the three major networks aired more than twice as many crime stories last year as in 1992—even though the nation's crime rate remained virtually unchanged. The surge in newscast violence was driven by several high-profile cases, but some charge that the networks are trying to mimic the crime-crazed tabloid shows. Whatever the explanation, the public's fear of crime is now at record highs.

In fact, crime has remained stable or declined, but to admit as much would interfere with the enactment of harsh gun laws to prevent crime, an unrealistic solution supported by the media.

The abuse of the media is not limited to inserting their personal political agendas into their own presentations; they block opportunities for opposing views to be presented and many even refuse to accept paid advertising that takes issue with their worldview.

In a 1984 referendum campaign on "handgun management" in Broward County, Florida, two of the TV network affiliates refused to take the National Rifle Association's TV spots, and the third agreed to take them at "double the price" in order to allow the station to provide free time to the gun control proponents. They cited the "Fairness Doctrine" as the reason for making such outrageous demands. The National Rifle Association was effectively muzzled, while the media proceeded to pitch for passage of the gun law and finally persuaded unwitting voters to approve it. Just whose speech was protected and where was the fairness?

In 1989, NRA and Unified Sportsmen of Florida sought to purchase radio time to correct the untruths, half-truths, and distortions concerning proposed Florida legislation. Several radio stations in South Florida refused to accept the paid ads even though some station general managers admitted that their attorneys said the NRA ads were "not inaccurate" and presented no legal problems. They claimed to refuse the ads solely because they felt the issue was "too controversial." Yet it was they who made it controversial. So much for the "market of ideas" our Founders sought to protect in guaranteeing First Amendment free speech rights.

In 1993, the National Rifle Association produced an issue ad for television and successfully purchased time slots through CNN to reach markets around the nation. The paid message supported the need for passing reform measures to straighten out America's criminal justice system rather than more ineffective anti-gun laws.

In Washington, D.C., home to 535 members of Congress who were debating these very issues, the ad was rejected by the NBC, CBS, and ABC network affiliates for these reasons:

> They "tend to inflame public responses" and present "a series of facts irrelevant to the efficacy of gun control . . ."
>
> CAROL POWELL, WJLA-TV

> "It is our right and privilege, for reasons unto ourselves, to reject the ads."
>
> SANDRA BUTLER-JONES, WUSA-TV

(Refused to provide written explanation for rejection of the commercial.)

ALLAN HORLICK, WRC-TV

Where was freedom of speech in our nation's capital—the cradle of freedom?

Why were the "thought police" afraid to let people see another side of the crime issue and decide for themselves?

Access to public airwaves was arbitrarily denied to the NRA because our viewpoints differed from those of the gun-hating media in metro Washington. That's not what the First Amendment is all about, and they know it.

If the media in Florida, Washington, D.C., and elsewhere had acted responsibly and been accurate in the first place, it would not have been necessary to buy ads to correct the disinformation. These stations used the First Amendment to attack the Second Amendment's right to keep and bear arms.

When the major news media, run by a tiny cohort, crank out a steady stream of distortions, ordinary citizens begin to feel isolated and disempowered, believing they're the only ones who feel differently from the news media. That is not accidental.

When the Brady Bill passed Congress last November, the evening network news shows gushed their praise. Leading the pack was NBC News, which praised passage of the handgun purchase waiting period as the "Moment of the Week."

Press coverage of the Brady Bill intrigued the staff at the Media Research Center (MRC) in Alexandria, Virginia, and prompted them to take an in-depth look at the network evening news coverage of the gun control debate. Results of their research were published in the December 1993 issue of the Center's *Media Watch* newsletter.

MRC analysts reviewed "every gun control policy story" that appeared on ABC's *World News Tonight*, the *CBS Evening News*, the *NBC Nightly News*, and CNN's *World News* during a two-year time frame from December 1, 1991, to November 30, 1993. Television network stories that focused exclusively on so-called "assault weapons" were excluded, MRC analyst Andy Gabron said, "because of the difficulty of classifying stories and time considerations."

In all, 107 network news stories were examined, and MRC reported that "a clear pattern emerged, emphasizing the agendas, spokesmen, labels, and academic research of gun control supporters. Overall, 62 percent of the stories devoted substantially more time to pro- than anti-gun control arguments; talking heads who endorsed gun control outnumbered opponents by nearly 2-to-1; in stories concerning the Brady Bill, the bias against gun control opponents was even greater, a ratio of 3-to-1."

The length of pro- and anti-gun statements in each story were timed exactly. Reports in which one side received more air time by a ratio greater than 1.5 to 1 were categorized as being either for or against gun control. Stories with a disparity of less than 1.5 to 1 were considered to be neutral.

Among statements considered for gun control were claims that:

- gun control would reduce crime
- violent crime occurs because of guns, not criminals
- those who oppose gun control efforts are partisan or obstructionist

Labeled as arguments against gun control were claims that:

- gun control would not reduce crime
- criminals, not guns, are the problem
- Americans have a constitutional right to keep and bear arms

MRC researchers examined seventy-eight gun control stories unrelated to the Brady Bill and discovered that in two years only three stories, a mere 4 percent, were devoted to firearm owners' rights. Twenty-nine news reports were considered to be neutral, while forty-six, or 59 percent, were judged to contain "an aggressively pro-gun control agenda."

When the Brady Bill was the topic, *no story* leaned to the pro-gun point of view. Pro-Brady coverage dominated 69 percent of the stories, while the remaining reports were judged neutral. "Soundbites" were just as uneven, as those favoring gun control during the Brady debate outnumbered anti-gun control "soundbites" by 75 to 34, a vast 3-to-1 disparity. *Media Watch* reported that "Brady bill supporters amounted to 69 percent of all the sources quoted, compared to 22 percent opposed and 8 percent who were neutral."

MRC analysis also counted the number of spokespersons who appeared on evening news shows in support of and against the Brady Bill. NBC allowed only six Brady opponents to speak, but aired thirty-four supporters. Law-abiding gun owners fared slightly better on CNN, where gun-control advocates were given a 4-to-1 advantage with sixteen speakers compared to four. The Bradys and supporters received twice as much coverage on CBS, where they outnumbered their opponents 13-to-6. At ABC the anti-gun tilt was 12-to-8.

ABC most closely approached objectivity in its Brady coverage. According to MRC research, "All five ABC stories gave both sides about equal time, although talking heads favoring gun control held a margin of 12-to-8. CNN ran six neutral stories and just one heavily pro-gun control story. Both CBS and NBC skewed their coverage and sources in favor of gun control. Five of six CBS stories favored the Brady bill. But NBC was the most egregious offender: pro-gun control themes dominated in 10 of 11 stories (91 percent)."

Media Watch noted also that NBC's White House correspondent Andrea Mitchell suggested in two stories that if the Brady waiting period had been in effect, presidential assassin "John Hinckley might have flunked that test." A little investigative research by Mitchell would have revealed that Hinckley had no felony convictions in any jurisdiction. Neither had Hinckley any public record of mental illness. Furthermore, since

Hinckley purchased two handguns at the same time, the transaction by law was reported to Bureau of Alcohol, Tobacco and Firearms, which has power to investigate such purchases.

In this era of "soundbite" television journalism, labels are used to define debate, a fact not lost on MRC analysts. As an example, *Media Watch* pointed to CBS reporter James Hattori's April 3, 1992, story in which he described doctors who call for gun bans as having a "clinical, apolitical view."

The same MRC study of network news' gun policy coverage turned up sixteen labels for gun control proponents. The term "gun control advocates" appeared fourteen times. On the other hand, "gun rights advocate" and "gun advocate" were each used once. Network reporters mentioned the "gun lobby" seventeen times, but the label "gun control lobby" only twice. "Two labels which often appeared together were 'fear' and 'NRA,'" *Media Watch* noted.

The research done by the staff at the Media Research Center confirms what most gun owners already know all too well—when it comes to the national media reporting the gun issue, objectivity and fact get lost in a torrent of emotion.

Ignorance also comes into play. The NRA has been aware for years that the overwhelming majority of reporters and editorial writers who deal with gun issues have absolutely no knowledge of or experience with guns. A *USA Today* cover story on December 29, 1993, acknowledged as much:

> *The USA's beginning gives context to the commonness of guns today. In many parts of the country, guns always were a part of home life; owning one posed no moral dilemma, teaching a child to use one, no sin.*
>
> *But elsewhere, guns are decidedly foreign objects.*
>
> *In the newsroom of* USA Today *for example, which prides itself on drawing its staff from a cross-section of the nation, it was hard to find editors and reporters who had ever owned a gun. In other workplaces, it would be difficult to find anyone who hadn't.*
>
> —TONY MAURO, *USA Today*

Yet the media aggressively "lobby" their point of view to millions of trusting Americans, sitting in their living rooms thinking they are watching the news.

The media spin doctors lobby the U.S. Congress and state legislatures just like any special interest group, but with a much greater advantage and without having to comply with lobbying and election campaign laws.

Politicians are heavily influenced by repeated media misrepresentations, if, that is, their constituents don't make their voices heard. Even then, fear lurks. Politicians who dare to hold a view contrary to the media lobby prefer not to argue "with someone who buys ink by the barrel." Name a politician who thinks he or she will get fair coverage for opposing media bias and you'll discover a politician who in time will no longer hold his office. No one can compete with the media, financially or otherwise. A candidate for office could funnel mega thousands of dollars into advertising, but there are no assurances that an organization's issue-oriented copy would be allowed to run.

Dare to challenge a media position, or call them to task for dishonest or unfair practices, and you risk personal attack. Your motives are impugned, your character assaulted, and even your sanity is called into question.

When the media call the NRA "merchants of death" or "the powerful gun lobby" or any number of other pejorative terms, they wish to make the public believe the organization is too extreme, too uncompromising, too far right, and out of touch with mainstream America. They want to make the NRA seem foreign to the majority of Americans. Fortunately, they have failed.

In August 16, 1993, Yankelovich Partners conducted a poll for *Time* magazine of five hundred adults. One of the questions asked was: "Do you think the National Rifle Association has too much, too little or just the right amount of influence over gun control laws in this country?"

The answer clearly was not what *Time* editors expected.

Thirteen percent (13 percent) of Americans polled weren't

sure one way or the other. But of the Americans who had an opinion, 55 percent said *the NRA had just the right amount or even too little influence over gun control laws in this country.* That's a better rating than Congress or most presidents get.

The NRA and its 3.3 million members believe gun laws against the rights of law-abiding citizens do not stop criminals from getting guns and will not reduce violent crime in America. Yet if you watch almost any TV news network, you will get the impression that just about everyone in America "knows" that new gun laws are desperately needed to keep guns out of criminal hands and reduce violent crime. All the propaganda notwithstanding, a national poll released by CBS in December 1993 asked: "Do gun control laws reduce violent crime?" And 64 percent of Americans said gun control laws *do not reduce crime.*

The media appear to believe that the public needs "expert advice" to think correctly, and that they are the right people to give the advice.

In January 1994, during the week before the Super Bowl game, NBC TV ran a continuing series called "America the Violent." Each day during the week, a poll was conducted on topical issues. Viewers were invited to call a "900" telephone number and register their opinions on the question of the day for a 55 cents per call charge. The computer answering system was set up to accept only one call per phone number to assure that no one could "stuff the ballot box."

The question was simple and straightforward: "Should all handguns be banned?" The results: *No = 61,051 (80 percent): Yes = 15,705 (20 percent).* NBC reported these numbers on the evening news, but stipulated that the results were not scientific, merely a "straw poll," and quickly moved on. Would the numbers have been played down had the survey shown the opposite results? It is most doubtful. If the NBC poll was designed to buttress a Gallup poll (1993) that claimed over 50 percent of the people support banning handguns, the effort backfired.

Validating the NBC "nonscientific" poll, a December 1993

poll commissioned by *Time* magazine (scientific poll) found that 74 percent of Americans are *opposed* to banning handguns.

Despite the plethora of evidence to the contrary, the news media push the view that law enforcement athorities are virtually unanimous in believing that gun control will stop criminals from getting guns and thus reduce violent crime in America. Those claims, of course, fly in the face of what police really believe.

Every year the National Association of Chiefs of Police conducts a survey of law enforcement leaders. In 1992, 15,800 command officers, chiefs of police, and sheriffs across America were asked some critical questions about gun control:

93 percent said *banning* firearms (handguns, shotguns, and rifles) will *not* reduce the ability of criminals to obtain firearms

90 percent said *banning* the private ownership of firearms will *not* result in fewer crimes with firearms

80 percent said that a *waiting period* to purchase a handgun or any type of firearm will *not* have any effect on criminals getting firearms.

Tired of hearing Sarah Brady, Handgun Control, Inc., and the media claim "virtually all police support gun control?" Tired of hearing a few "top brass" law enforcement administrators pretend to speak for all law enforcement while calling for all manner of gun control? Well, apparently so are the police. Take a look at another survey conducted for Southern States Police Benevolent Association (SSPBA). The group wanted to know what police really think so they commissioned a professional research firm (Spectrum Resources, Inc.) to survey police officers. The results are a major setback for Sarah Brady and the anti-gunners.

SSPBA, it should be noted, has traditionally maintained a neutral position on gun control, but it decided to commission the poll to resolve the burning controversy concerning the position of law enforcement people on gun control. SSPBA President Jack Roberts told reporters:

> We simply have had enough of every special interest group, including a number of national police organizations, claiming they spoke for rank-and-file officers on the subject of gun control. The only way to know how law enforcement feels about gun control is to ask them. And, that's exactly what we did. What our members told us may be quite an eye-opener for some people, but it won't be to anyone who is in touch with rank-and-file street cops.

Included in the survey results of police officers were the following:

- 95.8 percent oppose gun bans
- 96.4 percent say people should have the right to own guns for self-protection
- 89.5 percent say the criminal justice system needs major reform
- 84.5 percent say waiting periods won't stop criminals from getting guns
- 90.1 percent say the U.S. Constitution guarantees every law-abiding citizen the right to own firearms.

The SSPBA poll of law enforcement officers also asked police to identify the "most pressing cause" of crime in America today.

Their survey shows what NRA has been saying for years— and getting media-whipped for doing it. Police chiefs, sheriffs, and command officers have also been saying it but have been virtually ignored. Because what the people and law enforcement professionals believe doesn't fit with the media viewpoint. Law enforcement professionals were asked:

- Many gun-rights organizations suggest we need to build jails, prosecute cases under present laws, and target criminals instead of law-abiding gun owners. Would you agree with that statement?

Eight-nine percent said yes!

Remember, the NRA had nothing to do with that poll. Unfortunately, the news media will have nothing to do with it either.

The responses are overwhelmingly different from what the media wish to convey of law enforcement officials on this policy issue.

Jim Fotis, executive director of the Law Enforcement Alliance of America (LEAA), a national group affiliated with SSPBA, added: "Claims of police support for the Brady Bill are hollow, political shams."

Fotis, the most highly decorated officer in his department's history, retired from the Lynbrook, New York, Police Department after sustaining multiple injuries in the line of duty. He threw down the gauntlet to any police group whose officers claim support for the Brady Bill, saying:

> We challenge every police group supporting the Brady Bill and other restrictive gun control measures to *independently* survey its membership as the Southern States PBA did. Let the chips fall where they may. But, I'll guarantee the officer in the street will overwhelmingly reject gun control as realistic crime control.[2]

The overwhelming majority of law enforcement professionals said waiting periods won't work and that the Brady Bill itself was seriously flawed. Did this overwhelming rejection get any sort of news media coverage? Of course not. Media bias has destroyed objectivity, balance, and professionalism.

Why didn't more chiefs of police, sheriffs, and command officers speak out? How do we know they didn't? If a tree falls in the forest and there's no one willing to report it, did it happen?

NBC News itself conducted a national poll in January 1994 and said to Americans:

I would like to read you a list of some actions that have been proposed as ways to combat violent crime. For each one please tell me if you think it will make a major difference in reducing crime, a minor difference, or no difference at all.

There were nine items on NBC's list. Only two of them had to do with guns: placing higher fees on gun dealers; and raising taxes on ammunition.

The two gun-related items came in *dead last* at 17 percent and 18 percent.

> Toughening penalties for juveniles received 73 percent.
> More crimes punishable by capital punishment hit 64 percent.
> Life without parole for three time felons was 76 percent.

Everything on the list was *at least twice* as important as the gun-related items. But it seems not to have dampened NBC's passion for gun bans. Surely, they should at least relegate gun control to the back burner given these results.

Why, for that matter, wasn't a gun control question on NBC's list of major crime-stoppers? Perhaps NBC had already seen the results of the CBS poll rejecting gun control.

But NBC did ask one question that came close to a gun control question:

> Thinking about the causes of crime in America, which of the following do you feel is the ONE factor most responsible for the recent problems with crime in the country: unemployment, drugs, availability of handguns, breakdown of the family or lenient sentencing?

Not surprisingly, the "availability of handguns" came in dead last as the factor most responsible for crime. Four times as many said it was family breakdown. Three times as many said drugs. Twice as many said lenient sentencing.

NBC is like the Everready battery commercial with the pink

bunny—they just keep going and going and going on the gun control issue no matter how wrong they are, no matter what truth they uncover.

The network encounters a number of embarrassing moments as a result. Clearly that was the case on September 17, 1993, on the NBC-TV "Today Show."

Katherine Couric interviewed police officer Tina Dillard live from her hospital room at DeKalb Medical Center in Decatur, Georgia. Dillard, a black female police officer, had survived a criminal attack. She had become a familiar face to many Americans since appearing in the DuPont Survivors Club TV commercial with other police officers who credited bulletproof vests with saving their lives. In the commercial, Officer Dillard told viewers how she survived being shot twice at close range.

Several weeks before the interview with Couric, Officer Dillard had been ambushed and again shot at close range. Her physicians expected a 100 percent recovery and she planned to go back to work as a police officer.

During the interview Couric talked to Officer Dillard about her recovery, her commercial, bulletproof vests, and going back to work as a police officer. Couric then asked the following:

> COURIC: "Is there anything that you think should be done that would reduce the opportunities for this happening to other police officers across the country? Or does it basically just go with the territory?"
>
> DILLARD: "Essentially it does kind of go with the territory, but again we do have to watch our backs and we have to be real careful. And that's about all we can do."
>
> COURIC: "What about gun control laws? Would you like to see stricter gun control laws put in place?"
>
> DILLARD: "Personally, I don't think that would have any effect, because what it does is make it harder for law-abiding citizens who want to get weapons to protect their homes and families to get weapons; because criminals are going to get them if they want them."

COURIC: "Officer Tina Dillard, thanks so much for talking with us this morning. Best of luck to you. And hope you're feeling better very soon."

Katie Couric obviously didn't expect nor welcome Officer Dillard's candid opinion, and she dropped Dillard like a hot potato—probably too much reality for that early in the morning. Once again NBC didn't get the response it wanted—the only response it would willingly air.

During the debate over so-called semi-automatic "assault weapons," listen to the major news media. Read the daily paper and wide-circulation news magazines. Chances are you'll get the impression that professional law enforcement officials are 100 percent behind the effort to ban semi-automatic firearms. But it isn't true. This is what law enforcement professionals believe:

• A "military type" of long gun (rifle, shotgun, etc.) is now being described as one able to hold more that five rounds of ammunition. It must be fired by pulling the trigger each time. The legal description would cover many semi-automatic weapons. Do you believe that *banning* such types of weapons would reduce the chances of criminals obtaining them? *Eighty-nine percent said NO!*[3]

And there are other polls.

In 1993, Luntz Weber Research & Strategic Services, a firm that worked for independent presidential candidate Ross Perot, conducted a poll to find out what Americans really think about crime and criminals. The results of the poll clearly show that NRA and mainstream America are in lock-step on the issue.

• Americans were asked what they thought was the most important cause of violent crime. *Response*: Values (58.5 percent), Drugs/Alcohol (35.1 percent), and Economics

(14.9 percent) were the leading causes. What about guns? Only 7.3 percent indicated firearms were a leading cause of crime.

- Only 9.3 percent of those surveyed said "gun control" was the "single most important thing that can be done to help reduce violent crime in the United States today."
- By a margin of more than 2–1, respondents said "more gun control laws" would be "least effective in reducing violent crime." According to those polled, stopping early release of criminals from prison, the death penalty, more police on the streets, and tougher judges would all be more effective than gun control in curbing crime.
- 75.7 percent believe Congress has had little or no effect at all in dealing with violent crime.
- 70.3 percent said mandatory prison sentences would be more likely to reduce violent crimes than more gun control.
- 68.3 percent agreed that stopping plea bargains would be more effective than gun control laws in reducing crime.
- 87.8 percent believed the "whole criminal justice system is broken and needs major reform."
- 83.0 percent said "people have a right to protect themselves from violent crime, including the right to own a gun for self-defense."
- 81.6 percent said a waiting period would "only affect law-abiding citizens" and that "criminals will still be able to obtain handguns."
- 75.2 percent said it should be "your choice, not the government's, whether you own a gun or not."
- 92.4 percent believe "there should be an instant criminal background check on handgun purchases right at the gun shop."
- 88.8 percent surveyed said Yes, when asked, "Do you believe that you, as a citizen, have the right to own a gun?"[4]

The problem of media bias is complex. There are no easy answers.

Abuse of the First Amendment should be punished as severely as abuse of the Second Amendment. The media must exercise their freedoms more responsibly. They should consider the consequences to the First Amendment should we lose our Second Amendment rights.

And while doing so, they might also consider the CNN/USA Today Gallup poll conducted late in 1993. The Gallup organization asked Americans if they thought coverage of news about crime on TV was *actually encouraging* more people to commit crimes, or not. Of the respondents, 43 percent believed it was encouraging crime. That's *more* people than believe gun control will work and *fewer* people than those who believe the NRA has too much influence on gun control.[5]

The news industry has a lot of housecleaning to do before it takes its broom elsewhere. Nonetheless, it has a protected freedom, and we should fight to defend it.

One reason firearms owners fight so hard to protect Second Amendment freedom is that we see the Bill of Rights as a solid barrier between the freedoms of ordinary citizens and the power of tyrants—in government or the media—to strip away our civil liberties. Remove even one brick from that wall of protection and the entire structure would teeter on the brink of disaster.

The media themselves are swimming against the tide of public opinion because people no longer believe or trust them. The national media need to step down from their self-righteous pulpits and trust the American people—who trust the entire U.S. Constitution. They would do well to work to restore truth and accuracy to the news, and commit themselves to an honest pursuit: responsible reporting. As Theodore Roosevelt said in his address in Washington on April 14, 1906:

> The men with the muckrakes are often indispensable to the well-being of society; but only if they know when to stop raking the muck . . .

GETTING TOUGH: AN AGENDA FOR THE NINETIES

As THE MAXIM goes "all politics are local," and so it is with crime.

Since 95 percent of all crime that occurs is within the jurisdiction of state and local authorities, and not the federal government, reform of our criminal justice system must be carried forward at the state level. Indeed we need fifty criminal justice reform movements in this country, one in each of the states, if we are to restore integrity to our laws and order to our streets.

The National Rifle Association has identified twenty key elements that each state must have for its criminal justice system to be effective. These elements, taken together, form the bedrock for preserving the peace and freedom that are the great promises of this country.

With these reforms, Americans can reduce the violent crime that today terrorizes our lives; without them, the fear of violent crime will remain our children's most constant companion.

These twenty elements are built upon solid research of what works, and the common sense of the American people. An aroused and informed electorate in every state must step forward to demand action. Only through concerted and sustained action will the politicians get the message that the people expect more than hand-wringing speeches and stop-gap solutions.

We must work for a top to bottom reconstruction of our criminal justice system. Our children deserve nothing less.

TWENTY ELEMENTS FOR AN EFFECTIVE CRIMINAL JUSTICE SYSTEM

#1: Legal authority for the pretrial detention of dangerous defendants.

In almost every jurisdiction there is a horror story involving dangerous criminals who, set free while awaiting trial, go on to victimize more innocent people. The country mourned the loss of James Jordan, Michael Jordan's father, who was killed in North Carolina in July 1993, allegedly by two eighteen-year-old men. One of the men arrested, Larry Martin Demery, was out on bond awaiting trial for an armed robbery in which he and a thirteen-year-old boy fractured the skull of a convenience store clerk by bashing her in the head with a cinder block. In another instance, in Gouverneur, New York, a convicted rapist has been accused of assaulting a sixty-year-old woman forty-eight hours after posting a $3,000 bond that secured his release from jail on another sex offense.[1]

State statutes or constitutional provisions that prohibit a dangerous defendant from being held without bond must be changed. Laws similar to the Bail Reform Act of 1984, which allows federal judges to deny bail or pretrial release to defendants who pose a danger to an individual or to society, must be passed at the state level. In appropriate circumstances, trial judges must have the authority to keep criminals behind bars before trial. Without this power violent criminals, already under indictment for violent crimes, will continue to victimize society.

#2: Mandatory prison sentences for the most serious offenders including those who are:

  (A) convicted of a felony involving the use of a deadly weapon or dangerous instrument;
  (B) convicted of a felony involving the intentional or knowing infliction of serious physical injury;
  (C) convicted of felony sexual assault;
  (D) convicted of violent or sexual felony offenses committed against children;
  (E) repeat felony offenders, and enhanced terms for those who commit their offense while on release from another offense, either pending trial or after conviction;
  (F) convicted of felony offenses for using or involving minors in the activities of a criminal syndicate or street gang.

In 1990, of the estimated 147,766 people convicted of violent crimes including murder, rape, robbery, and aggravated assault, 20 percent—or about 29,553 violent offenders—received sentences that included no prison or jail time at all. Twenty-eight percent of those convicted of aggravated assault, and 14 percent of those convicted of rape, were sentenced to straight probation.[2]

The raging debate about the purposes served by imprisonment will not be resolved soon, but one consequence of incarceration is incontestable: a person confined in a secure facility does not have the opportunity to create additional victims.

Imprisonment must be mandatory where a deadly weapon

or dangerous instrument is used in the commission of a felony, where the criminal causes serious injury, or where the crime involves a sex offense, violence against children, or involves children in street gangs. Furthermore, there must be a graduated punishment scheme that imposes a mandatory prison term for repeat offenders or those who have violated their conditions of release, probation, or parole. If the law requires that dangerous offenders meeting this profile go to prison, the crime rate will be reduced.

#3: Sentencing laws that require the court to sentence for actual conduct, where it is shown at the time of sentencing by a preponderance of the evidence that the crime involved the use of a deadly weapon or dangerous instrument, or the intentional or knowing infliction of serious physical injury.

This concept, called "real-offense sentencing," requires a judge to take into account at sentencing that a defendant used a weapon or caused serious physical injury when the crime was committed even if the defendant pleads to a charge that does not reflect this conduct. Courts must be allowed, and in fact encouraged, to consider the actual behavior that has brought a criminal to the sentencing phase of the criminal justice process. "Real offense" sentencing restricts the discretion of both prosecutors and judges and makes it more likely that offenders are adequately punished and that society is properly protected.

#4: Mandatory life prison sentence without release, except for executive clemency, for the third conviction for a violent or serious felony including murder, manslaughter, sexual assault, armed robbery, aggravated assault, arson, child abuse or molestation, and kidnapping.

Certain predatory criminals repeatedly victimize our citizens without engaging in conduct that warrants the death penalty. Criminals who continue to manifest a blatant disregard for the rights of others and the norms of society must be

removed from that society for the rest of their lives. The benefits of such a policy are significant: study after study demonstrates that incapacitation has a significant impact on the
crime rate. Isolation of these obviously dangerous individuals
from society will save countless citizens the horror of becoming a victim of violent crime.

#5: *The death penalty for first degree murder with aggravating circumstances.*

The death penalty is necessary to deter and punish those
convicted of the most heinous, violent crimes—those who
have demonstrated their absolute disregard for human life. No
society should ask its citizens to risk allowing such criminals
to wreak havoc again.

State laws should require the judge or the jury to impose
death whenever it is determined that the aggravated circumstances outweigh mitigation. Furthermore, reform of federal
and state habeas procedures is long overdue. The endless appeals and delays in execution greatly reduce the deterrent and
incapacitating effect of the death penalty.

#6: *Determinate sentences with "truth-in-sentencing" laws
and prison release policies that require every inmate to serve
no less than 85 percent of the prison sentence imposed by the
court.*

On average, violent offenders released from prison in 1990
received a sentence of 7.8 years, but served only 3.1 years
before they were released. Over 47 percent of the violent offenders were discharged from prison in two years or less, and
nearly three-fourths were back on the streets in four years or
less.[3]

Parole and all other forms of early release must be severely
restricted. Every study on the subject shows that parolees have
a high recidivism rate. A 1987 study found that 69 percent of
parolees traced were rearrested for serious crimes within six
years of release. In 1989, 39,000 people, accounting for 10

percent of the jail population, had committed their current crime while on parole.[4]

The costs to society, both human and monetary, of the ill-advised release of convicted felons cannot be justified on any rational basis. To stop this insanity, states must pass "truth-in-sentencing" laws that abolish parole and prohibit any mechanism that even considers a prisoner eligible for release until at least 85 percent of the sentence imposed is served.

#7: *Prisons and jails that are safe and habitable but which do not allow their inmates to live better than law-abiding persons living at the poverty level and that require all able-bodied prisoners to work.*

A critical factor contributing to the increased expense of incarceration are the institutions in which prisoners live at a comfort level that exceeds the minimum standards required by the Eighth Amendment of the United States Constitution. The Constitution does not mandate comfortable prison conditions; it only demands that the minimum civilized measure of life's necessities is provided.

In determining an objective national standard for measuring the minimum decency of prison conditions, it is reasonable to look at the official measure of the poverty level. The Department of Health and Human Services has identified an income level that reflects a minimum income below which it is not possible for a free individual to obtain the minimum necessities of life such as food, clothing, and shelter. Criminals should not be entitled, by virtue of their imprisonment, to live better than these law-abiding poor. This poverty level should be a presumptive indicator for per-inmate expenditures in an institution.

All able-bodied prisoners should be required to perform some useful labor. If it is necessary to avoid displacing job opportunities for the law-abiding work force, prisoners should still be responsible for maintaining the correctional institution or perform other activities that offset the cost of incarceration.

#8: Mandatory drug testing for every person convicted of a felony offense and mandatory discipline for continued drug use by a person on any form of conditional release from prison or on probation.

Twenty-eight percent of state prisoners incarcerated for a violent crime, 28 percent of murderers, and 35 percent of property offenders reported that they were under the influence of drugs when they committed their crimes. Over a third of all inmates serving time in state prisons admitted to using drugs in the month before committing their offenses.[5] These figures clearly demonstrate a link between drugs and crime. States should implement drug testing of convicted felons to allow judges to make more informed decisions about sentencing and conditions of probation. With substance abuse involved in such a high percentage of criminal offenses, the criminal justice system must begin to mandate treatment for appropriate offenders. Random drug testing of all convicted felons should continue throughout their sentences, whether they are on some form of supervised release or imprisoned. Drug use on probation, parole, or conditional release must result in the automatic revocation of release.

#9: Computerized records containing data on crime and punishment for both adult and juvenile criminal justice systems that are reliable, accurate, and timely, and that publicly disclose how cases are handled from arrest to conviction.

The American people have a right to reliable, accurate, and timely information about the system whose responsibility it is to guarantee their safety. Without this information, citizens cannot evaluate how plea bargains, early releases from prison, and other factors are affecting their well-being. Procedures must be in place to provide this information so that citizens can intelligently exercise their right to self-government by demanding that the legislature respond to their concerns.

#10: Effective victim and witness protection programs.

Victim and witness cooperation is essential to the successful prosecution of criminals. But victims and witnesses are hesitant to become involved in the criminal justice process when they fear for their safety. Every victim or witness who remains silent increases the possibility of a violent offender escaping prosecution. Each state should have an effective victim and witness protection program so that citizens can be confident they will not suffer harm if they speak out against a violent criminal.

#11: A comprehensive and effective juvenile justice system that:

(A) provides early intervention strategies for "at risk" youth involved in status offense misconduct such as truancy, curfew violations, and so on;

(B) emphasizes discipline and responsibility for nonviolent first time offenders through programs that, depending on the age of the juvenile, may include informal and formal restitution, arbitration, mandatory community and public service, and boot camps;

(C) allows juvenile offenders to be treated as adults for committing serious offenses such as;

  (i) a felony involving the use of a deadly weapon or dangerous instrument;

  (ii) a felony involving the intentional or knowing infliction of serious physical injury;

  (iii) felony sexual assault;

  (iv) violent or sexual felony offenses committed against children;

  (v) repeat serious felony offenses, or serious offenses committed while on release from another offense, whether pending trial or after conviction;

(D) provides for the admissibility and consideration of juvenile criminal history in adult court proceedings.

The juvenile justice system must face the fact that a different kind of juvenile offender exists today. Between 1981 and 1990, murders committed by adults rose 5.2 percent. Murders committed by juveniles increased 60 percent in the same time period. In 1990, people under twenty-one were responsible for more than a third of all murders in this country.[6]

Certain recidivists and certain violent offenders committing adult crimes such as rape, robbery, murder, and drive-by shootings are hardened criminals who happen to fall below the age of majority. The juvenile justice system must have the ability to identify and respond correctly to these offenders as adult criminals with adult penalties.

Currently, the uncertainty of transfer to adult court reduces the deterrent effect of the threat of adult punishment. All states should enact legislation that provides for consistent treatment of juveniles as adults for appropriate offenders.

In many states, evidence of serious repeat or violent offenses committed by a juvenile may not be available or may not be admissible evidence during sentencing for adult crimes. This "clean slate" approach protects persons who continue a life of crime when they are legally classified as adults. States should amend their career criminal statutes to allow convictions of juvenile offenders for serious repeat and violent crimes to become factors in sentencing.

The Department of Justice has authorized the FBI to accept juvenile records from the states for inclusion in the national criminal records system. States should forward juvenile criminal history for serious offenses to the FBI. Where necessary, the states should change their expungement and confidentiality statutes concerning juvenile offenses to ensure that they are able to provide such information. States must also pass laws to ensure that juveniles convicted of serious offenses are photographed and fingerprinted, since records are useless without a reliable means of identification.

#12: Comprehensive and enforceable rights for victims which must include:

(A) The right to justice and due process;
(B) The right to be treated with fairness, respect, privacy, and dignity, and to be free from intimidation, harassment, and abuse throughout the criminal justice process.

As a defendant has the right to certain protections within the system, the victim must also have specified rights if the system is to be truly equitable, and these rights must be guaranteed by constitutional provisions.

A victim is forced into the criminal justice system through the voluntary actions of the defendant. Steps must be taken to ensure that the victim is not subjected to further victimization due to the adversarial nature of the criminal justice process.

Bestowing these general rights upon a victim will ensure that the victim will be treated like a human being, not a piece of tangible evidence. In addition to these general rights, the victim should also have specific guarantees:

(C) The right to be present at all proceedings where the defendant has the right to be present;
(D) The right to be heard at any proceeding involving a postarrest release decision, a negotiated plea, sentencing, or a postconviction release from confinement;
(E) The right to be informed of all proceedings, and to be informed of the release, transfer, or escape of the accused or convicted person.

Victims deserve the right to be present at any proceeding where the defendant has the right to be present so that they can judge for themselves whether justice is being served in their cases.

Victims must also be informed of the release, transfer, or

escape of the person who has victimized them. Many victims live in fear that, given the opportunity, the person who victimized them will pursue them. This fear is compounded if victims are uncertain of the offender's custody status. Assuring victims that they will be notified before the offender is released or transferred, or after an escape, will help alleviate this fear and will provide victims with an opportunity to take precautionary measures if necessary to protect their safety.

(F) The right to a speedy trial or disposition and a prompt and final conclusion of the case after the conviction and sentence.

The longer a case drags on the less likelihood there is of a conviction. Time negatively affects the strength of the state's case, and victims should be entitled to have their cases adjudicated when the facts are fresh in witnesses' minds.

There must be some finality to the process. In the current system a victim can never be sure that a case is actually over. Appeals and collateral attacks on convictions and sentences are never-ending. Without an end, there can be no closure for victims.

(G) The right to receive full restitution.

Many states have statutes that provide for victim restitution; however, these provisions are rarely mandatory. Requiring defendants to pay restitution to victims forces the defendants to accept some responsibility for their behavior. In order for a sentence to have an impact on defendants and on victims, the restitution order must be enforced. Most victims are not in a position personally to enforce the restitution order and they should not be led to believe that restitution is forthcoming if the state is not committed to collecting the money on the victim's behalf.

(H) The right to confer with the prosecution.

While victims are not entitled to interfere with prosecutorial discretion, they should have a right to confer with the prosecutor during the criminal justice process to ensure that they remain informed and that the prosecutor has been advised of their feelings concerning various aspects of the prosecution. Although the prosecutor is acting on behalf of the state and not the victims, victims must still have the right to speak to the persons charged with the responsibility of handling their cases.

(I)   The right to be informed of each of the rights established for victims.

If the protections afforded to victims are to be of any use, there must be a comprehensive scheme that ensures that victims are informed of their rights.

#13: Upon the victim's request, HIV testing for those arrested for sexual offenses or any other offense where there is a reasonable likelihood of transmission of the disease.
Victims suffer enough without the added burden of wondering whether or not the perpetrator exposed them to the HIV virus. If there appears to be a risk that a victim may have been exposed to the virus, the arrestee should be tested upon the victim's request.

No conviction should be required before testing is mandated. Given the latency of the virus, the arrestee should be tested as often as necessary to provide victims with a reliable HIV status. Testing and the results should be handled in a manner that protects victims' privacy.

#14: Adequate prison capacity including the legal authority for the states and localities to privatize prisons, jails, and other detention facilities.
The United States lacks adequate prison capacity. In 1991, state prisons in the aggregate were operating at about 123 percent of average capacity. In the same year, at least thirty-

four states had one or more institutions under court order, some of which included population caps, requiring states to release prisoners into the community due to the shortage of space.[7]

Resistance to increasing prison capacity is often related to the cost of building and administering the institutions. Studies have shown that having private companies build and maintain prisons can reduce the costs of incarceration. Since privatization can increase the number of prison beds while also reducing the cost, states and localities should be granted the authority to delegate this government function.

#15: No release pending appeal for high risk offenders and waiver of appeal as part of a guilty plea.

Once a defendant has been convicted of a crime and sentenced to serve time in a correctional facility, there is little cause for release pending appeal. A convicted offender who must serve time if the appeal is denied is a substantial flight risk. Furthermore, violent criminals or repeat offenders should not remain on the streets to commit more crimes before they begin their sentences.

Defendants should be required to waive their appeal rights as part of a guilty plea. A guilty plea is akin to a contract and the defendant is advised of its terms before the plea is accepted. The defendant's acceptance of the terms of the plea must be voluntary. If the defendant receives the benefit of the agreement into which he has voluntarily entered, there is absolutely no justification for permitting the defendant to challenge the conviction on appeal. This would also have the effect of encouraging them to take responsibility for their actions.

#16: No unsupervised furlough or other temporary or conditional release for violent or repeat offenders.

No system of justice designed to protect the public would release violent or repeat offenders on unsupervised furlough or other temporary or conditional release. Nearly 60 percent of prisoners who escaped from custody in 1990 did so from furlough or a work/education release program.[8] The escape risk is too high for violent or repeat offenders to be granted leave under these programs. The restriction on furlough and release must also apply to juveniles.

Both victims and citizens have the right to demand that violent or repeat offenders who have been sentenced to correctional facilities will remain in the custody of that facility, and will not be freed intermittently to roam the streets of the community, whether on "compassionate leave," work furlough, education release, or state-sponsored field trips. While these programs may have a place in the criminal justice system, they should not be available to violent and repeat offenders.

#17: Progressive community punishment programs for nonviolent first-time offenders that have the following elements:

(A) effective supervision, including electronic monitoring, for those offenders who pose the highest risk to reoffend;

(B) mandatory payment of restitution to victims;

(C) community service and work requirements to discharge fines and restitution; and

(D) mandatory revocation of release for violations of conditions of release.

Not all persons convicted of crime can or should be imprisoned. Community-based programs that are designed to instill responsibility and discipline are appropriate for nonviolent, first-time offenders. The program should employ various levels of supervision depending upon the probability that a particular offender will reoffend. The offenders must be required to pay their debt to the victim through restitution and their debt to society through community services. The program must ensure that these first-time offenders realize that there are unpleasant consequences for their deviant behavior and must attempt to dispel the notion that crime does pay.

A crucial element of a community-based program is the mandatory revocation of release for violations of program conditions. These programs must be designed to instill respect for the law and the criminal justice system. This respect can only be gained if offenders know that if they do not abide by the rules of their conditional release they will automatically be incarcerated.

#18: Protection against civil and criminal liability for a person's exercise of the right to use reasonable force, including deadly force where warranted, in self-defense, in defense of a third person, or to prevent a serious felony, where the use of force is legally justified.

The right to defend oneself from deadly attack is fundamental. At common law, a citizen had the right, if not the duty, to use force against an assailant who was committing a crime such as murder, robbery, arson, forcible rape, housebreaking, or mayhem. If force was used to repel, suppress, or resist these crimes, the victim was not required to demonstrate actual need for using force, even deadly force. The conduct of the criminal resulted in a presumption that the force was warranted. Citizens who used deadly force in these situations were viewed as not only protecting themselves but society as a whole.

Guns are not the only means victims use against a criminal attack, but they are the most widely documented methods. Whatever the means, victims who use force to resist crime must be protected by the criminal justice system. A citizen's inalienable right to protect life or prevent serious crimes must not be tempered by the threat of civil and criminal liability. A citizen must not be forced to chose between death or serious physical injury and prosecution when confronted by a dangerous criminal.

#19: Laws to prevent criminals from collecting damages from a private citizen for injuries sustained while committing, attempting to commit, or fleeing from the commission of a felony criminal offense.

No criminal should be able to collect damages from a private individual for injuries sustained during the perpetration of a criminal act. Burglars who are injured when they fall through sky lights or trip over items in the home they are burglarizing should not be allowed to sue their intended victims. Even the negligence or gross negligence of a citizen who is attempting to thwart the commission of a crime or to apprehend a criminal must not result in monetary gain to a criminal. Such lawsuits add new meaning to the idea that crime pays, and they must be prohibited.

#20: Effective laws to deter and punish stalking.

Since California passed the nation's first stalking law in 1990, numerous states have followed suit to enact what may well be the most popular criminal statute in years. This reform in the law is warranted. Nearly one-third of all women murdered in America are murdered by either their husbands, boyfriends, or former companions, and of this number, as many as 90 percent were stalked prior to being murdered.[9] Had stalking laws been in effect or enforced, many of these lives may have been saved. States that do not have effective stalking laws should pass legislation that will protect these victims.

LAW REVIEW ARTICLES ON EACH SIDE

THE FOUR POST–1980 law review articles on the Second Amendment cited in the *Encyclopedia of the American Constitution* that endorse the anti-gun states' right view and dismiss the individual rights view of the majority are:

(1) Dennis A. Henigan, "Arms, Anarchy and the Second Amendment," 26 VALPARAISO U. L. REV. 107 (1991).

(2) Keith A. Ehrman and Dennis A. Henigan, "The Second Amendment in the 20th Century: Have You Seen Your Militia Lately," 15 U. DAYTON L. REV. 5 (1989).

(3) Warren Spannaus, "State Firearms Regulation and the Second Amendment," 6 HAMLINE L. R. 383 (1983).

(4) Sam Fields, "Guns, Crime and the Negligent Gun Owner," 10 N. KY. L. R. (1982).

In addition, see Beschle, "Reconsidering the Second Amendment: Constitutional Protection for a Right of Security," 9 HAMLINE L. R. 69 (1986) (conceding that the amendment does guarantee a right of personal security, but arguing that that can constitutionally be implemented by banning and confiscating all guns).

The thirty-two pro-individual right majority include articles in the following law reviews:

(1) William Van Alstyne, "The Second Amendment and the Personal Right to Arms," forthcoming 43 Duke L. J. #6 (April 1994).

(2) Akhil Amar, "The Bill of Rights and the Fourteenth Amendment," 101 YALE L. J. 1193, 1205–11, 1261–2 (1992).

(3) Don B. Kates, Jr., "The Second Amendment and the Ideology of Self-Protection," 9 CONSTITUTIONAL COMMENTARY 87 (1992).

(4) Elaine Scarry, "War and the Social Contract: The Right to Bear Arms," 139 U. PA. L. REV. 1257 (1991).

(5) David C. Williams, "Civic Republicanism and the Citizen Militia: The Terrifying Second Amendment," 101 YALE L. J. 551 (1991).

(6) Robert J. Cottrol and Raymond T. Diamond, "The Second Amendment: Toward an Afro-Americanist Reconsideration," 80 GEORGETOWN L.J. 309 (1991).

(7) Akhil Amar, "The Bill of Rights as a Constitution," 100 YALE L. J. 1131, 1164ff. (1990).

(8) Sanford Levinson, "The Embarrassing Second Amendment," 99 YALE L. J. 637 (1989).

(9) Don B. Kates, Jr., "The Second Amendment: A Dialogue," 49 LAW & CONTEMP. PROBS. 143 (1986).

(10) Joyce Lee Malcolm, Essay Review, 54 GEO. WASHINGTON U. L. REV. 582 (1986).

(11) Smith Fussner, Essay Review, 3 CONSTITUTIONAL COMMENTARY 582 (1986).

(12) Robert E. Shalhope, "The Armed Citizen in the Early Republic," 49 LAW & CONTEMP. PROBS. 125 (1986).

(13) Stephen P. Halbrook, "What the Framers Intended: A Linguistic Interpretation of the Second Amendment," 49 LAW & CONTEMP. PROBS. 153 (1986).

(14) Don B. Kates, Jr., "Handgun Prohibition and the Original Meaning of the Second Amendment," 82 MICH. L. REV. 203 (1983).

(15) Glenn H. Reynolds, "The Right to Keep and Bear Arms Under the Tennessee Constitution," forthcoming in 61 TENN. L. REV #2 (Winter, 1994) (extensively discussing the Second Amendment in "Firearms Purchases and the Right to Keep Arms," 96 W. VA. L. REV. 1 (1993).

(16) Stephen P. Halbrook, "The Right of the People or the Power of the State: Bearing Arms, Arming Militias, and the Second Amendment," 26 VALPARAISO L. REV. 131 (1991).

(17) Stefan B. Tahmassebi, "Gun Control and Racism," 2 GEO MASON CIV. RTS.L. J. 67 (1991).

(18) Bernard J. Bordenet, "The Right to Possess Arms: the Intent of the Framers of the Second Amendment," 21 U.W.L.A. L. REV. 1 (1990).

(19) Thomas M. Moncure, Jr., "Who is the Militia—The Virginia Ratifying Convention and the Right to Bear Arms," 19 LINC. L. REV. 1 (1990).

(20) Eric C. Morgan, "Assault Rifle Legislation: Unwise and Unconstitutional," 17 AM. J. CRIM. L. 143 (1990).

(21) Robert Dowlut, "Federal and State Constitutional Guarantees to Arms," 15 U. DAYTON L. REV. 59 (1989).

(22) Stephen P. Halbrook, "Encroachments of the Crown on the Liberty of the Subject: Pre-Revolutionary Origins of the Second Amendment," 15 U. DAYTON L. REV. 91 (1989).

(23) David T. Hardy, "The Second Amendment and the Historiography of the Bill of Rights," 4 J. LAW & POLITICS 1 (1987).

(24) Nelson Lund, "The Second Amendment, Political Liberty and the Right to Self-Preservation," 39 ALA. L. REV. 103 (1987).

(25) David T. Hardy, "Armed Citizens, Citizen Armies: Toward a Jurisprudence of the Second Amendment," 9 HARV. J. LAW & PUB. POLICY 559 (1986).

(26) Robert Dowlut, "The Current Relevancy of Keeping and Bearing Arms," 15 U. BALT. L. FOR. 32 (1984).

(27) Joyce Lee Malcolm, "The Right of the People to Keep and Bear Arms: The Common Law Tradition," 10 HAST. CONST. L. Q. 285 (1983).

(28) Robert Dowlut, "The Right to Arms," 36 OKL. L. REV. 65 (1983); David I. Caplan, "The Right of the Individual to Keep and Bear Arms," DET. COLL. L. REV. 789 (1982).

(29) Stephen P. Halbrook, "To Keep and Bear 'Their Private Arms,'" 10 N. KY. L. REV. 13 (1982).

(30) Alan Gottlieb, "Gun Ownership: A Constitutional Right," 10 N. KY. L. REV. 138 (1982).

(31) Richard E. Gardiner, "To Preserve Liberty—A Look at the Right to Keep and Bear Arms," 10 N. KY. L. REV. 63 (1982). Note, "Gun Control: Is It a Legal and Effective Means of Controlling Firearms in the United States?" 21 WASHBURN L.J. 244 (1982).

(32) Stephen P. Halbrook, "The Jurisprudence of the Second and Fourteenth Amendments," 4 GEO MASON L. REV. 1 (1981).

ENDNOTES

CHAPTER ONE: That's Not What They Meant

1. Lyman H. Butterfield & Hilda B. Zobel, eds., *Legal Papers of John Adams*, III (Riverside, N.J.: Macmillian, 1965), page 248.
2. Ibid.
3. Stephen P. Halbrook, *That Every Man Be Armed* (Albuquerque, N.M.: University of New Mexico Press, 1984), page 59.
4. Ibid., page 61.
5. Jonathan Elliot, *The Debates in the Several State Conventions on the Adoption of the Federal Constitution*, III (Washington, D.C.: Printed by and for the editor, 1836–45), pages 425–426.
6. Samuel Adams, *Writings*, III (1906).
7. Robert D. Meade, *Patrick Henry* (Marietta, Ga.: Lippincott, 1969), page 34.
8. Stephen P. Halbrook, op. cit., page 62.
9. Proposed Virginia Constitution (1776), Thomas Jefferson, *Papers*, I, J. Boyd ed. (New York, N.Y.: Putnam, 1896), page 344.
10. Thomas Paine, *Writings*, III, M. Conway ed. (New York, N.Y.: Putnam, 1896), page 56.

11. James Madison, *The Federalist*, No. 46 (Rutland, VT: Charles E. Tuttle Co., Inc., 1992), page 245.

12. *Papers of the Presidents*, I, G. Richardson, ed., page 65.

13. Jonathan Elliot, *Debates*, op. cit., pages 425–426.

14. Noah Webster, "An Examination of the Leading Principles of the Federal Constitution" (1787), Paul Leicester Ford, ed., *Pamphlets on the Constitution of the United States* (Chicago, IL: 1888).

15. J. Elliot, *Debates*, op. cit., pages 425–426.

16. Benjamin Franklin, Motto of the Pennsylvania Historical Society, 1759.

17. C. S. Lewis, *The Abolition of Man* (Riverside, N.J.: MacMillian, 1978).

18. Dwight D. Eisenhower, speech to the English Speaking Union, London, England, 1944.

CHAPTER TWO: The Second Amendment: "The Right of the People to Keep and Bear Arms"

1. Don Shoemaker, "A nation of guns," *Evansville Press* (Indiana), December 7, 1990.

2. Leonard Larsen, "Bush quoting NRA hogwash is absurd," *Evansville Courier*, December 5, 1990.

3. Leonard W. Levy & Dennis J. Mahoney, *Encyclopedia of the American Constitution* (Riverside, N.J.: Macmillan, 1986).

4. Don Kates & Alan Lizotte, "Civilian Defense is Time-Honored," *Los Angeles Times*, November 29, 1993.

5. Alshil Amar, "The Bill of Rights As a Constitution," 100 *Yale Law Journal* (1991), pages 1131, 1166.

6. Robert Shalhope, "The Ideological Origins of the Second Amendment," 69 *Journal of American History* (1982), page 599; see also Robert Shalhope, "The Armed Citizen in the Early Republic," 49 *Law & Contemporary Problems* (1986), page 125.

7. Don Kates, "Forefathers Firm on Bearing Arms," *Chicago Tribune*, December 14, 1993.

8. From a 1775 article in *Pennsylvania Magazine* of which Thomas Paine was managing editor; quoted in A. J. Ayer, *Thomas Paine* (Chicago, Ill: University of Chicago Press, 1988).

9. Thomas Paine, *Writings*, Moncure Conway, ed. (New York: N.Y.: Putnam, 1894), page 56.

10. Cesare Beccaria, *An essay on crimes and punishments*, 3rd ed.(London: F. Newbery, 1770) pages 87–88.

11. *Debates and Other Proceedings of the Convention of Virginia*, convened at Richmond, on Monday the 2d day of June 1788 (Petersburg, VA: Printed by Hunter and Prentis, 1788).

12. James Madison, *The Federalist*, No. 46. (Rutland, VT: Charles E. Tuttle Co., Inc., 1992), page 245.

13. Don Kates, "Handgun Prohibition and the Original Meaning of the Second Amendment," 82 *Michigan Law Review* (1983), pages 203–224.

14. Ibid.

15. Steven Halbrook, "What the Framers Intended: A Linguistic Interpretation of the Second Amendment," 49 *Law & Contemporary Problems* (1986), page 153.

16. Robert Cottrol & Don Kates, "Founders Backed Gun Ownership," *Democrat & Chronicle*, Rochester, N.Y., March 3, 1993.

17. Ibid.

18. Ibid.

19. Ramsey Clark, *Crime in America* (New York: Simon & Schuster, 1970).

20. Pete Shields, *Guns Don't Die, People Do* (Morrow, 1981).

CHAPTER THREE: **Self-Defense: The Right and the Deterrent**

1. Gordon Witkin, "Should You Own a Gun?" *U.S. News & World Report*, August 15, 1994, page 27.

2. Gary Kleck. "Crime Control Through the Private Use of Armed Force," *Social Problems* 15 (1): 1–21, at 7 and 9 (February 1988).

CHAPTER FOUR: **Carrying Concealed Firearms: Who Will Protect the People?**

1. Suzanna Gratia, testimony given before the Texas House Public Safety Committee, February 18, 1993.
2. Ibid.
3. Florida Department of Law Enforcement, *Crime in Florida, 1993, Annual Report* (Tallahassee, FL: Florida Department of Law Enforcement, 1993).
4. Editorial, *Sun Tattler*, April 11, 1985.
5. *Palm Beach Post*, July 26, 1988.
6. *Gainesville Sun*, November 4, 1990.
7. Carol Ruth Silver & Don B. Kates, Jr., "Gun Control and the Subway Class," *Wall Street Journal*, January 10, 1985.

CHAPTER FIVE: **Waiting Periods: The First Step**

1. James D. Wright & Peter H. Rossi, *The Armed Criminal in America: A Survey of Incarcerated Felons*, U.S. Department of Justice, National Institute of Justice, July 1985.
2. *Centers for Disease Control: Suicide Surveillance, 1970–1980*, issued April 1985.
3. Philip J. Cook and Jame Blose, "State Programs for Screening Handgun Buyers," Annals, American Academy of Political and Social Science, Vol. 455, pp. 80–91 at 90 (May 1981).
4. Ibid.
5. Douglas R. Murray, "Handguns, Control Laws, & Firearm Violence," Social Problems, 23 (October 1975).

CHAPTER SIX: **"Assault Weapons": A Classic Case of Bait and Switch**

1. Testimony of Edward D. Conroy, deputy associate director, Law Enforcement, Department of the Treasury, Bureau of Alcohol, Tobacco and Firearms, U. S. Senate Judiciary Committee Sub-

committee on the Constitution, "Sales of Assault Weapons," February 10, 1989.

2. Testimony of Joseph Constance, deputy chief, Criminal Investigations, Trenton, New Jersey Police Department, the Maryland Senate Judicial Proceedings Committee, March 7, 1991.

3. James D. Wright and Peter H. Rossi, *ARMED AND CONSIDERED DANGEROUS: A Survey of Felons and Their Firearms* (New York, N.Y.: Aldine De Gruyter, 1986).

4. Testimony of Robert Butterworth, attorney general of Florida, Florida House of Representatives Committee on Criminal Justice, "Banning Assault Weapons," January 5, 1994.

5. State of Florida Commission on Assault Weapons, Final Report, May 18, 1990, issued by Department of State, Division of Licensing.

CHAPTER SEVEN: **Comparing Guns to Vehicles: A Flawed Tactic of the Anti-gun Crowd**

1. Florida Legislature, House of Representatives, 1994 House Bill–2171, page 1.

2. National Safety Council, *Accidental Facts, 1992 Edition*, Itasca, IL.: Author (1992), page 32.

3. Samuel Francis, "If you're going to make comparisons..." *Washington Times*, February 4, 1994.

CHAPTER EIGHT: **Guns-for-Cash, or Good Intentions—Bad Results**

1. Frank J. Murray, "Dole Calls for $30 Million Investment in Gun Swaps," *Washington Times*, February 2, 1994.

2. Bill Bryan, "Gung-Ho: Some Bring Guns In For $25 Buyback By City Police, But Too Soon," *St Louis Post-Dispatch*, September 27, 1991.

3. Larry Fiquette, "Question of What's Fit To Print," *St. Louis Post-Dispatch*, March 6, 1994.

CHAPTER NINE: **Children and Guns**

1. "Governor Assails N.R.A. for Opposing Gun Limits for Teen-Agers," *New York Times*, September 8, 1993.
2. National Safety Council, *Accident Facts 1992 Edition*, Itasca, IL.: Author (1992), page 32.
3. Ibid.
4. Marion P. Hammer, "Physician Heal Thyself," *The American Rifleman*, December 1993, page 27 (quoting Basil A. Pruitt, MD, president of the American Trauma Society from his letter to the Safety and Education Divison of the National Rifle Association, June 15, 1993).
5. National Safety Council, *Accident Facts*, op. cit., page 19.

CHAPTER TEN: **The Brady Bill II Agenda: Registration, Licensing, Gun Bans, and Taxes**

1. According to Cuban talk show host, Tomas Regalado, Fidel Castro first made this revealing remark on January 8, 1959, during his first Inaugural speech. Later, when confiscation of firearms began, it was used repeatedly in response to demands by angry citizens that they keep their firearms.
2. David B. Kopel, "Trust the People: The Case Against Gun Control," Cato Institute, Policy Analysis No. 109, July 11, 1988.
3. Testimony of Stephen Halbrook, U.S. Congress, House Committee on Judiciary, "Brady Handgun Violence Prevention Act," March 21, 1991 (Washington, D.C.: U.S. Government Printing Office, 1991).
4. *City of Cleveland v. Turner*, Cleveland Municipal Court, No. 75CRB22050, January 28, 1976.
5. *City of Cleveland v. Turner*, Ohio Court of Appeals 8th District, No. 36126, August 4, 1977 (unreported).

6. Federal News Service, August 3, 1993, quoting testimony of New Jersey Governor Jim Florio before the U.S. Senate Judiciary Committee hearing on "Proliferation of Assault Weapons."

CHAPTER ELEVEN: **Arming against Crime**

1. Testimony of Randolph N. Stone on behalf of the American Bar Association, U.S. Congress, House Subcommittee on Crime and Criminal Justice, "The Crime Prevention and Criminal Justice Reform Act" (H.R. 3315) and "Violent Crime Control and Law Enforcement Act of 1993" (H.R. 3355) February 22, 1994.
2. Ibid.
3. Ibid.
4. Bureau of Justice Statistics Special Report, U.S. Department of Justice, *Violent Prisoners and Their Victims*, July 1990.
5. Rorie Sherman, "Crime's Toll on the U.S.: Fear, Despair and Guns, NLJ poll finds self-defense replacing reliance on law enforcement," *National Law Journal*, April 18, 1994.
6. Ibid.

CHAPTER THIRTEEN: **The Criminal Justice System**

1. U.S. Department of Justice, U.S. Bureau of Justice Statistics, *Criminal Victimization in the United States, 1991* (Washington, D.C.: U.S. Department of Justice, 1993), page 102.

CHAPTER FOURTEEN: **Juvenile Justice**

1. *Montgomery Journal* (Maryland), August 31, 1979, page A7.
2. Charles A. Murray & Louis A. Cox, *Beyond Probation: Juvenile Corrections and the Chronic Delinquent* (Beverly Hills: Sage Publications, 1979).
3. Mack, "The Juvenile Court," 23 *Harvard Law Review* (1909), pages 104, 107.

4. *Kent v. United States*, 383 U.S. (1966), page 541.

5. James Q. Wilson, "'What Works?' revisited: new findings on criminal rehabilitation," *The Public Interest* 61:3, 11–13 (Fall, 1980).

6. *Washington Post*, November 19, 1979, page A4; Murray & Cox, *Beyond Probation*, op. cit.

7. Marvin Wolfgang, *Crime in a Birth Cohort* (Philadelphia: University of Pennsylvania, 1973).

CHAPTER FIFTEEN: **Prisons: Cruel and Unusual Punishment?**

1. Thomas H. Zoet, "Congress Spotlights Community Programs," *Corrections Today*, June 1991, pages 130–132.

2. Professor Michael K. Block, University of Arizona, based on "Crime in the United States, FBI Uniform Crime Reports," 1960–92; and "Correctional Populations in the United States," Bureau of Justice Statistics, Washington, D.C., 1992.

3. Ibid.

4. Ibid.

5. "Imprisonment Rates in 4 Countries," Bureau of Justice Statistics, Washington, D.C., 1987 (NCJ–103967).

6. Block, "Crime in the United States," op. cit.

7. "The Case for More Incarceration," U.S. Department of Justice, Washington, D.C., November 1992, pages 4–5 (NCJ–139583), citing "Historical Statistics on Prisoners in State and Federal Institutions, Yearend 1925–86," May 1986 (NCJ–111098).

8. Michael K. Block and Steven J. Twist, "Lessons from the Eighties: Incarceration Works," *Commonsense*, National Policy Forum, Washington, D.C., ————— 1994, page 78; for this and relevant passages. (Note: accepted for publication, not yet published. Page numbers based on galley proofs.)

9. National Center for Policy Analysis, "Why Does Crime Pay?" Heritage Foundation Backgrounder No. 110 (1991).

10. Block and Twist, "Lessons from the Eighties," page 80.

11. *Davenport v. DeRobertis*, 844 F.2d (7th Cir. 1988), pages 1310, 1313.

12. Joseph Henslik, John Shinners, and John Molenda (inmates at the Federal Correctional Institution in Oxford, Wisconsin), "An Insider's Guide to America's Top Ten Jails" (based on interviews of over seven hundred prisoners). Published in *Playboy*, July 1992, and in the *New York Times* Law Section, July 24, 1992.

CHAPTER SIXTEEN: **Death Penalty**

1. U.S. Congress, Senate Committee on Judiciary, "Establishing Constitutional Procedures for the Imposition of Capital Punishment," S. Rep. No. 251, 98th Cong., 1st Session, 1983.

2. Professor Christie Davies, "Safely executed: arguments in favor of capital punishment for repeat offenders," *National Review* Vol. 43, No. 14, August 12, 1991, page 44.

3. Ibid.

CHAPTER SEVENTEEN: **Crime and Morality**

1. U.S. Department of Justice, *Highlights from Twenty Years of Surveying Crime Victims. The National Crime Victimization Survey*, 1973–92, Washington, D.C., U.S. Department of Justice, 1992.

2. Ibid., page 6.

3. Steven A. Holmes, "Prominent Blacks Meet to Search for an Answer to Mounting Crime," *New York Times*, January 8, 1994, page 1.

4. Dorothy Gilliam, "Crime Through Race-Tinted Lens," *Washington Post*, December 4, 1993, page D1.

5. Courtland Milloy, "We Have Met the Enemy . . . ," *Washington Post*, September 19, 1993, page B1.

6. Ruben Castaneda & David Montgomery, "In King's Name, A Mandate; Blacks Are Urged to Take Responsibility for Violence," *Washington Post*, January 17, 1994, page D1.

7. Mary A. Johnson, "Crime: New Frontier; Jesse Jackson Calls It Top Civil Rights Issue," *Chicago Sun-Times*, November 29, 1993, page 4.

8. Lynne Duke, "Black Leaders Press Action on Crime, Youth; Rainbow Conference Urges Job Training," *Washington Post*, January 9, 1994, page A28.

9. As found in William Raspberry, "Stop Blaming and Start Solving," *Washington Post*, October 20, 1993, page A29.

10. As found in Charles V. Zehren, "Getting Tough on Unwed Moms; Proposals Target Teen Pregnancy," *Newsday*, May 9, 1994, page A7.

11. U.S. Department of Health and Human Services, *Vital Statistics of the United States*, 1991 vol. 1, *Natality* (Washington, DC: GPO, 1993).

12. U.S. Bureau of the Census, *Current Population Reports*, pages 60–181.

13. As found in Joe Klein, "Illegitimacy Becomes a Subject We Can Discuss," *Sacramento Bee*, December 13, 1993, page B7.

14. As found in Robert Rector, "Thumbs on the Scale When Poverty is Weighed," *Washington Times*, September 26, 1993, page B3.

15. M. Anne Hill and June O'Neill, *Underclass Behaviors in the United States: Measurement and Analysis of Determinants* (New York City: City University of New York, Baruch College, March 1990).

16. Charles Murray, "The Coming White Underclass," *Wall Street Journal*, October 29, 1993, page A14.

17. Elijah Anderson, *Sex Codes Among Inner-City Youth* (Philadpehia, Pa: University of Pennsylvania, 1993).

18. Charles Murray, "The Coming White Underclass," op. cit.

19. Robert Rector, "Thumbs on the Scale . . . ," op. cit.

20. Gregory B. Christiansen and Walter E. Williams, "Welfare Family Cohesiveness and Out of Wedlock Births," in Joseph Peden and Fred Glahe, *The American Family and the State* (San Francisco, Ca.: Pacific Institute for Public Policy Research, 1986), page 398.

21. M. Anne Hill and June O'Neill, *Underclass Behaviors*, op. cit.

22. Robert Rector, "Combatting Family Disintegration, Crime and Dependence: Welfare Reform and Beyond," Heritage Foundation Backgrounder No. 983, April 8, 1994.

CHAPTER EIGHTEEN: **Is America Too Free? An International Perspective**

1. Dr. David I. Caplan, "The Warsaw Ghetto; 10 Handguns Against Tyranny," *The American Rifleman*, February 1988.
2. U.S. Department of Justice, U.S. Bureau of Justice Statistics, *International Crime Rates*, Washington, D.C.: U.S. Department of Justice, U.S. Bureau of Labor Statistics, 1988.
3. Jeffrey Snyder, "A Nation of Cowards," *The Public Interest*, Fall, 1993, quoted by George F. Will, *Newsweek*, November 18, 1993, pages 84, 93.

CHAPTER NINETEEN: **BATF Abuses: Trampling on Civil Liberties**

1. U.S. Congress, Senate Committee on Judiciary Committee, Firearms Owner Protection Act, December 9 & 11, 1981, and February 8, 1992 (Washington, D.C.: U.S. Government Printing Office, 1982).
2. Film, *It Can't Happen Here,* narrated by Rick Jason, produced by MFC Film Production for the National Rifle Association, 1980.
3. Jim Oliver, "The Randy Weaver Case: A Federal Fiasco," *The American Rifleman*, November 1993.
4. Carol Vinzant, "ATF-TROOP," *Spy Magazine*, March 1994.

CHAPTER TWENTY: **Media Bias: The "Thought Police" in America**

1. Rush Limbaugh, *The Way Things Ought To Be* (New York, N.Y.: Simon & Schuster, 1992).
2. The Law Enforcement Alliance of America, News Release at

Press Conference in Mobile, Alabama, July 11, 1993, during the 47th Annual Southern Legislative Conference, July 11, 1993.

3. Seventh Annual National Association of Chief of Police (NACOP) poll conducted Spring 1994. Results published in PR Newswire story entitled, "U.S. Police Chiefs Rebut Sen. Feinstein's 'Misrepresentations'; Survey Shows Top Cops Overwhelmingly Doubt Effectiveness of Weapons Ban," May 2, 1994.

4. Luntz Weber Research & Strategic Services, Washington, D.C., Media Master & Focus Group Analysis, April 1993.

5. TV news encourages crime—CNN/USA Today, *Crime in America* Survey, Gallup, October 13–18, 1993; Gun laws don't work—CBS/New York Times Poll, December 5–7, 1993; NRS Influence—Time Magazine Survey, Yankelovich Partners, August 16, 1993.

CHAPTER TWENTY-ONE: Getting Tough: An Agenda for the Nineties

1. "Judge Defends $3,000 Bail In Rape," *Buffalo News*, New York, August 10, 1993.

2. *Felony Sentences in State Courts, 1990*, Bureau of Justice Statistics, U.S. Department of Justice (1993), page 2.

3. *National Corrections Reporting Program, 1990*, Bureau of Justice Statistics, U.S. Department of Justice (1993), table 2–4.

4. *Special Report, Profile of Jail Inmates, 1989*, Bureau of Justice Statistics, U.S. Department of Justice (1991), page 5.

5. *Survey of State Prison Inmates, 1991*, Bureau of Justice Statistics, U.S. Department of Justice (1993), page 22.

6. *Crime in the United States, FBI Uniform Crime Reports, 1990*, Federal Bureau of Investigation, United States Department of Justice (1991), tables 27, 36.

7. Bureau of Justice Sourcebook of Criminal Justice Statistics, 1991, table 1.120.

8. Derived from Bureau of Justice Sourcebook of Criminal Justice Statistics, 1991, table 6.123, for states reporting relevant figures.

9. Comments of Ruth Micklem, co-director of Virginians against Domestic Violence, reported in *Newsweek*, July 13, 1992.

INDEX